Facilitating Reflective Learning Through Mentoring & Coaching

**Anne Brockbank
& Ian McGill**

KoganPage

LONDON PHILADELPHIA NEW DELHI

Publisher's note

Every possible effort has been made to ensure that the information contained in this book is accurate at the time of going to press, and the publishers and authors cannot accept responsibility for any errors or omissions, however caused. No responsibility for loss or damage occasioned to any person acting, or refraining from action, as a result of the material in this publication can be accepted by the editor, the publisher or any of the authors.

First published in Great Britain and the United States in 2006 by Kogan Page Limited

Reprinted 2006, 2009, 2010

120 Pentonville Road	525 South 4th Street, #241	4737/23 Ansari Road
London N1 9JN	Philadelphia PA 19147	Daryaganj
United Kingdom	USA	New Delhi 110002
www.koganpage.com		India

© Anne Brockbank and Ian McGill, 2006

ISBN 978 0 7494 4448 8

British Library Cataloguing-in-Publication Data

A CIP record for this book is available from the British Library.

Library of Congress Cataloging-in-Publication Data

Brockbank, Anne, 1943–
    Facilitating reflective learning through mentoring and coaching / Anne Brockbank and Ian McGill.
        p. cm
    Includes bibliographical references and index.
    ISBN 0-7494-4448-7
    1. Employees—Coaching of. 2. Mentoring in business. 3. Organizational learning.
I. McGill, Ian. II. Title
HF5549.5.C53B76 2006
658.3'124—dc22
                                                2005030840

Typeset by Digital Publishing Solutions
Printed and bound in Great Britain by Henry Ling Limited, Dorchester, Dorset

Contents

Acknowledgements

We express our appreciation of our colleagues, mentors, clients, participants on our courses, friends and family, all of whom have contributed to this book in their own individual ways.

We are grateful to our academic colleagues, Professor Yvonne Hillier of City University and Professor David Megginson of Sheffield Hallam University for their patient and critical reading of the text before submission for publication, and their valuable and incisive guidance for useful changes to it. We recognize the role of our colleagues at City University where much of the material has been tried and tested by Masters students reading for the MSc in the Education Training and Development of Adults. In addition, we acknowledge the contribution of each and every participant who has taken the Mentoring Coaching and Supervision module from 1995 to 2005 for the challenges and development they provided.

We extend our appreciation to our mentoring and coaching clients and for the insights we have gained through our relationships with them which support many of the ideas we present here. In our preparation and training of mentors and coaches for corporate clients we have been made aware of the variety of contexts in which mentoring and coaching activities are carried out.

Once again, we are grateful to Gerard O'Connor for his provision of diagrams in Chapter 10 and Dr Alison O'Connor who advised us in our initial discussions about the map of mentoring and coaching approaches.

We appreciate the role of our case study authors or contributors in illustrating many of our ideas, including: Linda Smith, South East London Strategic Health Authority and organization development consultant; Judith Hunt, Chair of London Health Observatory and executive coach; Alison Lyon and Eve Bazely of NCH, the children's charity; Jan Kay and Les MacDonald for the First Nation case; Patricia

Easterbrook and Claire Siegel for the Professional Awarding Body case; Helene Donnelly, Forensic Paper Conservator and Founder of Data & Archival Damage Control Centre; Dorothea Carvalho, Director, Chartered Institute of Logistics and Transport; and Robert Clasper-Todd, Training Manager, Addaction.

Our own experience of mentoring and coaching has influenced the content of the book and we acknowledge our debt to our past mentors and coaches, although not named as such, who have influenced and inspired our endeavours. These include Anne's violin teacher Helen Hogg, her private mathematics tutor David O'Connor, her trainer/supervisor Eunice Rudman and academic mentor, Professor Gary Davies, as well as Ian's teachers T Broadhurst, Mrs E Cox, and tutors Brian Thomas and Jack Greenleaf.

We also recognize the support of the editorial team at Kogan Page, including Helen Kogan, Suzanne Mursell, Helen Moss and Caroline Carr, who have enabled us to bring the book to publication.

Anne Brockbank (Anne.Brockbank@mailbox.ulcc.ac.uk)
Ian McGill (Ian.McGill@mailbox.ulcc.ac.uk)

1 Introduction and route through the book

This book is for those who practice mentoring or coaching as well as for those clients[1] who are interested in the mentoring and coaching process and wish to make best use of their experience as clients. Amongst mentors and coaches we include those aspiring to these roles as well as those experienced in the field who may wish to review their practice. The book may also be useful for those responsible for staff and management development in organizations who are involved in creating mentoring and coaching programmes.

We have based our book on our experience in the field as mentors and as designers of mentoring or coaching programmes for corporate clients. In addition we bring our experience of designing and running postgraduate programmes in which we utilize our knowledge of theory and its application to practice. In this book we seek to build a theoretical base for professional practice in the field.

The terminology of mentoring and coaching in the literature has been confused and confusing. Sometimes the words are used interchangeably with little or no agreement on their meaning. Academics have tended to position coaching as an activity that aims at improvement only, often in an instrumental way, whereas they have linked mentoring to a transformational learning outcome. The recent emergence of the life coaching movement has hijacked the term 'mentor', insisting that it is life coaching that aims at transformation as a learning outcome, and mentors are simply company advisers or even inexpensive tutors. Organizational programmes unless clearly defined have the potential for disappointment for mentors, coaches and clients alike.

We wish to acknowledge the contributions of Ann Darwin and Rolland Paulston whose work has inspired this book. We aim to clarify the meaning of the terms 'mentoring' and 'coaching' by relating them to the following questions:

- Whose purpose?
- What process?
- Which learning outcome?

We are aware also of concerns about less-than-qualified practitioners, and seek to raise the question of a code of ethics that takes into account the purpose, the process and the potential learning outcome, in a clear statement of what is being offered. We discuss a code of ethics in Chapter 13.

Part I is about theory. We set out the origins of our work in a theoretical account that underpins our practice. Alongside theory we declare our values with which we approach mentoring and coaching. In Chapter 2 we assert that the process of mentoring or coaching has one clear purpose, the learning and development of an individual, a process that involves change, in this case social change. Thus we present a map of approaches to mentoring and coaching that identifies the activities by their purpose, process and hence their learning outcome. Because each mentor or coach will have an underpinning base, it is crucial that they take time to examine their philosophy, however embedded it might be, and make this known to prospective clients. We identify four categories of mentoring or coaching:

- functionalist mentoring or coaching;
- engagement mentoring or coaching;
- revolutionary mentoring or coaching; and
- evolutionary mentoring or coaching.

The remainder of Chapter 2 is designed to set three of the four categories (excluding revolutionary) in the context of the purpose, the method of achieving it – that is, the process – and the learning outcome of the activity. In setting the context we discuss ways of 'seeing the world', the nature of the discourse within those contexts, and the power horizon within which mentor and client operate.

We continue Chapter 2 with the underlying view that mentoring and coaching do not operate in a value-free or neutral form. Both parties to the process are influenced by their social context. Mentor, coach and client are all influenced by how factors of class, race, gender, role, identity and relative opportunity impact on learning. We conclude the chapter with an introductory perspective toward reflective learning and the notion of critical reflection.

In Chapter 3 we examine the nature and potential relevance of learning theories in each of the three categories of mentoring and coaching we have defined. We commence by examining the social context of learning, and the impact of power and passivity toward learning, and introduce three levels of reflective learning: for improvement; for transformation; and learning about learning. This chapter introduces the reader to single and double loop learning and the significance of emotion in relation to learning.

Chapter 4 builds on the previous chapter by addressing the significance of reflective dialogue for mentoring and coaching. We examine the notion of dialogue and the importance of working interactively as a means to seek improvement as well as personal transformation for the client.

Part II addresses the way mentoring and coaching are defined and poses three questions: Whose purpose? What process? Which learning outcome? The answers indicate which category of mentoring or coaching is likely to emerge and we discuss the benefits of a range of the models available.

Definitions of mentoring tend to be used without clarification of the philosophical basis of the activity, the approach taken and the intended learning outcome. Chapter 5 seeks to clarify the meaning and purpose of definitions of mentoring as well as explaining their implicit philosophical approaches, the process used and learning outcomes. We examine the importance of diversity in mentoring by reference to relationships between mentors and clients who differ in gender, race, ethnicity, sexual orientation, class, religion, disability and any other groups associated with power in organizations.

Chapter 6 addresses the question: what is coaching? The confusion about naming a coaching activity replicates the difficulty with the term 'mentoring' discussed in the previous chapter. There are various definitions available, which again tend to be used without clarification of the philosophical approach, the purpose and hence the learning outcome. This chapter seeks to clear up some of the confusion around the term by categorizing coaching as functionalist, engagement or evolutionary, depending on the purpose, the process or method used, and the learning outcome that is implied in the definition. We discuss life coaching and executive coaching in the context of evolutionary coaching while noting that many functionalist approaches claim to be life coaching. We complete the chapter with diversity issues and intercultural coaching.

In Chapter 7 we return to mentoring. We review existing and well-tried mentoring models before recommending a cyclical model that can be used for all types of mentoring, from functionalist to evolutionary. The traditional mentoring model maps against the passage of time and charts changes or stages in the relationship from its beginning to its end, but tends to be silent on how to structure each session. Our recommended cyclical model is holographic in that it offers mentors a plan for a single session or a programme to be used over a long time period. The chapter concludes with a description of an additional in-depth mentoring model for evolutionary mentors, the double matrix model.

In Chapter 8 we return to and review existing coaching models before recommending the Egan model, which can be used for all types of coaching from functionalist to evolutionary. Traditional coaching models start from a definable goal, which may or may not be owned by the client, and proceed to methods of achieving that goal. Such models are likely to be used for basic or functionalist coaching. For evolutionary coaching, that is, executive coaching or life coaching, we recommend the Egan model because it enables clients to generate their own goals as well as their own methods of achieving them.

Part III defines the skills needed for clients and mentors in three categories, functionalist, engagement and evolutionary. These chapters are practical with numerous examples of how the skills 'work' in practice. This part also deals with the preparation of mentors and coaches.

Chapter 9 examines in detail the skills that contribute to being effective as a client in three contexts: in a functional mentoring or basic coaching relationship; in an engagement mentoring or coaching relationship; and in an evolutionary mentoring or life coaching relationship. We identify the skills used by the client and we describe them, indicating how they might be used to get the most out of a mentoring or coaching relationship. The purpose of this chapter is enhancement of the mentoring or coaching relationship by focusing on the client's skills.

In Chapter 10 we discuss the basic skills that you will need if you are acting as a functionalist mentor or coach. By this we mean coaching or mentoring that is primarily for the purpose of improvement. A company seeking to improve its customer complaints record may use coaching for this, or an organization wishing to raise the qualification standard of its membership may use mentors. 'Functionalist' means that the coaching or mentoring has a function for the organization in question, in particular to maintain the status quo. Hence functionalist coaching or mentoring does not seek to disturb things or enable transformation as described in Chapter 2. A functionalist coach or mentor is seeking to improve performance without altering the underlying system. The skills described in this chapter are contracting, listening, restatement, summary, primary empathy, questioning and feedback. Many readers are equipped with further skills, and we discuss these in Chapter 11. Chapter 10 suggests a minimum level of skill for workplace mentoring or coaching.

In Chapter 11 we locate the skills needed as an evolutionary mentor or life coach. By this we mean mentoring or coaching that aims to achieve reflective learning and transformation. A company seeking to launch a culture change may use evolutionary mentoring for this, or an organization wishing to develop key personnel may use external mentors or life coaches. Evolutionary mentors and life coaches seek to enable their clients to question the taken-for-granteds (tfgs) in their work environment, recognize the prevailing discourse and transform their view of the world, as described in Chapter 2. An evolutionary mentor or life coach, whilst attending to day-to-day performance, seeks, through reflective dialogue, to challenge clients to look beyond their immediate horizon and transform their view of the system in which they live and work. The skills appropriate here include mentor presence and speech, levels of listening, restatement, summary, empathy, questioning, feedback, challenge, immediacy and confrontation.

In Chapter 12 we discuss the rationale for preparing mentors and coaches for their role, the initial stages of the relationship in terms of agreeing a contract and goal setting, and the development of mentoring and coaching skills through a range of experiential exercises. The chapter also includes a workshop outline and some guidance on selecting mentors and coaches as well as mini case studies for trainee practice.

Part IV deals with the boundary between mentoring or coaching and therapy, the desirability of supervision and codes of practice.

Chapter 13 explores the boundaries between mentoring or coaching and therapy, that is, psychotherapy or counselling. Again the literature is confused and confusing, as neither counselling nor psychotherapy is a clearly defined concept. It is important to be aware of where the boundaries lie, as most mentors and coaches are anxious not to stray into a therapeutic situation without professional support and training in the field. Finally we address the importance of mentors and coaches having appropriate supervision in order to ensure and maintain safe conditions and boundaries for clients.

Readers who are more interested in practice than theory may choose to leave aside Part I and Part II, and go straight to the development of skills in Part III, possibly returning later to the chapters dealing with theory at their leisure. Readers who are new to mentoring and coaching theory may want to absorb the material in Part I and Part II before moving on to the practical chapters in Part III. Part IV takes the reader into the potential problem areas in mentoring and coaching, and hence the need for ethical standards.

WHERE WE ARE COMING FROM

It will be apparent to the reader that whilst we operate on occasion as functionalist mentors and coaches we tend to work with clients who wish to work in evolutionary mode. We recognize that day-to-day work requires a degree of functionalist activity, which will therefore feature in all mentoring or coaching. However, we offer clients the possibility of considering and reconsidering their ways of being-in-the-world through evolutionary mentoring and coaching. Both incorporate the idea of dialogue, the first with a view to improving performance, the latter as an encounter that is interactive and reflective in enabling the client to engage in dialogue that has the potential to uncover 'taken-for-granteds' that may not emerge for the client through personal reflection without the interaction with another.

Our purpose in this book is to promote an understanding and rigorous use of both approaches. Where mentors or coaches are using exclusively functionalist approaches we recommend that this is made clear from the start so that clients do not expect an evolutionary approach and experience disappointment when this does not happen. Our experience has led us to recognize that all clients have the potential to think outside the box and reveal the 'taken-for-granteds' in their life and work. A characteristic of our practice is that it gives clients the opportunity to reflect on their ways of being-in-the-world and the support to achieve a degree of transformation if that is their desire. Our clients may embark on a journey, starting from a functionalist purpose that evolves into personal and professional development.

NOTE

1   For ease of definition, throughout the book we use the term client to include mentee, coachee, protégé, and learner, except where we are discussing the work of another author.

Part I
LEARNING THEORIES AND VALUES

2 A map of mentoring and coaching

Mentoring or coaching has one clear purpose, the learning and development of an individual, a process that involves change, in this case social change. The method of mentoring or coaching is likely to be influenced by the philosophy that underpins it, and in general the theoretical base is implicit and undeclared. Mentoring has been described as 'a practice that remains ill-defined, poorly conceptualised, and weakly theorised, leading to confusion in policy and practice' (Colley, 2003: 13). Because the philosophy that underlies any approach will impact on its outcome, we recommend that practitioners take time to examine their philosophy, however embedded it might be, and make this known to prospective clients.

We draw on two sources for our map of social or educational change: the sociologists Burrell and Morgan (1979) and the philosopher Rolland Paulston (1996). Ann Darwin (2000) has developed their ideas in the context of mentoring, and we continue the analysis to include coaching below.

Burrell and Morgan (1979) developed a map of how organizations operate in the social world, using two dimensions: the objectivity/subjectivity dimension, which describes reality; and the transformation/equilibrium dimension, which describes the social or educational change, ie the learning outcome. The map can be seen in Figure 2.1.

Before continuing our analysis let us define what some of these terms mean.

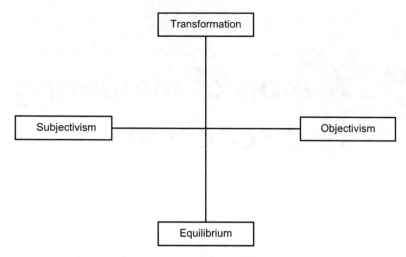

Figure 2.1   *Map of reality views and learning outcomes*

REALITY DIMENSION

An objectivist view assumes the existence of a reality 'out there', which can be captured by scientific method. Social reality is assumed to be similar to the natural world whose properties are believed to remain constant and unchanging. A typical objectivist understanding of reality would be revealed in mentoring or coaching by an emphasis on the rational elements of mentoring or coaching issues, with less consideration of the personal and social world of the learner. Such mentoring or coaching favours imposed objectives, based on perceived objective reality, and may use personality profiles and learning styles inventories because they assume a set of fixed qualities.

A subjectivist view assumes that social realities like learning and development are fundamentally different from natural phenomena and therefore cannot be captured by so-called objective instruments. The social world of a client is understood to be continuously constructed, reproduced and transformed through interaction with others. A typical subjectivist understanding of reality would be revealed in mentoring or coaching where the personal and social world of the client is acknowledged as the basis of the developmental process. Such mentoring or coaching recognizes the socially constructed nature of reality.

These are idealized types, and it is possible to recognize both views.

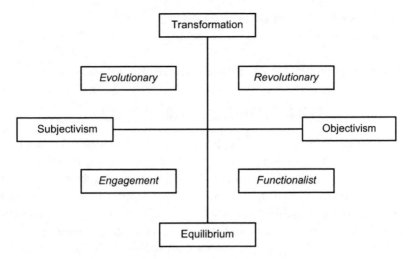

Figure 2.2 *Map of mentoring or coaching approaches*

LEARNING OUTCOME DIMENSION

Equilibrium as a learning outcome suggests that the status quo is maintained with essential factors being unchanged. The power structure in the workplace remains unaltered by new ideas, and the taken-for-granteds (tfgs) remain unchallenged behind what is known as 'the prevailing discourse' (Burr, 1995). Such mentoring or coaching has been described as 'the recycling of power' (Darwin, 2000) because of its tendency to replicate existing power relations.

Transformation as a learning outcome suggests that either the individual or organization (or both) is radically changed as a consequence of learning and development. To achieve transformation it is necessary to reconsider existing views, challenge the status quo and question the tfgs within the life/work environment. Such mentoring or coaching invites clients to identify the prevailing discourse and look beyond their power horizon (Smail, 2001), explained on page 16. We also discuss 'the prevailing discourse' on page 14.

In Figure 2.2, following Ann Darwin's analysis, these two dimensions are used to describe four approaches to the learning and development that occurs as a consequence of mentoring or coaching.

Figure 2.2 offers four quadrants, each with its different approach to mentoring or coaching:

■ functionalist mentoring or coaching;
■ engagement mentoring or coaching;[1]

- revolutionary mentoring or coaching;
- evolutionary mentoring or life coaching.

What are the characteristics of these different approaches?

FUNCTIONALIST APPROACH

Functionalist mentoring or coaching focuses on efficiency and equilibrium, assuming an objective real world, aiming at improved performance and, in order to maintain the status quo, tends to suppress challenge and questioning. The necessity of maintaining equilibrium leads mentors or coaches to socialize their clients, ensuring that existing values and norms are preserved, thereby 'guaranteeing' career advancement. This approach ensures grooming for career advancement, recycled power relationships and less diversity, resulting in 'a successful core of white middle class successors to organisational hierarchies' (Darwin, 2000: 205). For many individuals the imposed objectives are easily aligned with their own and the approach can be described as 'functionalist' for the individual. The approach tends to reinforce existing power relations and even overtly and/or covertly reproduces social inequalities. The equilibrium or status quo achieved with functionalist mentoring or coaching relies on what has been termed 'the prevailing discourse'. We discuss the prevailing discourse on page 14. The functionalist mentor or coach serves the perceived 'needs' of the organization or society by ensuring (without necessarily realizing this) that power structures remain intact and the tfgs continue to inform the prevailing discourse, regardless of the career advancement of the client. In fact, 'from a functionalist perspective, mentoring is associated with recycling of power within workplace relationships' (Darwin, 2000: 203). Traditional mentoring and traditional coaching of apprentices can be identified as functionalist, and some modern mentoring programmes designed to meet primarily organizational needs are recognizably functionalist. We discuss such a programme in Chapter 10.

Where there is non-conformity with the existing consensus, a social control mechanism comes into play, and this is described as 'engagement mentoring'.

ENGAGEMENT APPROACH

Engagement mentoring or coaching recognizes the subjective world of the learner, and uses a non-directive approach to maintain the status quo. Organizations seeking to effect cultural change or restructuring may use mentoring or coaching programmes that are broadly humanist in their approach in order to minimize opposition. We discuss such a programme in Chapter 10. Where the distribution of power remains unaltered we have termed this 'engagement mentoring or coaching', following Colley (2003), as it is a humanistic version of functionalist mentoring or coaching. While the mentoring or coaching couple are 'engaged', ie there is a relationship, nevertheless the power horizon remains invisible to the client. We discuss the power horizon on page 16. The idea of engagement mentoring or coaching includes interventions responding to disaffection and social exclusion: 'positive action' or 'community mentoring' aimed at supporting young people from oppressed groups, eg young men from black and Asian communities. In her description of engagement mentoring, Colley (2003: 151) suggests that 'it seeks to reform young mentees' dispositions in line with employers' demands for employability' and that for their mentors 'it seeks to engender devotion and self-sacrificing dispositions in mentors through its discourse of feminine nurture'. Dispositions are the habitual unconscious ways of thinking and feeling; ways of being – habitual states – are named 'dispositions' by Bourdieu (quoted in Grenfell and James, 1998) because they are believed to 'dispose' individuals to do or think or feel in particular ways. They are our unconscious tendencies and are revealed in our inclinations towards particular ways of being.

REVOLUTIONARY APPROACH

Revolutionary mentoring or coaching seeks to promote the transformation of society and radical change. Here the aim is to transform the structure of society according to a grand narrative such as Marxism; hence the approach adopts the objectivist view of reality. The subjective world of the individual is not important here, only the cause, which seeks to illuminate the 'false consciousness' or mistaken ideas of the individual through rational argument and persuasion. The revolutionary intent can be addressed (slowly) through one-to-one mentoring or coaching that, although it adopts an objective view of reality, seeing it as fixed and unchanging, is seeking to enable individuals to transform their beliefs and only in the fullness of time become part of a larger, changed world for which they may aspire to be agents. The process seeks disturbance and ultimately liberation from 'false consciousness'. Examples of such an approach are the conversion of hostages and the radicalization of some young Islamic men.

In this book we are going to concentrate on the other three approaches.

EVOLUTIONARY APPROACH

Evolutionary mentoring or life coaching acknowledges the subjective world of individuals as clients, respects the clients' experience and, by generating ownership of their objectives, invites an examination of embedded power structures that may inhibit learning. By working with individuals' social reality, which may include oppression and varieties of discriminatory behaviour, clients are enabled to evolve into their power, taking responsibility for their own learning and development as well as challenging the tfgs in their environment. Evolutionary mentoring, executive coaching or life coaching offers clients a chance to identify the prevailing discourse and challenge it, through reflective dialogue. In this recognition of clients' socially constructed worlds there are opportunities for transformation for both individuals and organizations. Evolutionary mentoring or coaching is usually (but not always) found in private arrangements, often quite separate from the workplace, where professional mentors or coaches work with clients over time, to an agreed contract. For evolutionary mentoring or life coaching, the necessary and sufficient conditions are the ownership of goals by the client and the potential for transformation through reflective dialogue. We discuss such case studies in Chapters 7 and 11.

We move now to explore the meanings of the terms 'prevailing discourse' and 'power horizon' used in the definitions above.

THE PREVAILING DISCOURSE

The idea of a prevailing discourse comes from social constructivist ideas, which depart from traditional approaches to personal development by challenging the presumption of objective reality and focusing on language or discourse as the medium through which individuals construct new understandings (Burr, 1995). Thus learning contexts, like mentoring or coaching, are themselves socially constructed, so that 'we create rather than discover ourselves' and we do this through engagement-with-others, using language in discourse (Burr, 1995: 28). Discourse is said to be an element in all social contexts, and includes language, visual images and body language (Fairclough, 1992), and the powerful role of language and discourse lies in its taken-for-granted nature. The prevailing discourse in any system is invisible to its users, being beyond the power horizon (Smail, 2001), which we discuss below. For clients, the context is defined by the concepts and 'givens' of the prevailing discourse. An example of an invisible prevailing discourse is the executive washroom, where only those above certain grades are admitted and this is accepted without question by those excluded. How does a prevailing discourse become established?

The prevailing discourse is defined as 'a set of meanings, metaphors, representations, images, stories, statements etc that in some way together produce a particular version' of events, person or category of person (Burr, 1995: 48). The power of discourse in learning contexts is explained by Stephen Ball (1990: 2) as follows:

> Discourses are about what can be said and thought, but also about who can speak, when, and with what authority. Discourses embody meaning and social relationships, they constitute both subjectivity and power relations. Discourses are 'practices that systematically form the objects of which they speak'... In so far as discourses are constituted by exclusions as well as inclusions, by what cannot as well as what can be said, they stand in antagonistic relationship to other discourses.

Examples of how such discourse is used can be seen in terms like 'attitude problem', 'downsizing', 'regulating', 'on-message', 'globalization', 'unionized', 'eco-warrior' and, as above, 'executive washroom'. Hence, we exist in a system or paradigm that is not value-free, where power is exercised that can influence our progress and affect our development. If we accept that our context is defined by the prevailing discourse, this has implications for our understanding of self. Existing in an ever-changing social context, the self is ever-changing, responding to and influencing its environment, being constructed continuously through interaction with others. Smail (2001: 23) maintains that 'our environment has much more to do with our coming-to-be as people than we do as authors of our own fate'.

Evolutionary mentoring and life coaching, through reflective procedures, which we describe in detail in Chapter 11, seeks to offer clients an alternative discourse. Such a paradigm shift has the potential to challenge the taken-for-granted assumptions of the prevailing discourse in which clients are embedded. Evolutionary mentoring or life coaching, a context of acceptance and challenge without judgement (itself an alternative prevailing discourse), allows clients to reconsider some of the givens of their situation.

It is important here to recognize that we are not proposing an either/or argument, but we do say that evolutionary mentoring and life coaching begin from clients' ownership of their goals, and allow for environmental influences to be acknowledged and their subjective effects given voice. In such a mentoring or coaching relationship, the recognition that 'the self' can take an infinite variety of forms enables clients to access their potential and challenge what constrains their learning.

Evolutionary mentoring or life coaching is at its best when clients are able to challenge the dominant paradigm in which they are living and working. An example of this is 'presenteeism', the practice whereby employees believe that working long hours over their working day makes them more productive and will get them promotion. Within such mentoring or coaching relationships, the subjective experience of clients is recognized and valued, giving them the option to seek improvement or transformation. Where clients are struggling with their work/life balance, the realization of 'presenteeism' as nothing more than an aspect of the prevailing discourse may lead them to transform their approach to work.

THE POWER HORIZON

In a functionalist context the organization and control of employees require them to perform specific and regulated roles. An important consequence of this is the cult of individualism, where the individual is identified as the source of disorder and the only resource for curing it, making the individual solely responsible for outcomes in the workplace. Whilst recognizing the importance of individual responsibility at work, the dogma of individualism may lead to a work environment where clients feel helpless, confused and stressed. Why should this be?

Where individualism is the only theory available, the social context, with its power nexus, is largely ignored and kept invisible, particularly to those who are powerless. This is known as a 'power horizon' (Smail, 2001: 67) and is kept in position by offering a version of objective reality as truth, known as 'the prevailing discourse', a version that maintains the sources of power invisible. The arch-proponent of individualism was Margaret Thatcher, who famously declared 'There is no such thing as society.'

The idea of a power horizon that is always just out of our sight suggests a prevailing discourse that maintains it in position, not unlike the situation of the unfortunate hero in the film *The Truman Show* who was kept unaware that his life was actually a TV show. The power horizon divides our real-life experience at work, the nearby power effects on an individual, from the distant power effects exerted by larger political and social factors, keeping the latter invisible (Smail, 2001: 67). The individual's power horizon, through the prevailing discourse, ensures that distant power effects are out of sight, leaving the individual no option but to concentrate on closer agents who are often themselves powerless and held within their own power horizon. An example of this is a client's perception of a manager as 'difficult' when he or she makes demands, whilst the manager is struggling to meet targets set by a superior, who is responding to board-level panic, a consequence of share price insecurity. The client's power horizon ensures that he or she attends primarily to the manager, without 'seeing' the more distant causes of the difficulty.

Evolutionary mentoring or coaching has the potential, through reflective dialogue, discussed in Chapter 4, to expand the power horizon for an individual, enabling him or her to see, often for the first time, where the source of a difficulty or frustration lies. This is achieved by recognizing the individual's goals, acknowledging the individual's subjective world and challenging the prevailing discourse within his or her social context.

LEARNING FOR IMPROVEMENT OR TRANSFORMATION?

Evolutionary mentoring and life coaching support both reflective learning for improvement and reflective learning for transformation (Brockbank, McGill and Beech, 2002). Cox (1981) has identified the limitation of moves towards change that seek only improvement of existing practices. Such learning he maintains is 'discursively bound' and knowledge outcomes from them are rational, efficient, controllable and fixed. We concur with this view but accept that such learning for improvement is part of the larger picture of learning. We have discussed reflective learning for improvement and reflective learning for transformation elsewhere (Brockbank, McGill and Beech, 2002) and recognize the value of both. In order to achieve transformation, there needs to be a learning process that addresses the subjective world of the individual, challenges the tfgs (which maintain the power horizon) and thereby problematizes the dominant framework, rather than the individuals within it.

Such reflective learning for transformation can offer alternative paradigms with the potential to transform institutions and social meanings. Individuals, as clients, who engage in such transformation have been able to see beyond, above, below and beside the taken-for-granted assumptions; the outcomes may be threatening to the status quo, and sometimes the consequence is that the individuals choose to leave or are excluded. Organizations that aspire to learning are likely to cope with such challenges and benefit from them. The concept of learning as additional insight is replaced by learning as 'outsight' where clients have identified the environment, beyond their power horizon, as part of their difficulty or frustration (Smail, 2001: 8–9), and this might enable people to 'live their lives as themselves, and understand their own experience as valid' (Smail, 2001: 8–9).

POWER AND ORGANIZATIONAL LEARNING

For effective organizational learning there is a need to recognize power relations rather than power as a 'given' commodity that leaves the individual feeling helpless. All social and personal relationships, including work relationships, have a power element, and the mentoring or coaching relationship is no exception.

Every mentoring or coaching relationship has a political dimension, in that it represents interpersonally the sense of power and powerlessness that is found in any other pairing within the organization. Individuals can feel a sense of power or powerlessness vis-à-vis others and may not be aware of their position or role but nevertheless live it. Issues of power can be implicit in the relationship as well, and when these are made explicit they offer the mentor or coach an opportunity for his or her own learning and development.

Examples of such power issues could include: a male mentor or coach matched with a female client, who is unaware that his use of language inadvertently puts down women; and a white mentor or coach matched with an ethnic minority client, who is unaware of his or her racist remarks. Training is likely to challenge the mentor or coach. If the conditions are appropriate, training can help the person in a direction that promotes learning and empowerment for both mentor or coach and client.

A mentoring or coaching couple that is aware of these political dimensions is, despite the uncertainty felt and the risk taken, potentially more likely to move into the process described above, leading to insight and new learning that empowers. Working implicitly, without recognizing this political dimension, may mean that the couple collude with power relations that limit the effectiveness of their relationship. Furthermore, if mentoring or coaching relationships implicitly replicate power relations elsewhere, the opportunity to work on the 'external' power relations will also be limited, as the couple will simply mirror that which is often implicit in organizations.

It is important to acknowledge the interrelationship between emotional feelings and political power in a mentoring or coaching relationship. Emotions promoting or discouraging learning are affected by the power balance of the relationship as well as the emotional atmosphere. In our example above of the male mentor with a female client, if training does not disturb the 'innocence' of the aspiring mentor or coach about his sexism, his client is likely to experience feelings of resentment and anger that either remain silent or are expressed in another way. The relationship moves into the limiting mode of learning and the politics remain as they were.

Many writings on learning and development, particularly management development, have treated that development in an individualistic and decontextualized manner (Covey, 1989; Reeves, 1994). In other words, the idea that individual managers are responsible for their own development suggests that their progress is a product of their own motivation, commitment and drive. Some of the tools for enabling managers to determine their progress, eg learning styles, assume a neutral context, as if managers were somehow the same gender, class and race and that the notions of diversity, status and relative opportunity did not exist. There is also a tendency to ignore the impact of the prevailing discourse on individuals.

In fact the organization is not neutral territory. Organizations have their formal and informal power structures and relationships in which employees are actors, as well as organizational agents and respondents. Engaging in reflective learning and development, which challenges the dominant discourse, may impact upon those structures and relationships, particularly if development is related to promotion or job retention as well as operational effectiveness. The organization will learn to the degree that 'it can reconcile individual and organisational needs to release and support the inherent energy and creativity of its individual members' (Pedler, Burgoyne and Boydell, 1990: 172). The assumption that individual and organizational learning goals are compatible has been questioned and the complexity of negotiating within the tension explored. Antonacopoulou (1999) has identified the positive and negative attitudes of managers towards the need to learn. Her findings illustrate how the interaction of personal and organizational factors creates conditions that affect an individual's receptivity to learning, and are situation-specific, so that individuals respond differently depending on the situation. The managers in her survey reported that they were more significantly affected by organizational culture and the attitude of top managers than personal barriers to learning. Also the way that the interaction between personal and organizational factors was perceived by managers was identified as one of the issues that determine an individual's attitude towards learning. These findings should alert us to the danger of assuming that responses to learning are, like the concept of 'learning styles', simplistic and uniform (Reynolds, 1997).

This brings us to the essential tension that exists between organizational purpose and self-development. How the organization generates its purpose may influence the commitment of its members. There will be difference and conflict in any organization, particularly about its purpose and chances of survival. The inevitable conflict between individual need and corporate purpose has been noted by John Heron as follows: 'what makes an organisation enlightened is that it has built-in procedures for acknowledging such conflict and working constructively with it' (1977: 7).

The political process of learning from difference, challenge and conflict is unfortunately dubbed as 'politicking' and viewed negatively, an example of how discourse can silence voices. The power of discourse lies in its connection with how an organization is run. A discourse is so embedded in our work or life culture that it is invisible and hidden from us, beyond the power horizon (Smail, 2001) and therein lies its power. As Foucault put it, 'Power is tolerable only on condition that it masks a substantial part of itself' from us (1976: 86). The challenge of embedded discourse is the 'uncovering' of its taken-for-granted status, often by drawing on alternative discourses and considering multiple meanings and others' stories. These processes are typical of evolutionary mentoring or coaching activity.

Where the embedded discourse is resistant to challenge, the organization will be unaware of its culture, convinced of the 'truth' or validity of its position, and this ideological belief will be enjoyed by many of its members. Organizations that seek culture change and transformation are seeking to dislodge the prevailing discourse and generate a new 'view of the world'. A difficulty is that the very structures and procedures that maintain the prevailing discourse may work against the prospect of transformation. French and Vince describe this paradox as 'that organisations espouse and want learning and change at the same time as they prevent themselves from embracing them' (1999: 18). For example, judgemental appraisals and a blame culture will resist openness and honest debriefing as too risky. Additionally, it can be argued that discourses are really powerful when they are not perceived and, therefore, not perceived as a problem. Under these circumstances there would be no intention to change them, and hence they continue to be 'natural' or 'the only way to do things'. Evolutionary approaches, in revealing them as not the only way, may open a Pandora's box for organizations. If individuals and groups are encouraged to challenge existing ideologies then they may become aware of some of the other realities of their corporate system. Those enlightened organizations that have the courage to open up their culture to reflective learning will be taking a risky step towards transformation and future survival.

VALUES OF REFLECTIVE LEARNING

In evolutionary mentoring and coaching, humanistic values are married to some ideas of critical theory to promote reflective learning. Reflective learning adopts the humanistic values as follows:

- A belief that people are driven to grow and develop rather than stagnate.
- A person is a whole person, not just the part that is doing the job.
- Goodwill is how most people operate.
- People are abundant in their resources rather than an assumption that they are in deficit.
- People have spiritual dimensions in their lives.

The humanist values above are usually recorded within the ground rules agreed by mentors and coaches and their clients at the start of a relationship when a contract is created. Examples of such a contract are given in Chapters 7 and 10. The values above have been described as 'person-centred' (Rogers, 1983). 'Person-centred' means that the learning approach recognizes every individual as a unique whole and in possession of the resources he or she needs to learn and develop. Rogers's conditions promote a person-centred climate in a mentoring or coaching relationship, thereby making possible the release of the individual's capacity for learning and development. His person-centred conditions are:

- congruence – genuineness, being real, sharing feelings and attitudes rather than opinions and judgements;
- unconditional positive regard – acceptance and 'prizing' of the other;
- empathy – understanding the other's feelings and experience, as well as communication of that understanding.

These three conditions are described in detail in Chapter 11. Rogers also gave some interesting insights into 'conditions of worth' as part of his model of personality.

Rogers's conditions of worth

Rogers's model of the person stipulates that we are influenced by how we are nurtured from the day of our birth. He maintains that all human beings are reared under 'conditions of worth', so that their self-concept is based on conforming to behaviour that is 'approved of' by the significant others in their life (usually parents or parent-substitutes). This socially acceptable self, formed for fear of losing the love of the parent, is often in opposition to the true 'organismic self' that is suppressed by conditions of worth. The struggle to live up to this idealized self is carried forward into adult life, and we discuss the two selves in Chapter 3. In evolutionary learning situations the idealized self-concept is revealed in the 'shoulds' and 'oughts' and 'got tos' that may appear in clients' issues. The use of 'should' suggests that clients may be speaking under conditions of worth – rather than from their true organismic self (Rogers, 1992). In a mentoring or coaching relationship, when Rogers's three conditions above are met, such conditions of worth are undermined, allowing clients to access the energy of their organismic self. (Note: clients may well choose to follow the path of their 'should' but have made the choice themselves after reflecting on it.) Carl Rogers, in his book *Freedom to Learn for the 80s*, emphasized the importance of relationships in this process, as 'the facilitation of significant learning rests upon... qualities that exist in the personal relationship between the facilitator [in this case, mentor or coach] and learner (1983: 121), and that this is not an easy option, as 'the person-centred way... is something one grows into. It is a set of values, not easy to achieve, placing emphasis on the dignity of the individual, the importance of personal choice, the significance of responsibility, the joy of creativity. It is a philosophy built on the foundation of the democratic way, empowering each individual' (1983: 95).

A full understanding of Rogers's thought suggests that any learning approach should include a recognition of the social, cultural and political contexts (mentioned above) as part of empathy and unconditional positive regard. However, the usual interpretation of Rogers tends to leave invisible the significance of the sociopolitical context, and this has been identified as engagement mentoring or coaching. Where the relationship includes the ownership of individual goals, together with a critically reflective awareness of the social context, described above, we have identified the relationship as evolutionary mentoring or life coaching.

Levels of reflection

In order to achieve the reflection needed for both improvement and transformation, Kemmis (1985) offers three types of reflection:

1. instrumental – concerned with achievement of goals or solutions, for example improvement;

2. consensual – questioning ends as well as means, for example culture change programmes;
3. critical – challenging assumptions and the prevailing discourse.

The recommended type for functionalist mentoring or coaching is 1, for engagement it is 2, and for evolutionary mentoring or life coaching number 3 is needed, a critical process that 'seeks to encourage the questioning of taken-for-granted assumptions so to reflect critically on how the reality of the social world, including the construction of the self, is socially produced and therefore open to transformation' (Alvesson and Willmott, 1992: 435). The characteristics of critical approach 3 that promotes such transformation are:

■ questioning the tfgs;
■ analysing power relations;
■ collaborative learning.

In evolutionary mentoring and coaching relationships these characteristics achieve transformation for the client by:

■ exposing unequal power relations in the field – previously hidden behind the power horizon;
■ challenging what is deemed 'natural';
■ accepting the reality of conflict through dialogue;
■ appreciating the power of language and the prevailing discourse.

Reflection offers opportunities for clients to reflect with their mentor or coach for both improvement and transformation. For functionalist and engagement approaches, instrumental and consensual reflection is appropriate. For evolutionary approaches, challenging embedded power relations through revealing a prevailing discourse enables critical reflection for clients.

Our map of mentoring and coaching will now be placed in the context of learning theory.

NOTE

1 The term 'engagement mentoring' has been coined by Helen Colley (2004) in her publication entitled *Mentoring for Social Inclusion*, Routledge-Falmer.

3 Learning theories

How can learning theories inform our understanding of mentoring and coaching? In Chapter 2 we presented four approaches to mentoring and coaching:

- functionalist mentoring or coaching, which focuses on efficiency and equilibrium, assumes an objective real world, aims at improved performance and, in order to maintain the status quo, tends to suppress challenge and questioning;
- engagement mentoring or coaching, which recognizes the subjective world of the client and uses a non-directive approach to maintain the status quo, thereby promoting a functionalist agenda;
- revolutionary mentoring or coaching, which seeks to promote the transformation of society through radical change (as we noted in Chapter 2, this approach is not developed further in this book);
- evolutionary mentoring or coaching, which acknowledges the subjective world of the client, respects ownership of the individual's goals and invites an examination of embedded power structures that inhibit learning.

What are the implications for learning of these different approaches to mentoring or coaching? Before exploring this question, we review learning theory and consider the significance of single and double loop learning and its outcomes.

THE NATURE OF LEARNING

There is no science or theory of learning that embraces all the activities involved in human learning. Most of what we do, think, feel and believe is learnt so the field of activities is wide and varied. There is little agreement among researchers about what learning is. For example, the behavioural psychologist tends to identify learning in changed behaviour, while cognitive psychologists seek for change *inside* the client as evidence that learning has taken place. Traditional academic learning has tended to emphasize learning as exclusively a mental process, whereas progressive approaches to learning assert that clients must also be active and learn by doing. Recent progressive ideas include emotional elements in learning. We recommend that all three domains of learning are considered, that is *doing, thinking and feeling*, for deep and significant learning.

Research suggests that deep, holistic learning is preferable to surface learning, and is likely to be achieved by clients who take responsibility for their own learning and are motivated by their own learning ambitions, as in evolutionary approaches to mentoring and coaching (Marton, Dall'Alba and Beaty, 1993; Prosser and Trigwell, 1999; Biggs, 1999). The importance of interactive reflections has been stressed by researchers (Kelly, 1955), allowing clients to create their own constructs and meanings in describing their learning, as well as recognizing that learning and knowledge are created within a social context. When clients themselves are consulted about their learning, they are revealed as active, responsible adults who are capable of sharing their meanings and justifying their understandings. The socially constructed nature of knowledge has been explored at length elsewhere (Berger and Luckmann, 1966; Brookfield and Preskill, 1999), and we discuss this further below. The social systems in which a client is embedded will dominate learning, as 'no human thought is immune to the ideologizing influence of its social context' (Burr, 1995: 21). The workplace has its own ideology, often invisible to clients. However, the power of the learning context can be used to enable development through recognition of others as sources of knowledge, and reflective learning offers a method for doing this. The cultural, emotional and value contexts of learning can vary considerably, and this highlights the importance of raising such issues for consideration in mentoring and coaching designs.

Functionalist approaches (including engagement) are likely to have the characteristics of surface learning, described originally by Saljo (1979) and confirmed by Marton, Dall'Alba and Beaty (1993) as:

■ a quantitative increase in knowledge;
■ memorizing;
■ acquisition of facts or methods.

Evolutionary approaches are likely to have the characteristics of deep learning, described by Prosser and Trigwell (1999) as:

■ the abstraction of meaning;
■ the interpretive process aimed at understanding reality;
■ learning as developing as a person.

Most modern learning theories promote the concept of reflection as essential for deep and significant learning. Boyd and Fales (1983) see reflection as a key element in learning from experience in such a way that the individual is cognitively changed or affectively changed. Boud, Keogh and Walker (1985) offer a comprehensive account of the role of reflection in deep learning and, finally, Steinaker and Bell (1979) suggest a reflective process believed to be of value in any situation in which change of behaviour is the objective. The theory underpinning our approach to learning, and in particular reflective learning, begins from the definition of reflective learning as: 'an intentional process, where social context and experience are acknowledged, in which clients are active individuals, wholly present, engaging with others, and open to challenge, and the outcome involves transformation as well as improvement for both individuals and their organization' (Brockbank, McGill and Beech, 2002: 6).

The reflective learning process is inherently complicated, and for mentors and coaches our definition indicates that there are several important factors to consider in what we know about learning. We consider some of them now.

HABITUS, FIELD AND DISPOSITIONS

The idea of dispositions and habitus is important for evolutionary mentoring and life coaching because such mentoring or coaching recognizes individuals' subjective worlds, acknowledges their particular realities and respects their goals. For functionalist or engagement mentoring or coaching, the concepts may assist practitioners trying to make sense of their situation. We draw on the work of Pierre Bourdieu to explore the meaning of these terms.

'Habitus' is a Latin word referring to a habitual or typical condition, state or appearance. Bourdieu tells us that habitus exists 'inside the heads' of learners; through their interactions with others; in their ways of talking and moving; and in other aspects of humanity, eg male/female, up/down and hot/cold. For all individuals, their habitus is the combination of their previous life experience, their sense of identity, lifestyle, personality, class, gender and cultural background. So the habitus inhabits body and mind and by extension the learner's environment, the 'field' described as 'a critical mediation between the practices of those who partake of it and the surrounding social and economic conditions (Bourdieu and Wacquant, 1992: 105). This idea is confirmed by observation of how a boardroom is laid out; how managers exhibit seniority in their stance; and how gender differences are acted out in positioning and gesture. The habitus is believed to be 'beyond consciousness', and Bourdieu (quoted in Grenfell and James, 1998: 14) tells us that 'when habitus encounters a social world of which it is the product it finds itself as a fish in water. It does not feel the weight of the water and takes the world about itself for granted'. However, habitus is not fixed and unchanging, for 'Habitus is not the fate that some people read into it. Being the product of history it is an *open system of dispositions* that is constantly subjected to experiences, and therefore constantly affected by them in such a way that either reinforces or modifies its structures' (Bourdieu and Wacquant, 1992: 133, original italics).

These unconscious ways of thinking and feeling, ways of being or habitual states are named 'dispositions' by Bourdieu, because they are believed to 'dispose' individuals to do, think and feel in particular ways. They are our unconscious tendencies, inclinations and even attitudes and they compose our habitus. The habitus provides a basis for practice (by which Bourdieu means what we actually do), and this is further influenced by the constraints, demands and opportunities of the social field in which the individual exists. Bourdieu further suggests that the habitus directs the conscious mind 'by a strategic calculation of costs and benefits which tends to carry out at a conscious level the operations which habitus carries out in its own way' (cited in Jenkins, 1992: 77).

How does this affect mentoring or coaching?

For functionalist mentors or basic coaches the field is likely to be a given, within the global 'field of power' (Bourdieu and Wacquant, 1992: 76), and an individual's habitus and dispositions are not considered relevant. An example of this would be a manager coaching staff on a new procedure in a context where only the manager speaks and staff do as they are told without question.

For engagement mentoring or coaching, the power relations within the field itself will influence the learning outcome so that subordination or superiority in either party, even with the best of intentions, may lead to disappointment. The intention in engagement mentoring or coaching is to ' transform the habitus of those on both sides of the dyad, to produce and reproduce habitus in a form determined by the needs of dominant groupings, rather than by the needs and desires of mentees or mentors' (Colley, 2003: 152). The idea of altering dispositions is a tall order and for many a questionable objective, and also anything unconscious is difficult to influence by education: hence the failure of so many engagement mentoring programmes (Colley, 2003). For evolutionary mentors or life coaches, an understanding of the role played by the habitus in people's practice or work will enable their mentors or coaches to collaborate with their dispositions to enable the transformation they seek. The process of reflective learning offers clients the possibility of drawing on their habitus and 'developing dreams and ideals into realities' (Pollard, 1997: 69). For instance, mentors or coaches using evolutionary approaches will attend to the 'dispositions' in their clients of past experience, gender, race and class. We discuss in Chapter 11 the skills a mentor or coach will need in order to reach such an understanding with a client.

LEARNING AS A SOCIAL ACTIVITY

We start from the value that people are abundant in their resources. They bring their experience to learning situations. This contrasts with the rather crude view that people are 'empty vessels' to be filled. But learning does not occur in a vacuum. The context in which learning may happen is crucial. Learning is a social process, which will influence the degree of 'agency' experienced by the client. The social process is critical to learning. By 'social process', we mean the context and conditions in which learning takes place, which will influence how intentional learning situations are created and undertaken.

A social constructionist stance holds that our view of reality is deeply influenced by our life experience. So learning contexts are themselves socially constructed by learners who create meaning through their interactions with each other (Kim, 2001; Kukla, 2000). In addition, the social constructivists tell us that 'we create rather than discover ourselves' and we do this through engagement-with-others, using language in discourse (Burr, 1995: 28). For reflective learning, the recognition that our conceptual space is created through our language, and that our context is defined by the prevailing discourse, enables clients to access their potential and challenge what constrains their learning.

The prevailing discourse is defined in Chapter 2 as 'a set of meanings, metaphors, representations, images, stories, statements etc that in some way together produce a particular version' (Burr, 1995: 48) of events, person or category of person. Identities are constructed through discourse; for example, how intelligent someone is judged to be may relate to that person's physical appearance and to how he or she is allowed to talk without interruption. The operation of discourses is not power-neutral, but rather discourses are imbued with power relations that impact on how people are defined and whether they are granted a voice, resources and decision-making powers. The individual is not a given, as the self is continuously constructed through the social relationships, discourse and practices of the organizational or family culture in which he or she is embedded. This is nicely put by Maturana and Varela as 'We who are flesh and blood people are no strangers to the world in which we live and which we bring forth through our living' (1987: 129).

Hence as clients we enter a system that is not value-free, where power is exercised that can influence our progress and affect our learning context. These contexts exist across the whole spectrum of organizations from public companies to formal educational institutions and voluntary organizations. In-house learning is explicitly aimed at fulfilling the purposes of the organization; these are generated by 'leaders', and these leaders are likely to influence the creation of mentoring or coaching programmes.

The social nature of learning offers opportunities for clients to reflect upon their learning not only by themselves, but with others. Being able to undertake reflection alone is necessary but not sufficient. The tendency to self-deceive, collude and be unaware is ever present. When others are present, clients have potentiality for challenge that may not be available alone. As meaning is created in relation to others, then reflection and the creation of meaning are inevitably a social process. The context in which such reflection occurs is the learning relationship.

The learning relationship is one that can occur formally or informally, explicitly or implicitly. When people in an organization find themselves in an enabling learning role, like mentor or coach, the stance they create with clients is crucial. Without explicit recognition of the interaction as embodying a relationship, then in working with these conditions we may be less effective. There is a tendency for knowledge to be treated as static and disembodied, as a product rather than a process. In this case functionalist coaches may also treat their clients as detached, disembodied and passive. This is a very limited form of relationship, inhibiting learning for the client. In recognizing the interaction as constituting a relationship between mentor and client we are saying that the learning outcome of the activity comes through their interactions. Julie Hay has described such a relationship as a developmental alliance that depends on genuine connection, and she asserts it 'will not work properly unless those involved believe that it is normal for people to want a close connection with each other' (Hay, 1995: 47).

INDIVIDUAL LEARNING IN ORGANIZATIONS

As we noted in Chapter 2, many writings on learning and development at work start from the idea that individuals are responsible for their own development, and this suggests that their progress is a product of their own motivation, commitment and drive. Some assessment tools, for example learning style questionnaires, assume a neutral context, as if all clients are the same gender, class and race and the notions of diversity, status and relative opportunity did not exist. As discussed in Chapter 2, there is also a tendency to ignore the impact of discourse, culture and ideology on clients.

For mentoring and coaching it is necessary to recognize and articulate the power relations in the client's environment, rather than treating power as a 'given' commodity, which leaves the individual feeling helpless. Where mentoring and coaching procedures recognize such power relations and the client becomes aware of the reality of such discourse and identifies practices that dominate relationships in the workplace, there is hope of personal and ultimately organizational transformation.

Enlightened organizations will generate development programmes likely to deliver managers and others with the high-level skills needed to support reflective learning, and these will be the coaches and mentors of the future. Whilst emphasizing the need for taking organizational responsibilities seriously, it is important that the responsibility of the client remains just that, the individual's responsibility to manage his or her own learning, whilst keeping in sight 'the greater good', that is, the needs of the organization as a whole.

If clients feel powerless in a learning relationship, then there will be a lack of trust. Lack of trust means that the clients will not feel able to trust the learning context or any enabler of learning in that context. Given that reflective learning will involve feelings or emotion in addition to thinking and action, a lack of trust will inhibit any display of emotion or vulnerability and therefore openness to learning. When we really learn, particularly that which is potentially transformatory, we lay ourselves open to uncertainty and can be (temporarily) unstable. For the feelings that uncertainty can engender, we need conditions of safety that ensure those expressed feelings are not taken advantage of. Determining who is part of the learning relationship will be important, and it is therefore inappropriate to match clients with their line manager as mentor.

Levels of learning

When individuals learn, they may improve their performance and they may also transform themselves. This has been described as not only doing things right, but also, more challenging, doing the right things (Flood and Romm, 1996: 10). In addition, an organization whose members are capable of reflecting on the learning process, ie learning about learning, is likely to develop, prosper and survive. We can identify these three levels as improvement, transformation and learning about learning:

- Improvement. Reflective learning will deliver improvement, as clients process their work, assessing and reconsidering for improved performance, that is, 'doing things right'. This we identify as reflective learning for improvement.
- Transformation. Reflective learning for transformation offers the potential for clients to move one step further and reconsider their work in strategic terms, questioning and challenging existing patterns, thereby opening the door to creativity and innovation, that is, doing the right things.
- Learning about learning. We also offer the idea of a further level of reflection, which can only occur as a consequence of the first two, and that is reflective learning about learning. This entails an individual or organization standing back from its improvements and transformations and seeking to identify 'how we did that' so that this knowledge can be transferred to future situations.

Reflective learning for improvement is a necessary component for organizational success but it is no longer sufficient for organizations that hope to survive in the world continually subject to change. The ever-changing market environment demands learning that can keep up, developing and creating ever-new ideas and products, whilst keeping in mind the organization's responsibilities to its stakeholders and not just its shareholders. The increasingly globalized economy impacts, along with the rapidity of social change, upon the public and voluntary sectors. In order to keep in the race, the organization needs collectively to stop and reflect, critically, on the organization's purpose. Reflective learning for transformation occurs when clients are enabled to pause and reconsider, preferably with others, the nature of what they are doing. This means more than re-examining the task in hand. It means re-examining the rationale behind what is being done. When such a dialogue with others is enabled throughout a system, the organization collectively reflects, reconsiders and ultimately transforms itself from within.

We move now to discuss what is meant by reflective learning for improvement, reflective learning for transformation, and learning about learning. This can be usefully elaborated by recourse to notions of single and double loop learning.

SINGLE AND DOUBLE LOOP LEARNING

The terms 'single loop learning' and 'double loop learning' were first used by Argyris and Schon (1996) to distinguish between learning for improving the way things are done and learning that transforms the situation. Single loop 'instrumental' learning, whilst it achieves immediate improvement, leaves underlying values and ways of seeing things unchanged. Improvement learning may involve reflection on the given task but is not likely to change it. Double loop learning is learning where assumptions about ways of seeing things are challenged and underlying values are changed (Brockbank and McGill, 1998). Double loop learning, in questioning 'taken-for-granteds' (tfgs), has the potential to bring about a profound shift in underlying values by cracking their paradigms or 'ways of seeing the world'.[1] In the context of evolutionary mentoring, 'In order to see how ideas different from ours exist in their own legitimate framework, it is necessary to leap out from our shell of absolute certainty and construct a whole new world based on some other person's ideas of reality, other assumptions of truth' (Daloz, 1986: 228).

Single loop learning or day-to-day maintenance learning for improvement, meeting goals and altering practice on the basis of experience, enables progress to be made. The concept of effective single loop learning has been described graphically in a well-known diagram by Kolb (1984), where goals are set on the basis of theory, action is taken and, on the basis of this experience and reflection, a new action or plan is devised. For day-to-day learning, the loop is productive and the client gains competence and confidence, ie this is reflective learning for improvement. The process is illustrated in Figure 3.1.

Single loop learning has been identified by Stacey (1993) as typical of what is known as 'ordinary management', which:

■ translates the directives of those higher up in the hierarchy into goals and tasks;
■ monitors the performance of the task in terms of goal achievement;
■ ensures that staff are motivated to perform the task;
■ supplies any skills or efforts that are missing;
■ articulates purpose and culture, so reducing uncertainty.

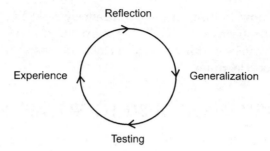

Figure 3.1 *Single loop learning*

Ordinary management is important because 'No organisation can carry out its day-to-day tasks effectively, no organisation can continue to build on and take advantage of its existing strengths, unless it practices ordinary management with a high degree of skill' (Stacey, 1993: 306): hence the justification for single loop learning in day-to-day work. Functionalist mentoring and basic coaching are characterized by single loop learning as their outcome, and they mirror ordinary management in their objectives.

What about evolutionary mentoring and life coaching? We refer now, with permission, to Peter Hawkins's original diagram to illustrate double loop learning in Figure 3.2.

The arrows in the lower circle indicate day-to-day functioning in single loop learning. When conditions are favourable, in reflective dialogue, assumptions or tfgs are questioned, and the client may swing out of the lower circle orbit and begin to traverse the upper circle in double loop learning mode. The client has 'come outside of the box'. The option remains of returning to the single loop when appropriate, perhaps to test a new theory in the normal way, in order to achieve improvement with a new understanding. The single loop orbit is contained and can be traversed within, say, a coaching contract, setting goals within a given cycle of activity or achieving a level of understanding within a professional field. The double loop orbit would occur when reconsidering the whole project with a view to major change, or even reconsidering an organization's purpose, structure or culture, ie learning for transformation. Such an outcome is characteristic of what is known as 'extraordinary management' where:

■ new knowledge is created when the tacit is made explicit and crystallized into an innovation, that is a *recreation* of some aspect of the world according to some new insight or ideal;

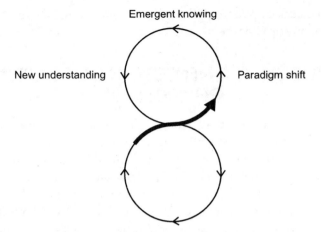

Emergent knowing

New understanding

Paradigm shift

Source: Adapted from an original idea by Peter Hawkins, 1997, in Brockbank and McGill (1998).

Figure 3.2 *Double loop learning*

■ innovative organizations accept the paradox and use their informal organization such as mentoring or coaching as the tool for destroying old paradigms and creating new ones that lead ultimately to concerted action;
■ when they operate informally rather than using formal structures in the organization, people are likely to achieve extraordinary management.

Stacey describes extraordinary management as double loop learning: 'Extraordinary management is concerned with how managers *smash the existing paradigm* and create a new one... create the chaos required to destroy old patterns of perception and behaviour... create new paradigms of perception and behaviour' (Stacey, 1993: 337, original italics).

For individuals, evolutionary mentoring and life coaching are characterized by the transition from single to double loop learning that enables clients to move beyond their existing way of seeing the world with the support and challenge, using reflective dialogue, of their mentor or coach. We should note here that many of our assumptions about life are useful, and the tfgs for reconsideration are those that emerge from clients' own objectives.

What is needed to enable clients to shoot out of the single orbit and traverse the exciting and potentially disturbing orbit of double loop learning? If we were to pursue our analogy of orbits and trajectories, the answer suggests that what is required is *energy* to fuel the 'burn' of a changed trajectory. Where is this energy to come from? There is evidence that emotion supplies the required fuel for double loop learning.

EMOTION IN A MENTORING OR COACHING RELATIONSHIP

The evidence suggests that 'emotion and motivation are inherently connected' (Giddens, 1992: 201) and that double loop or transformative learning can be triggered by strong emotion, through trauma or 'peak' experiences (Brookfield, 1987: 7). The language used to describe such learning indicates the strong emotive content in comments like 'passion to learn', 'hunger for truth' and 'thirst for knowledge'. In addition, the process of questioning and challenging the tfgs can stimulate strong emotions, disturbance, distress and also joy and exhilaration (Brookfield, 1987: 8). We are told that a certain degree of energy or excitement is necessary for learning to occur, so that a crisis may generate transformative learning.

How can mentors enable their clients to access their emotions?

The capacity to deal with emotion appropriately, known as 'emotional intelligence' (EQ), together with IQ is a predictor of future success in business (Dulewicz and Higgs, 1998: 42–45). EQ has been defined as 'the ability to understand and reflectively manage one's own and other people's feelings' (Mayer, 1999: 49), and those who are emotionally adept are those who 'know and manage their own feelings well and who read and deal effectively with other people's feelings' (Goleman, 1995: 36). The traditional overemphasis on action and thinking has left a gap in our understanding of the learning process, and mentoring and coaching when used in an evolutionary form will redress the imbalance.

The idea that transformative learning can occur where emotional material is ignored, whilst favoured in many rationalist contexts, fails to appreciate the nature of the changes that take place when a meaning structure is transformed through reflection. Jack Mezirow clarifies how our meaning *schemes* or patterns may be refined and elaborated by reflecting on the content and process of what we do, in single loop mode. However, he maintains that the deeper meaning *perspectives*, which grow from psychological and cultural codes, are not nearly so responsive to simple or self-reflection. What is needed for transformation of perspectives, based as they are on cultural codes, is a process involving 'a critique of assumptions... by examining their origins, nature and consequences' (Mezirow, 1994: 223). The recommended method for such learning to occur is dialogue, as 'dialogue is central to human communication and learning' (Mezirow, 1994: 225). The chances of such a critique being achieved without generating emotion are remote and, where emotion is denied or suppressed, transformative learning is unlikely. Other no-go areas in organizational discourse have been identified by Fineman and Gabriel as chaos, uncertainty, emotionality, humour, grief, sexuality and the boundary between work and non-work, all of which the mentor/client relationship may address (1994: 376).

In order to recognize the existence of emotion in learning situations, we turn again to Argyris and Schon (1996), as they identify the phenomenon of defensive reasoning.

Defensive reasoning

The tendency to overlook the obvious, the tfgs in life, is supremely human. Some of the tfgs form quite powerful defences, known as 'defensive reasoning', which are difficult and painful to dislodge. As clients, the prospect of really looking at what is taken for granted in our work and analysing our defensive reasoning is threatening on four counts:

- ■ We may lose control.
- ■ We may not win.
- ■ We may not be able to suppress negative feelings.
- ■ We may not be rational.

For managers trained in the Western rational system, such threats are real and powerful, and the managers resort to defensive reasoning in order to protect against these threats, maintaining comfort and, in the process, cloning another generation of managers in their own image. For managers to engage in reflection they need to be confident in themselves and able to tolerate doubt and uncertainty about their decisions. Managers who can face up to the possibility that they might have so-called irrational feelings, and express them, are prepared to display their vulnerability. This is done by naming what is taken for granted in the work context and staying with the discomfort that may be engendered by such naming. An example is the recognition that a punitive appraisal system is demotivating employees and a commitment to replace it with a developmental programme. Needless to say, such moves can generate differences in the organization, and this may lead to conflict. Where conflicts arise, the political process in organizations rarely offers facilitation for resolving differences, thereby inhibiting organizational learning.

Argyris and Schon (1996: 78) offer a method of analysing the tfgs in our work, which transfers well to the mentoring or coaching situation, known as 'the left-hand side of the page method'. Here the client revisits or anticipates a problematic event. The page is divided into two columns and the facts of the story are entered on the right-hand side. In the left-hand column the client is invited to note the thoughts and feelings associated with each stage of the story. The content of the left- hand-side column is highly illuminating, as strong feelings are revealed that are not likely to be said. When clients become aware of some of their left-hand-side material, they are at the cusp of double loop learning.

Evolutionary mentors or life coaches acknowledge the left-hand side of their clients' material and, through reflective dialogue, offer them opportunities for double loop learning. The process is helped by attending to the three domains of learning, ie feeling as well as thinking and doing, and the five senses, hearing, seeing, touching and even tasting and smelling, as carriers of emotional information. If the learning process is limited to one of the three domains, the others are affected and learning is not so effective. To accommodate the full range of human potential, development should address all three domains of learning, ie thinking, feeling and doing. The importance of *integrating* all three domains of learning for learning at work has been emphasized by Ronnie Lessem: 'The all round quality that we are bringing to bear upon our learning enterprise is represented in the marriage between thought, feeling and action' (1991: x).

Mentoring that concentrates on one or two out of the three domains will be less effective, and an effective process should seek to 'tease out' learning in the missing domains, monitoring the balance between the three domains and guiding our questioning or explorations to cover all three as fully as possible. In particular, as a mentor you may have a tendency to avoid the emotional content of learning and this would disadvantage your client, as 'An emotional content to learning is inevitable, because learning begins in that part of the brain' (Rose and Nicholl, 1997: 31).

For example, where a client is discussing an aspect of his or her work and the coach notices some negative body language, uncovering how the client is feeling may assist his or her development. This suggests that all the human senses are brought to bear on the learning endeavour. An awareness of touch and smell, as well as hearing, sight and voice, is likely to enhance and enlarge the learning experience. Eric Jensen in *Brain Based Learning and Teaching* (1995) suggests that 'all learning involves our body, our emotions and our attitudes'. Hence the time and place where mentoring occurs may affect the learning process. A noisy or uncomfortable environment will inhibit learning, and mentoring is best undertaken in a quiet restful place, without interruption. We discuss learning and the body further on page 40. We now address some of the psychology that underpins learning in mentoring and coaching.

PSYCHOLOGICAL PRINCIPLES OF LEARNING

Humanist approaches to learning recognize the power in every human being to learn in a self-directed way, finding the appropriate method and medium for whatever the self desires to learn, and they begin from the following beliefs:

1. People are OK; they are fundamentally good.
2. A person is a whole person.
3. Human beings are driven to change and grow.
4. The 'abundance' model rather than the 'deficiency' one is suitable for personal development.
5. Humans operate with a spiritual dimension.

Evolutionary mentoring and life coaching require trust in the client and confidence in the client's capacity for development. Evolutionary mentors and life coaches hold the belief that clients are fundamentally sincere and desire to change and develop. In addition, humanist principles of learning emphasize the importance of being authentic rather than being impersonal, and we discuss mentor congruence in Chapter 11.

Carl Rogers (1983) described the conditions for learning and development as 'person-centred', a statement that grows from the humanistic belief in the 'actualizing tendency' of human beings, the striving towards growth and development present in every person. What psychological climate in a learning relationship makes possible the release of the individual's capacity for learning and development? Rogers offers three conditions for a person-centred climate:

■ congruence, ie genuineness, realness, sharing feelings and attitudes rather than opinions and judgements;
■ unconditional positive regard (UPR), ie acceptance and 'prizing' of the other;
■ empathy, ie understanding of the other's feelings, experience and attitudes and communicating that understanding.

We must not leave psychological principles of learning without mentioning defence mechanisms, which, like boundaries, are not strictly part of a humanistic approach, coming as they do from traditional psychology. We discuss boundaries in Chapter 13. The typical defence mechanisms that are likely to appear in mentoring or coaching relationships are the following:

- denial – unconsciously being unaware of what is happening;
- displacement – unconsciously expressing a feeling to the wrong person;
- projection – unconsciously sending away aspects of the self to another;
- identification – unconsciously taking on aspects of an admired other;
- introjection – unconsciously becoming what an important other says;
- transference – unconsciously projecting aspects of self on to another based on past experience.

For many, the idea of defence mechanisms is not relevant to mentoring or coaching. However, there is plenty of evidence that defence mechanisms are alive and well in such relationships, as transference is now understood to be 'an entirely natural occurrence in any relationship... a form of projection... involving archetypal material' (Jacoby, 1984: 19). We discuss handling defence mechanisms in Chapter 11 and move now to another mainly unconscious aspect of learning.

LEARNING AND THE BODY

In this section we aim to explore a hidden dimension in modern learning theory – the body. First, we introduce the idea of two selves, identified by Gallwey (1974), and discuss how they interact in a learning situation like mentoring or coaching. Second, we explore the 'typological error' of Descartes, which has divided mind and body for centuries (Ryle, 1983) and discuss how this dominates learning approaches like mentoring and coaching. See also Antonio Damasio's (1995) powerful description of Descartes' Error. Third, we identify what has been called the headquarters of emotional evaluation, the limbic system or the emotional brain, and discuss how this supports transformational learning.

The two selves

This idea came from Tim Gallwey's (1974) analysis of his tennis clients who he noticed 'talked to themselves'. This usually silent dialogue is common to most adults. The 'I', or self 1, seems to give instructions, while 'myself', or self 2, seems to perform the action (Gallwey, 1974: 13).

When a typical dialogue between self 1 and self 2 is analysed, what emerges is a self 1, the thinker, that does not trust self 2, the doer, although self 2, because it includes the unconscious mind and nervous system, hears everything, forgets nothing and is anything but stupid. When people struggle to improve their performance (be it tennis or giving presentations or delegating) by thinking too much and trying too hard, self 1 sabotages the innate competence of self 2 to do the job. The thinking activity of self 1 interferes with the natural 'doing' activity of self 2. In a mentoring or coaching situation an understanding of the effects of this internal dialogue assists both parties to identify barriers to learning and development. The skilled mentor or coach will enable the client to articulate the inner dialogue and submit it to rigorous inspection and evaluation so that judgemental self-talk like 'I'm just no good as a manager' and 'I'll never do it' can be recognized as interference from self 1 and addressed in the mentoring or coaching relationship.

How did self 1 get to be so dominant? The answer is historical and although the concept of mind versus body goes back to Plato and Aristotle it has been blamed on Descartes (Ryle, 1983) and referred to as Descartes' Error (Damasio, 1995). The Western way of understanding the mind separated it from the body, categorizing its activities as totally unconnected and different from bodily experience. Modern surgery has established that this is not the case, and that the mind and body are linked by continuous electrical and chemical communication (Rothschild, 2000). In addition, because the mind differed from the corporeal body (thought to be a site of sinfulness) it was believed to be innately superior. Western educators have not caught up with science and still operate as though the mind can be addressed by directly ignoring the body and is the superior partner in learning and behaviour. Hence self 1 has been led to believe that it can order self 2 about and that self 1 should decide what happens without reference to self 2. Needless to say, self 2 asserts itself and we find ourselves behaving in ways we don't understand and are sometimes ashamed of. For learning, the dominance of self 1 means that bodily information is neglected, leaving only half the story to be learnt. Modern person-centred approaches to learning and development have the potential to reverse this and reconnect self 1 and self 2.

To address the tendency of self 1 to criticize and undermine self 2 destructively, Gallwey recommends that, first, we persuade self 1 to trust self 2 to do what is asked of it and relax its surveillance of self 2 and, second, we instruct self 2 with images rather than words.

Quieting the mind and self 1

The process of quieting the mind means less thinking, with all its attendant judging, worrying, hoping and fearing. The stilled mind is aware of the here and now, and connected to self 2 in harmony, so that learning can occur. How to quiet the mind?

Some people use meditation to practise quieting their conscious mind by deep relaxation and concentration on an object or word, which disallows the 'buzzing' of stressful thinking. Letting go of judgements and negative thoughts is associated with a quieter, calmer mind. Positive thinking techniques seek to replace negative thoughts with positive ones, and because these are judgements too they agitate rather than quiet the mind. The state of stillness we seek has been called 'mindfulness', as the mind is full of the present, excluding the judgements and fears, concentrating on the here and now. Mindfulness is 'about being aware of what is happening in the present, on a moment by moment basis. It is an intentional becoming aware of our bodies and minds and the world around us whilst not making judgements about what we like or don't like in what we find there' (Landale, 2005). We present a mindfulness exercise in Appendix 2.

In addition, for transformative learning it is necessary to revise the destructive core beliefs embedded in the emotional brain, which informs self 2. The emotional brain learns negative core beliefs from uncaring or threatening messages from childhood, and associates them with feelings like hurt, anger, fear and envy. Positive core beliefs are learnt from caring and supportive environments and are associated with feelings like joy, trust, confidence and contentment. The emotional brain learns in order to survive. When under threat or perceived threat, the emotional brain overrules reason in order to survive and takes us into a trance-like state where only the core beliefs are relevant. The influence of this on advanced or transformative learning is obviously powerful, as effective reflective dialogue is a challenge to just those core beliefs that are lodged within the emotional brain. The calming of the self 1 part of us enables us to 'hear' our self 2, which is lodged in our emotional brain, and we discuss how to access self 2 below.

Images for self 2

Imagery is a thought process that invokes and uses the senses – a communication between perception, emotion and bodily change. Imagination affects the body in powerful ways, both positively and negatively. The connection between image and health is well documented (Rothschild, 2000), and we believe that image may also influence learning and is therefore relevant in mentoring and coaching. Aspects of imagery that mentors and coaches may want to be aware of include the following:

- Images relate to physiological states, eg sweating, blushing or feeling sick.
- Images may either precede or follow these changes.
- Images can be induced by conscious, deliberate behaviours, eg closing eyes, as well as by subconscious acts, eg reverie or dreaming.

(Achterberg, 1985: 115)

We look now at details of the systems mentioned above, and discuss the scientific evidence for the statements.

Evidence

There are two parts of the brain sending messages to the body, and the right and left hemispheres have developed specialized functions, through evolution or a person's own experiences. The left brain is thought to attend to language for 87 per cent of right-handers and 50 per cent of left-handers (Bogen, 1969; Sperry and Gazzaniga, 1967). In addition, the left brain processes information in linear fashion and specializes in analysis rather than synthesis. The right hemisphere stores and processes images, so that non-verbal representations rather than words are used here. Physiological evidence supports the idea that imagining oneself engaging in a physical activity like running or golf triggers activity in our motor neurons, as well as changes in blood glucose and gastrointestinal activity (Jacobson, 1929). The evidence concludes that the image effect connects with both the voluntary part of the autonomic nervous system and the involuntary part, not normally under conscious control. For learning, the most important finding is that images create a bridge between conscious processing of information and physiological changes in the body. These changes provide the energy and will that precede action, as well as the 'burn' for double loop, transformational learning, which we discussed earlier.

How does this relate to learning and development in a mentoring or coaching context?

It seems likely that, when clients in a mentoring or coaching relationship can access their self 2 and visualize what they want to achieve, success is more likely. The two selves described above are equivalent to the thinking brain and the emotional brain. How can mentors or coaches enable their clients to access their emotional brain and quieten their thinking brain for long enough for this to happen? We believe that the relationship forged between mentor or coach and client will support the process, as the couple learn to trust and respect each other. The person-centred approach implicitly promotes communication that values the messages from self 2 and builds a gentle but solid relationship. Mentors and coaches may like to learn the approach by taking a course in horse-whispering (Gqubule 2005), where managers are persuaded, by working with a horse, to leave their 'command and control' practices aside and learn to trust the non-verbal body messages from their staff and adopt patient and affectionate styles of leadership. It seems likely that most mentors and coaches will opt for more conventional learning and development methods, and we discuss the training and development of mentors and coaches in Chapter 12.

Learning can be perceived in a variety of ways: new knowledge and understanding; a change in behaviour; or a revision of attitude. As a consequence, mentoring may lead to improvement in performance, or it may lead to transformation and then perhaps to learning about learning itself. When clients dare to traverse the double loop by confronting their taken-for-granteds (tfgs), they may transform their view of the world. A clever organization builds on such individual transformation and indeed will encourage and enable it to happen through executive mentoring or coaching. The complex power of discourse and culture is recognized by such an organization, and development programmes including mentoring are likely to reflect this. A learning environment that nurtures single and double loop learning and offers clients a chance to reflect on their learning demands high-level skills in those enabling learning, either formally or informally. We move now to explore how best to achieve the reflection needed for all types of learning through reflective dialogue.

NOTE

1 Here 'world' is used to denote the realities of an individual, group or organization.

4 Reflective dialogue and learning

We now connect learning theory to practice through the use of reflective dialogue, the basis of successful mentoring or coaching. First, we differentiate reflective dialogue for learning from everyday dialogue, and explore how it leads to the different levels of learning. We review research that corresponds with different levels of learning and discuss how to achieve them. Reflective dialogue is compared with internal dialogue, and intentional dialogue is recognized as part of the mentoring and coaching process.

Reflective dialogue is an exchange between mentor and client that promotes learning. The theory set out below provides the underpinning that reveals evolutionary mentoring or life coaching as a valid and relevant approach to learning and development. The aim here is to show how dialogue itself contributes to learning and development. The second aim is to distinguish learning that leads to improvement from learning that leads to a transformation of one kind or another. Dialogue is an integral part of the mentoring or coaching process. It is important to explain the particular meaning we give to dialogue and how dialogue within a mentoring or coaching relationship can differ from other forms of interaction. We distinguish dialogue, as that which takes place between people, from internal dialogue within individuals. Internal dialogue is important but it may not lead to the kind of learning and development to which we will refer. We return to this point on page 53.

Dialogue does occur quite naturally between people. Dialogue in the form of discussion where the speaker's intention is to hold forth in order to convey his or her knowledge is unlikely to lead to some new understanding. This form of dialogue is often characterized by one party claiming to be expert in interaction with another who may not be.

For the receiver, what is received may be significant, but the mode is primarily one way.

Dialogue has been explored by Bohm (1996), who contrasts dialogue with the word 'discussion'. For him, discussion really means to break things up:

> It emphasises the idea of analysis, where there may be many points of view, and where everybody is presenting a different one – analysing and breaking up. That obviously has its value, but is limited, and it will not get us very far beyond our various points of view. Discussion is almost like a ping-pong game, where people are batting the ideas back and forth and the object of the game is to win or to get points for yourself.
>
> **(Bohm, 1996: 7)**

On the other hand, Bohm offers a definition of true dialogue as a process where 'meaning is not static – it is flowing. And if we have the meaning being shared, then it is flowing among us' (1996: 40).

This is a useful point at which to introduce the notion of 'separated' and 'connected' knowing, originally set out in Belenky et al (1986) and developed further in the writing of Tarule (1996), a sequel to Belenky. Separated knowing leads to 'a kind of dialogue that values the ability to pronounce or "report" one's ideas, whereas [connected knowing] values a dialogue that relies on relationship as one enters meaningful conversations that connect one's ideas with another's and establish "rapport"' (Belenky et al, 1986: 277).

Separated knowing is very similar to Bohm's didactic discussion. Connected knowing is that which suggests the creation of that flow of meaning suggested by Bohm (1996: Chapter 2). It is appropriate here to introduce the work of Belenky at al (1986), who are central to our concepts of learning and development.

STAGES OF LEARNING

Belenky et al wrote *Women's Ways of Knowing* in 1986. The original research behind their book was undertaken to bring attention to the 'missing voices of women in our understanding of how people learn'. Prior to their work the only scheme of personal learning and development in adults was conducted by Perry (1970) and he only recorded the results amongst Harvard men. Belenky and her colleagues argued that this represented a major failure in not examining closely women's lives and experience. Their project was both an extension of Perry's work and a critique of his scheme.

They undertook research with a group of 135 women of different ages and ethnic and class backgrounds from urban and rural communities and with varying degrees of education, not just higher education. They included high school dropouts as well as women with graduate or professional qualifications. This was itself a breakthrough, given that most research in this area at the time was restricted to white, middle-class groups, often male. They intentionally sought a diversity of backgrounds in order 'to see the common ground that women share, regardless of background' (Belenky et al, 1986: 13). Their aim was stated thus: 'Let us listen to the voices of diverse women to hear what they say about the varieties of female experience' (Goldberger et al, 1996: 4). Five perspectives emerged:

1. Silence – a position of not knowing in which the person feels voiceless, powerless and mindless.
2. Received knowing – a position at which knowledge and authority are construed as outside the self and invested in a powerful and knowing other from whom one is expected to learn. We recognize this as an objectivist view of reality, discussed in Chapter 2.
3. Subjective knowing – in which knowledge is personal, private and based on intuition and/or feeling states rather than on thought and articulated ideas that are defended with evidence. We recognize this as a subjectivist view of reality, discussed in Chapter 2.
4. Procedural knowing – the position at which techniques and procedures for acquiring, validating and evaluating knowledge claims are developed and honoured. Within this sub-head they also described two modes of knowing (which are crucial for our purposes as authors):
   – separated knowing, characterized by a distanced, sceptical and impartial stance toward that which one is trying to know (reasoning against), which is another objectivist take on reality;
   – connected knowing, characterized by a stance or belief and an entering into the place of the other person or the idea that one is trying to know (reasoning with), which we recognize as another subjectivist stance.
5. Constructed knowing – a position at which truth is understood to be contextual; knowledge is recognized as tentative, not absolute; and it is understood that the knower is part of what is known and has a share in constructing it. In their sample of women, constructed knowers valued multiple approaches to knowing (subjective and

objective, connected and separate) and insisted on bringing the self and personal commitment into the centre of the knowing process.

(Goldberger *et al*, 1996: 4–5[1])

The first learning stage of silence, where women had yet to discover their mind, is a position of powerlessness. Many mentoring programmes seek to rescue people perceived to be in this position, and an example of this is given in the First Nation case study on page 90.

The second stage of received knowing is reminiscent of 'received wisdom', the term that suggests the presence of a prevailing discourse, and here basic coaching can be found. When the third stage of subjective knowing is reached, where the subjective world is recognized for the first time, then mentors are edging towards engagement mentoring although their functionalist agenda is likely to remain in place.

The fourth stage, described as 'procedural knowledge', was realized in two forms: separated and connected. Researchers found the connected mode as more typical of female conditioning, whilst the separated mode was akin to men's. When Perry's men moved towards an understanding that all knowledge is relative, they are thought to have adopted a strategy, also found among college women, entitled 'separated knowing'. The separation strategy, known as 'the doubting game', is characterized by the objectification of the other (Elbow, 1973: 148). A powerful account of relationships based on such objectification can be found in Buber (1994), where seeing the other as a thing-to-be-used is characteristic of an I–It orientation, whilst an aspiration to connect with the other as a person reveals an I–Thou orientation. Traditional training tends to engage in separated knowledge, where discussions often become adversarial interactions, and 'It's not personal' is something to be proud of. The adversarial jousting has been called 'ceremonial combat' and is a style peculiarly attractive to men, as to many women it seems silly. Indeed the feminist Adrienne Rich declares that 'rhetoric is a masculine adversary style of discourse' (1979: 138).

Connected knowing, which can be described as the 'believing game' (Elbow, 1998: 149), is learnt through empathy, being without judgement, and coming from an attitude of trust is quite the opposite of separated knowing. However, connected knowing differs from simple subjectivism as it is 'the deliberate imaginative extension of one's understanding into positions that initially feel wrong or remote' (Belenky *et al*, 1986: 121). There is no reason to suppose that connectedness is the preserve of women only, and connected knowing is available to men as well as women. The principle of connectedness is essential to evolutionary mentoring or coaching, as it involves the client as a whole person, rather than a recipient of facts and figures, and acknowledges his or her hopes and desires, as well as offering a mutuality of understanding.

Connected knowing prepares learners for their fifth and final stage of development, the adoption of constructivist approaches to knowledge. For the constructivist, 'all knowledge is constructed, and the knower is an intimate part of the known' (Belenky et al, 1986: 137). In this category of learning, there is passion and participation in the act of knowing, which, as a philosopher, Sara Ruddick knew only too well: 'instead of developing arguments that could bring my feelings to heel, I allowed my feelings to inform my most abstract thinking' (1984: 150). Such a stance alters one's orientation to experts, as 'an expert becomes somebody whose answers reflect the complexity... the situation holds' (Belenky et al, 1986: 139), and constructivist learning is characterized by empathy and connectedness, so relationship is a key ingredient in what is a completely holistic stance towards knowledge and learning. The components of constructivist knowledge are those that lead to a recognition of relationship in learning, ie connectedness to another, as above, empathy and awareness of feelings, all characteristics of evolutionary mentoring or life coaching.

For Belenky et al (1986), the use of the terms 'separated knowing' and 'connected knowing' is intrinsic to their work. We want to explain these terms more fully, for they are a valuable way of understanding mentoring relationships based as they are on particular forms of dialogue. By going to the root of how we discourse with each other we can understand how a mentoring and coaching dialogue is an appropriate format for transformational learning and development.

Separate[2] and connected knowing

We can now return to the terms 'connected knowing' and 'separate knowing' within the context of mentoring and coaching. 'Connected knowing' means the mentor suspends judgement in an attempt to understand clients' ways of making sense of their experience. In the words of Elbow (1998: 149), mentors 'play the believing game', with questions like 'What do you see?... Give me the vision in your head' and 'You are having an experience I don't have. Help me to have it' (Elbow, 1986: 261). The mentor is seeking to understand where a client is coming from and what it means to the client as 'knower' of that experience.

In contrast, when conducting a dialogue through separate knowing mentors or coaches will relate in a different way to the client. They will, in Elbow's words, 'play the doubting game' (1998: 148), looking for flaws in the client's reasoning, examining the person's statements with a critical eye and insisting that the client justify every point he or she makes. With separate knowing the dialogue is about testing the validity of propositions or statements or stories against some objective criterion and/or view of the world. It tends to be an adversarial stance – the mode of discourse is argument. Functionalist mentoring and basic coaching is typified by separate knowing. With connected knowing the dialogue is about understanding what the person is saying – his or her experience. The mode of discourse is 'one of allies, even advocates, of the position they are examining' (Clinchy, 1996: 208).

The key for us is the context. Evolutionary mentoring or life coaching is a particular context where understanding where their client is 'coming from in their experience' is significant in enabling mentors to work with that experience. '"Playing the believing game" becomes a *procedure* that guides the interaction with other minds. It is not the *result* of the interaction' (Clinchy, 1996: 209). In other words, I do not necessarily have to agree with the person's stance, but I suspend my judgement in order to understand that person's stance.

Connected knowing as a procedure

Clinchy refers to connected knowing as originally a serendipitous discovery when they undertook the research leading to their publication, *Women's Ways of Knowing* (Belenky *et al*, 1986): 'Connected knowing was originally a serendipitous discovery. We did not ask the women we interviewed to tell us about it; they did so spontaneously, and from their comments we constructed the procedure as a sort of "ideal type"' (Clinchy, 1996: 205).

Similarly, when mentoring we have found that the interactions that lead to increased understanding of the client's experience rather than attempt to 'knock it' actually worked, and clients shifted their understanding of their worlds without having to be convinced by the 'rational' arguments of another. A very ordinary example here will be given.

In an early mentoring session one of the authors listened to his client wishing to sort her work priorities. To this end she brought a long list of things she was attempting to do currently in her work. As a separate knower, I might have challenged the list and no doubt have sought to get her to order the list according to some logic and criteria. In fact I listened to her explanation of what she was doing, not doing, frustrations, blockages and feelings toward her work. The purpose here, rather than seeking clarification, was simply to ascertain what she found important and how she felt about it all. At the end of our session she had done some sorting but there was a sense of the unfinished about it. Slowly, at our subsequent meetings the list became a recognition of something wider and deeper – her recognition of a shift in the potential direction of her career. We could not have foreseen this and it would have been inappropriate at an earlier stage to have drawn that conclusion.

As our experience as mentors and coaches developed we realized that getting into the world of our clients was not only effective from their standpoint, but it was also, in Clinchy's words, a useful *procedure* to adopt to enable the learners to understand their world and to work from there.

Procedure as transformation

The procedure we are adopting in our mentoring is a shift in culture by moving away from the prevailing discourse in the worlds of work that we live in – be it business, education or training. In reflective learning there is an explicit aim through the process to get into the world of our client. This does not mean a subjective immersion in that world. It is to try to understand where the other is coming from. The emphasis here is on the word 'try'. It is not easy or natural. Clinchy quotes the anthropologist Clifford Geertz (1986) here:

> Comprehending that which is, in some manner or form, alien to us and likely to remain so, without either smoothing it over with vacant murmurs of common humanity... or dismissing it as charming, lovely even, but inconsequent, is a skill we have arduously to learn and having learnt it, work continuously to keep it alive; it is not a natural[3] capacity, like depth perception or the sense of balance, upon which we can complacently rely.
>
> **(in Clinchy, 1996: 209)**

In early mentoring or coaching sessions, it is easy to endeavour to get into the client's world and there may be a temptation to make assumptions about that world and to base interventions upon those assumptions without checking if they are accurate. Having made assumptions about the other's world, we may then proceed to ask questions that detract from his or her world on the basis that we now know the client's world. In fact the dialogue may be nearer our world than that of our client.

We should emphasize that getting into the client's world through connected knowing does not mean that mentors are acritically accepting that world. This would mean a subjectivism that would suggest that the mentor accepts whatever the client says as a valid view of the world. The point for the connected knower is to understand the client's world, not necessarily to accept it. Understanding what the learner expresses doesn't mean that mentors have to agree. Geertz (1986) explains this as: 'understanding in the sense of comprehension, perception and insight needs to be distinguished from "understanding" in the sense of agreement of opinion, union of sentiment, or commonality of commitment... We must learn to grasp what we cannot embrace' (in Clinchy, 1996: 217).

To be really heard as a client in connected knowing terms is to be affirmed and validated, and this is achieved by the mentor 'swinging boldly into the mind' of the client. Clinchy (1996: 218) suggests that by 'swinging boldly into the mind of another', two perversions of connected knowing are prevented. The first, known in the USA as the 'Californian fuck-off', is typified by a response like 'Well, given your background, I can see where you're coming from', which is simply patronizing and a totally negative response. The second is typified by a quick response like 'I know how you feel' when in fact the person has little idea or quite the wrong idea.

The relatedness that arises when connected knowing occurs has echoes in a story we have of a recent week-long workshop introducing mentoring to senior government personnel. Following the first day, when we arrived at the start of the next day of the workshop (and each day thereafter) we would ask the participants for their overnight thoughts. The purpose of this was to address any concerns or reflections about the previous day and was useful in grounding the workshop at the beginning of the day. We asked on the third morning for overnight thoughts. One of the participants told a story to us and his colleagues. He had telephoned his partner late the previous evening and she had relayed to him her upset at how she had been treated very negatively by her manager that day despite undertaking all that had been required of her. Our storyteller asked questions essentially about what had happened and tried to understand how she felt. She worked through on the phone her feelings about the event and created her own picture about the interaction with her manager. Our participant told us that this was the first time he had ever done this with his partner. Usually on hearing her woes he would have launched into giving her solutions. He was surprised by his change in behaviour, which he attributed to the work he was doing at the workshop. He had swung boldly into the mind of his partner without being judgemental and had endeavoured to understand her world of work and the relationship with her manager, a good example of connected knowing.

We can now summarize the story so far.

As evolutionary mentors or life coaches, we enter into a dialogue with our client. The dialogue that we engage in can be termed one of connected knowing, that is, we endeavour to enter our client's world in order to understand where the client is coming from. It is a procedure to enable mentors to enter the world of their client and possibly to learn from it as well. The form the dialogue takes represents a cultural shift from that prevailing in many work situations. We now explore how this dialogue enables reflection and reflective learning.

REFLECTION AND REFLECTIVE DIALOGUE

There are many definitions of reflection, and they tend to say what reflection is but not how to do it. For instance, 'reflection is a generic term for those intellectual and affective activities in which individuals engage to explore their experiences in order to lead to new understandings and appreciation' (Boud, Keogh and Walker, 1985: 3) or reflection is 'the process of internally examining and exploring an issue of concern, triggered by an experience, which creates and clarifies meaning in terms of self, which results in a changed conceptual perspective' (Boyd and Fales, 1983: 100).

Our definition describes not only what reflection is but also how to achieve it: 'We define reflective learning as an intentional process, where social context and experience are acknowledged, in which learners are active individuals, wholly present, engaging with another, open to challenge, and the outcome involves transformation as well as improvement for both individuals and their organisation' (Brockbank, McGill and Beech, 2002: 6).

The idea of reflection as an individual activity, pursued in private, in isolation, is a persistent one. It belongs to the rational model of learning that suggests that the cognitive mind alone can solve any problem, sort out any confusion, because the mind is all-powerful and any contribution from anywhere else is dismissed. However, we maintain that, while intrapersonal reflection is effective and may offer opportunities for deep learning, which may or may not be shared with another, *it is ultimately not enough to promote transformatory learning*. On the other hand, providing for interpersonal reflection in reflective dialogue with another in a mentoring or coaching relationship guarantees that learners are challenged, that double loop learning is an option and that the transformatory learning that results from dialogue is a real potential outcome.

The importance of reflection for individual learning is understood at all levels of learning, from reflective learning for improvement (single loop or maintenance learning), through reflective learning for transformation (double loop or evolutionary learning), to our third level of learning, that is, where the learner goes one step further to consider and reflect upon how the single and double loop learning was achieved, in other words reflective learning about learning (Argyris and Schon, 1996: 20).

Reflection has been identified as part of the mentoring process by David Clutterbuck, who refers to the personal reflective space (PRS) of a client, which occurs in private and is the result of intrapersonal dialogue, ie a dialogue with the self.

Internal dialogue

Clutterbuck's reference to personal reflective space suggests that it usually happens:

> with the mind cluttered with all sorts of issues, concerns and thoughts. When the learner makes the transition into personal reflective space (PRS), he or she is usually responding to a learning trigger. For some (relatively few) people, this can be closing the office door and shutting the world out. For another it can be a repetitious activity (for example, jogging, ironing, driving a familiar route home), a period of enforced inactivity (for example in an aeroplane or train), or simply relaxing in the bath! However they achieve PRS, people... focus their thinking down on one issue for a period of quality time... An 'inner dialogue' takes place...
>
> Rearranging the problem more clearly often leads to significant insight and understanding. This in turn allows the learner to reframe a problem in a way that makes it easier, or at least clearer, to deal with. Alternative solutions give way under examination to some specific actions that the learner can take.
>
> **(1998: 16, parentheses in original)**

Clutterbuck's diagram in Figure 4.1 conveys how in that space the effect of internalized energy releases the learner to deal with the issue now that he or she understands it better.

Clutterbuck acknowledges that, when a learner is with another in dialogue, dyadic reflective space (DRS) adds 'external dialogue' to the inner dialogue by providing another perspective, asking questions not previously considered and drawing on other experience. We acknowledge the value of PRS. However, we consider that, by virtue of the dialogue in the mentoring or coaching relationship, which resembles Clutterbuck's DRS, the client is more likely to leap beyond his or her 'tfgs' and therefore have a better chance of moving into double loop learning.

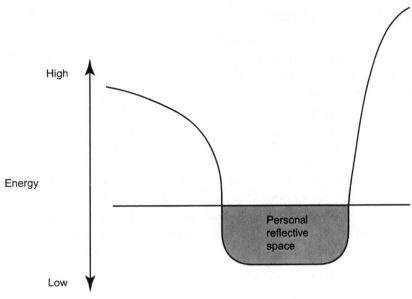

Source: Clutterbuck (1998: 16)

Figure 4.1 *Personal reflective space*

We distinguish internal dialogue, within individuals, from dialogue with another. For, without dialogue, reflection is limited to the insights of the individual (which are not to be underestimated, as Clutterbuck has shown). Personal reflection demands detachment on the part of self, to look at another part of self, and in this there is a danger of self-deception (Habermas, 1974). On the other hand, dialogue that takes place with another reflects our view that learning is not merely an individualistic process. Jarvis (1987) stresses that 'learning always takes place within a social context and that the learner is also to some extent a social construct, so that learning should be regarded as a social phenomenon as well as an individualistic one'.

Clients as learners do not operate in a social vacuum and hence their learning does not take place in a vacuum. We are all imbued with the influences of our personal biography and the social and economic forces that mediate the way we see the world and ourselves in it. We describe these in Chapter 2 as our 'dispositions'.

We attend now to the detail of reflective dialogue and its potential for transformatory learning.

Reflective dialogue

Reflective dialogue or reflection-with-another is distinguished from internal dialogue, where reflection is limited to the insights of the individual. The detachment of self required to look critically at the self is difficult to achieve, and there is a danger of self-deception. Individualistic learning isolates learners and leaves them to their own view of the world, a view that is mediated by personal biography and social and economic forces; these give rise to 'assumptions, beliefs, perceptions and ways of construing and acting on experience' (Weil and McGill, 1989: 247). The learners are at the subjective stage of learning described earlier. Such assumptions, beliefs etc tend to remain untouched by internal dialogue, but may be challenged by reflective dialogue-with-another, through connected learning. Dialogue-with-another offers opportunities for reflective learning at all three levels (described on page 32):

1. Reflective dialogue-with-another may lead to a reconsideration of how things are being done and how things can be improved. This we name 'reflective learning for improvement' and place it in the functionalist quadrant of our map in Figure 2.2.
2. Reflective dialogue-with-another also offers the possibility of engaging at the edge of those assumptions and beliefs, reconsidering the tfgs in relation to self-generated goals, and this we have identified as 'reflective learning for transformation'. We place such connected knowing, with the possibility of constructivist learning, in the evolutionary quadrant of our map in Figure 2.2.
3. Reflective dialogue-with-another, when improvement or transformation has occurred, can take learning one step further, so that clients learn about learning itself, from their experience as reflective learners in mentoring or coaching relationships. For example, the realization that a particular method of production is economically sound but environmentally damaging may lead to altered methods, a transformation perhaps. In addition, mentors, coaches and clients may choose to identify what factors enabled the realization to emerge and the change to be implemented, that is, the client reflects upon his or her reflective learning. Consideration of what issues were considered in dialogue and how they were processed would enable clients to pinpoint the key elements of their learning for future reference, and this applies to organizations too.

What is dialogue-with-another?

For effective reflective learning, intentional dialogue that occurs in a mentoring or coaching session is necessary. Naturally occurring dialogue may reflect the power differences in a situation and this can inhibit learning. So the mentor whose dialogue with a client takes the form of a monologue about how things should be done, with which the client is obliged to agree, is unlikely to promote reflective learning for improvement or transformation! In addition, the casual conversation does not carry the requisite safety needed for reflective dialogue leading to transformative learning.

We identified the characteristics of reflective dialogue (Brockbank and McGill, 1998) as dialogue that 'engages the person (who is in dialogue) at the edge of their knowledge, sense of self and the world'. Intentional dialogue provides the safety for voicing the realities of the client's world, and ensures that the implications for the client and his or her learning are attended to by means of what has been called 'inclusion' (Buber, 1965). We draw on Buber (1965: 97) for an explanation of inclusion:

> Its elements are first, a relation, of no matter what kind, between two persons, second an event experienced by them in common, in which at least one of them actively participates, and third, the fact that this one person, without forfeiting anything of the felt reality of his activity, at the same time lives through the common event from the standpoint of the other. A relation between persons that is characterised in more or less degree by the element of inclusion may be termed a dialogical relation.

Dialogue implies that there must be more than one, because meaning and new understanding come 'through us and between us' (Bohm, 1996: 6). Intentional dialogue has a purpose, which is clear to both parties. Hence the process is agreed from the start. Reflective dialogue engages the learner's realities and subjective experience, giving space for the learner to consider and reconsider, without haste. This form of discourse we referred to earlier as 'connected knowing' as against 'separated knowing' where the dialogue seeks to analyse and itemize rather than to understand and connect with the learner (Goldberger et al, 1996).

In addition, intentional dialogue supports the perturbation or disturbance that may occur when existing assumptions are challenged, and deals with the emotional material flowing from such challenges. We discuss the management of emotion in Chapter 11. The engagement with another at the edge of awareness, although sometimes painful and possibly difficult to maintain, may generate new learning, forged from the discomfort and struggle of dialogue, which emerges as the reflective learning we seek as an outcome of the mentoring relationship. The power of such a relationship can be summarized in the words of Martin Buber, referring to the I–Thou relationship: 'the reciprocal essential relationship between two beings signifies a primal opportunity of being… indeed, that only with this and through this does he attain to that valid participation in being that is reserved for him; thus, that the saying of Thou by the I stands in the origin of all individual human becoming' (1965: 209).

So to conclude, definitions of reflective practice venerate the process of reflection, urging professionals to indulge in it, before, during and after their practice, with a view to improvement, transformation and, hopefully, learning about the learning process (Schon, 1987). Such definitions often imply self-reflection, and this, we suggest, seriously limits the quality of learning achieved. We noted above the limitations of self-reflection, and recommend that any system of reflective practice should include intentional dialogue-with-another, in order to optimize potential transformation through challenging the assumptions, the tfgs, the embedded beliefs that constrain the learner who is not 'connected' to another through dialogue: hence the value of an evolutionary mentor or life coach who engages in this connected form of dialogue with his or her client.

What do we dialogue about?

The material for dialogue in the mentor–client relationship is often about the content of work, the tasks and processes that form the work we do. To reflect on the task we begin from a description of what is being or going to be done. To reflect on the process we work with a description of how the task is being done or is going to be done. The content of dialogue is dictated by the client in evolutionary mentoring and life coaching (but may not be with basic coaching or functionalist mentoring), who brings material from a current, past or future project, and it is likely to cover the three domains of learning:

- doing;
- feeling;
- thinking.

Doing and thinking are familiar areas for modern organizations. The commitment to emotional literacy is less significant, and here we maintain the key to effective learning lies. We noted above that a dialogue that gets below the surface to 'defensive reasoning', in Argyris's term, is likely to stimulate double loop learning and enable the tfgs to be questioned and challenged. Such dialogue may incorporate and stimulate emotion and feeling for both learners and dialoguers. In evolutionary mentoring or life coaching relationships, the dialogue should be followed by a reflective learning review. This ensures learning at levels 1, 2 and 3 taking the form of questions and comments about what has been described. Reflection can occur at three levels as before:

1. For reflection for improvement, coaches will analyse and discourse with the learner about what has been described (the task) and how (the process), a model often found in good project management or basic coaching. We offer suggested questions for such a dialogue in Appendix 5.
2. For reflection for transformation, evolutionary mentors need to proceed with care, and here the learning relationship and trust are crucial. Examining the tfgs in a process uncovers material that may be uncomfortable and destabilizing, so mentors need to have skills in the emotional arena, be comfortable in it and have a clear grasp of appropriate boundaries in the workplace. Typical relationships for transformative learning include one-to-one executive mentoring, executive coaching and life coaching. For reflective dialogue, the client uses learner language and the mentor uses reviewer language. We give examples of such language in Appendix 5.
3. Where reflection for understanding the learning process is an additional aim (for CPD records perhaps), a step back from the two earlier processes is required, and consideration needs to be given to how the reflective learning was achieved, whether it was for improvement or transformation. This can be done as part of the mentoring or coaching session or even by keeping a journal (see Rigano and Edwards, 1998). We offer a self-coaching journal in Appendix 2 and some suggestions for a learning review in Appendix 5.

The reflective dialogue process demands structured time, space, clear boundaries, tolerance of uncertainty and competence in dealing with emotional material for the relationship to prosper for the client and stimulate transformatory learning. An example of a reflective dialogue exercise is given in Appendix 4. We discuss the details of a mentoring model in Chapter 7 and offer techniques for training in Chapter 12.

We move now to definitions of mentoring and how they relate to the four quadrants of our map in Figure 2.2.

NOTES

1 This summary of the five perspectives is drawn from Goldberger *et al* (1996) rather than the original (Belenky *et al*, 1986). The summary is essentially the same except that the later version is probably intended to be more accessible to the reader. In Goldberger *et al* (1996), the original authors and invited contributors explore how the theory introduced in Belenky *et al* (1986) has shifted and developed over the years.

2 The original term in the Belenky research was 'separated'. In the later review of their work, Goldberger *et al* used the term 'separate'.

3 In the original quotation, Geertz uses the term 'connatural'. We take this to mean the same as 'natural'.

Part II

MENTORING AND COACHING MODELS

5 What is mentoring?

Definitions of mentoring tend to be used without clarification of the philosophical basis of the activity, the approach taken and the intended learning outcome. Our purpose in this chapter is to clear up some of the confusion around the term by placing definitions on the mentoring map as functionalist, engagement or evolutionary, depending on the purpose, process and learning outcome that are implied in the definition. In addition, we review what are considered potential barriers to mentoring, dysfunctional mentoring and diversity in mentoring, which we illustrate with a Canadian case study.

Mentoring has been defined recently as 'a relationship between two people with learning and development as its purpose' (Megginson and Garvey, 2004: 2). In addition, Megginson and Garvey state that mentoring is primarily for the mentee, as 'the mentee's dream' (Caruso, 1996) is central to mentoring. This refers to Caruso's use of Levinson and Levinson's term 'dream' in their 1996 publication *The Seasons of a Woman's Life*, quoted in full on page 75. Here we see how the concept of mentoring is constantly changing and changeable. In an earlier work, Caruso (1992) reported that 'mentoring help' functions were identified in the mentoring literature as:

1. learning technical skills and knowledge;
2. learning the current job;
3. learning organizational culture;
4. learning organizational policies;
5. preparation for a future job.

Following Chapter 2, we can recognize this as a functionalist approach, and it has been described as an old-fashioned model of mentoring (Darwin, 2000). The advantage of such an approach is that it makes evaluation possible, as success is measured by how far these objectives or outcomes have been achieved. However, the 'outcome' approach has been critiqued as: 'it is effective in getting us to where we want to go but it cannot develop our awareness of the different sorts of destination available' (Megginson and Garvey, 2004: 12).

We now examine available definitions under each of the three approaches under consideration and admit our preference for the evolutionary approach.

FUNCTIONALIST MENTORING

We define 'functionalist mentoring' in terms of its purpose, process and learning outcome as 'an agreed activity between mentor and client with a prescribed purpose that may or may not be assented to by the client, using a directive process, and the learning outcome is improvement'. Functionalist mentoring adopts a rational reality model, promotes objectivity and is instrumental, maintaining an equilibrium in the work context, and the mentoring purpose is to keep this reality unchanged. The approach is typically hierarchical, and the process has been described as the 'recycling of power' (Darwin, 2000); it is clearly evident in this description of a mentor written nearly 30 years ago: 'A good enough mentor is a transitional figure who invites and welcomes a young man into the adult world. He serves as guide, teacher and sponsor... The protégé has the hope that soon he will be able to join or even surpass his mentor in the work they both value' (Levinson *et al*, 1978: 323).

The functionalist intention, ie grooming the junior to adapt and conform to the work context within a hierarchical structure (an older mentor with more power than the client), is revealed in this description of mentoring: 'A relationship between a young adult and an older, more experienced adult, that helps the younger individual learn and navigate in the adult world and the world of work' (Kram, 1988: 2). The process is typically didactic, emphasizing the transmission of knowledge, and is typified by advice giving and direction, in contrast to humanistic approaches described in Chapters 2 and 3, which characterize engagement or evolutionary mentoring.

The recycling of power has echoes in the historical roots of mentoring, which lie in the Greek myth of Ulysses, who in preparation for his lengthy sea voyages entrusted his young son Telemachus to the care of his old friend Mentor (alias Athena in some versions of the story). The purpose here was to enable Telemachus to become his father's son, to achieve political, military and sexual domination, and this was achieved through slaughter and torture (Colley, 2000: 7). Thereafter the name has been identified with a more experienced person who forms a relationship with a less experienced person in order to provide that person with advice, support and encouragement (Megginson and Clutterbuck, 1995), and the mentor role has been mythologized to one of nurture and self-sacrifice.

Kram (1988) identified two broad functions within mentoring. Firstly, career functions including sponsorship and coaching that enhance career advancement (of the client) were identified. Where career functions are the primary focus, which is often the case in formal mentoring programmes, the model tends to be knowledge-based, instrumental and carefully controlled, ie functionalist. Secondly, psychosocial functions, including friendship, counselling and role modelling, were identified as enhancing a sense of competence, identity and effectiveness in a professional role. The benefits of career functions come largely from the experience, seniority and organizational ranking of the mentor, who is able to help the mentee to 'navigate effectively in the organisational world' (Kram, 1988). When psychosocial functions are actively present, the purpose is different, and we discuss this under 'Engagement mentoring' on page 73.

The difference between mentoring in US contexts and the equivalent in UK contexts has been identified by Clutterbuck and colleagues (Megginson and Clutterbuck, 1995).

The UK approach replaces the sponsorship element in the US context with career support but limits this to professional development. The psychosocial functions identified in Kram's US research are replaced by personal development functions. In addition, the details vary as shown in Table 5.1.

Table 5.1 Mentoring in US and UK contexts

The US approach	The UK/European approach
Career functions:	*Professional functions:*
Sponsorship	Career development but not sponsorship
Exposure and visibility	Sharing knowledge (connection with study)
Coaching	Improving performance through coaching
Protection (source of the term 'protégé')	
Challenging assignments	

The US approach	The UK/European approach
Psychosocial functions:	*Personal functions*:
Role modelling	Work-related 'counselling'
Acceptance and confirmation	Social contact typified by distance and British reticence
Counselling	
Friendship	

David Clutterbuck (1998: 87), while describing mentoring as 'one of the most powerful developmental approaches available to individuals and organizations', contrasts the North American concept of mentoring with that currently practised in the UK. In particular, he points out that US business mentors are likely to be older, more powerful and usually in a line relationship with their protégé. UK business mentors on the other hand are more likely to be off-line and more experienced rather than more powerful. Where only career functions or professional functions are present, the mentoring is functional, and this is typical of many mentoring programmes where the purpose is linked to corporate objectives and the approach lacks either the psychosocial (US) or personal (UK) functions listed in Table 5.1.

The contribution to the field of US researchers like Ragins, Scandura and Kram has been invaluable.

Parsloe and Wray (2000), using a broad definition of mentoring as 'a process that supports and encourages learning to happen', identify three types of mentor:

■ corporate – in a business context;
■ qualification – as part of an educational process;
■ community – as support for disadvantaged or oppressed groups in society.

The improvement model of learning offered by Parsloe and Wray (2000: 25) positions corporate and qualification mentoring in the functionalist quadrant, as the Kolb cycle limits learning to single loop with less potential for transformation, and offers an appropriate model for robust environments where the mentoring objective is functionalist and the desired outcome is maintenance of equilibrium (2000: 117).

The corporate mentor echoes Clutterbuck's US business mentor, the qualification mentor fits the UK model and the community mentor fits neither. We identify the community mentor as an engagement mentor, which is discussed on page 73.

In a nursing context, functionalist purposes can be detected in the classification by Morton-Cooper and Palmer (2000), as shown in Table 5.2.

Table 5.2 Mentoring approaches

Type	Nature
1. *True mentoring relationships* (i) Classical mentoring – informal (primary mentoring) A natural, chosen relationship. Purposes and functions are determined by the individuals involved. An enabling relationship in personal, emotional, organizational and professional terms.	– Self-selection of individuals, persuasive influences; attraction with a shared wish to work together. – No defined programme. – Less specific purposes and functions as set by the individuals, circumstances and context. – No explicit financial rewards for mentors. – Probable duration 2-15 years.
(ii) Contract mentoring – formal (facilitated mentoring/ secondary mentoring) An artificial relationship created for a specific purpose that is essentially determined by the organization. Some elements of mentor function, with focus on specific helper functions.	Programmes are identified by: – clear purposes, functions, defined aims or outcomes; – selected individuals with assigned mentors, forced matching or choice of mentors from mentor pool; – explicit material rewards; possibilities of financial incentives for mentors; – probable duration 1-2 years.
2. *Pseudo-mentoring relationships* (quasi-mentoring/partial mentoring/sequential mentoring) Mentoring approaches in appearance only – as offered by academic involvement in thesis preparation, orientation and induction programmes.	– Focus on specific tasks or organizational issues of short-lived duration. – Guidance from several mentors, for short periods. – Relationships do not demonstrate the comprehensive enabling elements of the true classical model. – Specified clinical placements. – Probable duration 6 weeks to 1 year.

Source: Morton-Cooper and Palmer (2000: 46)

The definition of contract mentoring places it in the functionalist corner with pseudo-mentors and minor mentors (discussed below). Contract mentoring by its nature will be semi-formal or formal and is functionalist in purpose, seeking for conformity and adaptation to existing structures and norms. The method is likely to be instructional and advice-driven, especially where qualification or accreditation is the aim, and this places contract mentoring firmly in the functionalist section of the mentoring map. The processes adopted in mentor selection, choice and support structures, as well as mentor training and skills, differentiate the true mentors from pseudo-mentors. We discuss mentor and coach training in Chapter 12.

Darling (1984) also identifies mentor types in the nursing context in terms of three components, attraction, action and affect:

1. Attraction means admiration and/or a desire to emulate the mentor.
2. Action means that the mentor invests time and energy for and on behalf of the protégé.
3. Affect means that the relationship has an emotional component, ie the couple respect and like each other, and the mentor offers encouragement and support as well as challenge.

A minor mentor is defined by Darling (1984) as having fewer than three of these components present; for instance, a mentor who is admired and invests time and energy but is unconnected emotionally to the client is likely to be functionalist, as the relationship is focused on prescribed outcomes that are not informed by a close emotional bond. Some minor mentors fit the engagement quadrant, and we discuss these below.

Situations of power imbalance that may occur in mentoring situations can adversely affect the relationship. In particular, where the mentor has hierarchical authority over the mentee, the psychosocial functions that support a developmental relationship may be inhibited by the power inherent in the relationship and the mentoring remains functionalist.

Other researchers in the UK context have reported similar findings in education and business. Carruthers (1993) suggests as above that functionalist mentor relationships are those that emphasize the professional development of the client only, without an emotional bond or the presence of psychosocial functions.

Norman Cohen (1995) identifies six principles for adult mentoring in US contexts, either in post-secondary education or in business or government, as follows:

- relationship emphasis – building rapport and trust;
- information emphasis – offering tailored advice;
- facilitative focus –introducing alternatives (TAANA v TINA[1]);
- confrontive focus – to offer challenge;
- mentor model – to motivate;
- mentee vision – to encourage initiative.

This model, with its single loop emphasis, lies within the functionalist quadrant. However, the focus on trust and relationship edges it towards the engagement field and, while the confrontive focus leaves a door open to the evolutionary corner, the presence of advice leaves it indisputably as a functionalist perspective. The scale provides for 55 specific mentor behaviours clustered into the six categories, and Cohen provides a self-assessment questionnaire for potential mentors to rate themselves on the six principles. An adaptation of this questionnaire was used in the CILT case study given below.

CASE STUDY

CILT: logistic mentors

The Chartered Institute of Logistics and Transport (CILT) is the professional body for those industries and organizations that are involved in, are working in or have an interest in the logistics and transport sectors. As an international organization, the Institute has 30,000 members in 28 countries. The Institute in the UK has a membership of 22,000.

'Logistics' is the process of designing, managing and improving supply-chains, which might include purchasing, manufacturing, storage and, of course, transport. Transport remains a major component of most supply-chains. Logistics services and other transport companies need to understand logistics and supply-chain management in order to tailor their services to meet their customers' needs.

The mission statement of the Chartered Institute declares that the Institute seeks 'To be the focus for professional excellence, the development of the most relevant and effective techniques in logistics and transport, and the development of policies which respond to the challenges of a changing world'. Members are independent qualified practitioners in their own right, working in a variety of contexts, and the Institute offers a programme of continuing professional development, part of which was their mentoring scheme inaugurated in 2001.

The declared purpose of the mentoring scheme, in an industry where members need to be prepared constantly to reskill to meet the demands of the knowledge economy, was as follows: 'To help our members to meet the challenges of a changing world of work and to provide a source of advice on professional development.'

The scheme was designed to offer members an incentive to join the Institute, to remain with the Institute and advance within the Institute, because of the career and professional development, advice and support available through the scheme. Hence it was decided that the quantifiable outcome for the Institute would be enhanced membership figures.

The scheme defined the mentor as 'an experienced and trusted advisor and guide', and the Institute launched the scheme by providing training and support for 30 senior practitioners working with 60 protégés for one year. The mentoring scheme was offered as an aid for new members, to help with upgrading membership, career advice or progression, and academic support with the purpose of maintaining and enhancing performance or knowledge.

The Director of Professional Development and her team approached the scheme with care, informed by and taking into account the mentoring literature.

The selection process was thorough, using a customized questionnaire (adapted from Cohen, 1995), and both mentors and protégés had choice. This was achieved by the provision of mentor profiles (including personal pen portraits) from which potential protégés were asked to choose their best three. On the basis of these, mentors were then offered a number of protégé profiles and made their choice. The questionnaire proved to be an ideal method of selection, as the only trainee mentor who had not completed it successfully alone had difficulty in accepting the training.

The chosen mentors were offered a two-day residential training workshop in three different locations, which aimed to:

■ consolidate knowledge;
■ recognize skills and practice;
■ engage in reflective learning;
■ peruse documentation for mentors;
■ discuss requirements for accreditation;
■ establish support structures;
■ agree a review process.

The overall aim of the workshop was to prepare members for taking up a mentoring relationship. The objectives of the workshop, which drew on the six functions for adult mentoring in business and government (Cohen, 1995), were that on completion of the workshop members would :

1. be familiar with the CILT mentoring programme;

2. have an understanding of the six mentoring functions;

3. appreciate the skills needed for mentoring;

4. have experienced 'hands-on' practice in mentoring skills;

5. have received feedback on their mentoring skills;

6. be familiar with mentoring documentation;

7. have begun to review their learning.

The mentoring package tailored to the Institute included notes for mentors and notes for protégés. Accreditation documents were obtained from the European Mentoring Council for mentors who chose to seek accreditation.

The outcome of the mentoring programme, which is still running, is enhanced membership and commitment to the Institute, as well as a plentiful supply of mentors but, surprisingly, less demand from protégés.

The CILT aimed to achieve a functionalist objective and used a person-centred approach to achieve it. The learning outcomes were difficult to identify, as each mentoring couple would have devised their own, but the tendency was to address career development issues. We believe that the programme offered clients an experience of mentoring where they benefited in a functional way and their learning was improvement in career terms.

E-mentoring

When the mentoring relationship is conducted electronically, by e-mail or other method, the term 'e-mentoring' has been coined. E-mentoring, using asynchronous e-mail to communicate, is being adopted by an increasing number of organizations with global reach, because of its practical advantages for geographically distant mentoring couples (Hall, 2005). Can learning be achieved electronically? The method is in its early stages, and outcomes from similar programmes suggest that learning for improvement can be achieved by the use of virtual classrooms and e-mail coaching and support, an approach known as a 'blended solution' (Brockbank, McGill and Beech, 2002). We would identify such a learning outcome as functionalist, but is this the case for e-mentoring?

Bierema and Merriam offer a definition of e-mentoring as: 'a computer-mediated, mutually beneficial relationship between a mentor and a protégé which provides learning, advising, encouraging, promoting and modelling, that is often boundaryless, egalitarian, and qualitatively different than traditional face-to-face mentoring' (2002: 214).

Is e-mentoring functionalist?

How is e-mentoring different from face-to-face mentoring? There is plenty of evidence to support the generation of significant relationships online with support for the idea that the medium itself generates intimacy (McKenna and Bargh, 1998). Hence mentoring online exists and has the potential to be evolutionary but the evidence to date suggests otherwise.

The 'boundaryless' claim made in the quotation above suggests that e-mentoring will be neutral and not be influenced by an individual's race, gender, age or status or where he or she lives. The naivety of this claim is supported by Russell (2001), who suggests that e-mentoring may perpetuate 'cultural imperialism' where existing cultural values are replaced by values from the far-from-egalitarian 'adviser'. Alternatively, the potential of e-mentoring to reach marginalized populations is reported by Burgstahler and Nourse (1999), and we discuss this further in 'Diversity in mentoring' on page 86.

The benefits of e-mentoring have been stated by Andrew Cardow as 'the elimination of noise due to personal bias' and 'only precise, simple and clear instructions were given to the protégé from the mentor' (1998: 35). Among the declared advantages reported here were that, in spite of the mentor giving guidance and instructions, the relationship was described as non-hierarchical, which seems unlikely. In addition, the much-discussed issue of conveying empathy electronically is ignored, as 'both the protégé and mentor are part of the same institutional field', which unfortunately is not a guarantee of empathy being present, electronically or otherwise (Cardow, 1998: 37; Anthony, 2000). We discuss the significance of empathy in mentoring and coaching in Chapter 10. There is evidence that online relationships generate higher levels of disclosure (Anthony, 2000) but, as with face-to-face relationships, this will depend on the mentor's degree of responding skills, like empathy and restatement/summary, discussed in Chapter 10.

We conclude therefore that, in general, e-mentoring is functional in intent and in practice, with equilibrium as the desired outcome and mentoring online being deployed for economic rather than developmental reasons.

Can e-mentoring be evolutionary?

Research suggests that, far from being a 'cold' medium, e-mail mentoring can be a rich but different form of communication (Hall, 2005). This is also reported by Megginson and Clutterbuck in their evaluation of MentorsByNet (Hall, 2005). This programme has 555 mentoring relationships in place, servicing small and medium-sized businesses. However, evaluation reveals that the method is seen as 'a teaching medium' and 'a valuable learning tool' to promote skill development or help new recruits to adapt to the 'ways of an organization', all suggestive of a functionalist perspective on the process. The structured nature of other e-mentoring programmes, in IBM and HP, including PowerPoint presentations and mini-lessons, confirms the use of technology in the form of e-mentoring for what are essentially teaching purposes (Hall, 2005). However, Clutterbuck (Hall, 2005) seeks to promote a 'learning dialogue' in e-mentoring, which may lead to personal development, and finds himself surprised by the quality of the mentoring relationships that emerge online. He calls attention to the importance of personal reflective space (PRS) (see Figure 4.1 on page 55) in truly reflective learning, where the learner has the opportunity, by internal dialogue, to 'step outside the box'. We refer to this as 'challenging the tfgs' in Chapter 3, with the potential for transformation.

We have found no evidence of e-mentoring that resembles evolutionary mentoring with transformation as a learning outcome. Why should this be? We believe that the participants in e-mentoring programmes, both mentors and protégés, are primed for functionalist outcomes, whatever they may say about their method. The process is cheap and does not entail commitment in time and space to another individual so must seem attractive to busy managers who prefer to keep a distance between themselves and potential protégés. There is no reason why potential evolutionary mentors should not use technology to support their relationships with clients and when this occurs there will be evidence of transformative outcomes achieved online.

ENGAGEMENT MENTORING

We define 'engagement mentoring' as an agreed activity where the purpose is prescribed, which the client may or may not be made aware of, which takes a humanistic stance that respects the client's subjective world and where the learning outcome is improvement leaving underlying values and systems unchanged.

In this book we are using the term 'engagement mentoring' to describe mentoring in the subjective/equilibrium quadrant where, although the approach is humanistic and respects the subjective in nurturing ways, the intention is maintenance of the status quo and a continuing equilibrium in the working environment. We identify the characteristics of engagement mentoring in a variety of corporate programmes (some are described in our case studies) where the purpose is functionalist, maintaining the status quo, or equilibrium, and the approach utilizes a nurturing or humanistic approach. The stated objectives of such programmes include development of particular skills related to the business concerned and enabling transitions or change initiative that may be problematic or meet with resistance. These objectives mirror the goals of 'employability' initiatives, where aims for young clients include 'to sign on to the values and ethos of the business and to fit into its organisational structure, culture and work ethics' (Colley, 2003: 25), ie transformation of personal dispositions and overcoming resistance to change.

The support and encouragement in some programmes of engagement mentoring mask its hidden functionalist purpose and is defined by Colley as: 'the re-engagement of young people with formal learning and the labour market, and the transformation of their personal attitudes, values and beliefs' (2003).

Helen Colley (2003) reports her in-depth study of one mentoring scheme, 'New Beginnings', for 'disaffected' youngsters mentored by volunteer university undergraduates. 'Engagement mentoring' is the term Colley devised as an intervention responding to disaffection and social exclusion. Engagement mentoring projects targeted groups of young people 'at risk' of disengaging or already disengaged from formal systems of education, training and employment. The programmes explicitly seek to re-engage young people with these systems in preparation for entry to the labour market. Other versions of engagement mentoring are the business/education partnerships and community mentoring (see Parsloe and Wray (2000), page 66) programmes focusing on oppressed groups. Colley positions UK engagement mentoring as a development from the historic 'Big Brothers Big Sisters' in the US, which currently claims a quarter of a million volunteer mentors and seeks to recruit 14 million young people 'at risk' (2003: 11). In the UK in 2003, the National Mentoring Network had 1,500 affiliates, a third of British schoolchildren are offered mentoring, and government initiatives include 'Excellence in Cities' and 'Connexions' (DfEE, 2000).

Colley's conclusions however state that, 'despite its popularity, there is little evidence to support the use of mentoring on such a vast scale' (2003: 13) and 'there is alternative evidence that mentoring may be counter-productive to policy intentions for interventions with socially excluded young people' (2003: 13).

The multiplicity of roles required in a community mentor are identified as guidance, good parent, case worker and learning facilitator, not a skill set that is present in the typical workplace. In addition, the community mentor is likely to be an instrument of regulation and surveillance, while being required to commit to a concept of empowerment that has been described as an 'impossible fiction' (Colley, 2003).

Engagement mentoring can be seen as a key aspect of staff and management development (Whitely, Dougherty and Dreher, 1991), as it is an integral part of a properly defined human resource strategy, which must be concerned with the development of people in the most effective manner (Keep, 1992). Formal and informal mentoring have increasingly been seen as part of a human resource strategy in which organizations seek to develop their human resources in a way that leads to competitive success (McKeen and Burke, 1989; Wright and Werther, 1991; Cunningham and Eberle, 1993). This understanding is associated with a 'soft' human resource strategy and management style that is concerned to develop abilities, competencies and concepts in people and to facilitate and encourage their use, rather than creating a functionalist system of control and extrinsic motivation, the latter being seen as 'hard' human resource strategy. However, engagement mentoring sustains a state of equilibrium and maintains the status quo, suppressing the possibility of transformative learning for the individual and the organization.

In Kram's research, when psychosocial functions are present the mentoring experience can include an intensity of emotion, risky self-transformation and development for both parties (Baum, 1992). Psychosocial functions rely on the quality of the interpersonal bond between mentor and client, and the degree of trust that exists within the relationship. Factors identified by Kram (1988) that influence the psychosocial bonding include mutual liking, respect, exclusivity, counselling skill and the desire for friendship intimacy. The presence of psychosocial functions differentiates engagement mentoring from functionalist mentoring.

EVOLUTIONARY MENTORING

We define 'evolutionary mentoring' as 'an agreed activity between mentor and client, where goals are generated by and for the client, the process is person-centred and the learning outcome is transformation'. We will now examine typical definitions of mentors and mentoring in terms of their purpose, process and learning outcome. Let us consider the nature of a 'true' mentor, described as follows: 'A true mentor fosters the young adult's development by nourishing the youthful Dream and giving it her or his blessing, believing in the young woman, helping her to define her newly emerging adult self in its newly discovered adult world, and creating a space in which she can move towards a reasonably satisfactory life structure that contains the Dream' (Levinson and Levinson, 1996: 239).

In this near-perfect definition of evolutionary mentoring, the 'dream' is a Jungian term referring to lifetime hopes held in early adulthood, and nourishing the 'dream' ensures that the client's goals are his or her own. The process has person-centred characteristics, and the learning outcome is identified as the transformation into a 'satisfactory life structure that contains the Dream'.

In the nursing profession a mentor is described as: 'Someone who provides an enabling relationship that facilitates another's personal growth and development. The relationship is dynamic, reciprocal, and can be emotionally intense. With such a relationship, the mentor assists with career development and guides the mentoree through the organisational, social and political networks' (Morton-Cooper and Palmer, 1993: xix).

The purpose of the relationship described here is the development of the client; hence the goals can be assumed to be the client's own. The presence of emotion suggests a person-centred approach, and the learning outcome, if and only if the goals are the client's own, is likely to be transformational, placing the definition in the evolutionary sector.

The European Mentoring and Coaching Council offers its definition of mentoring as 'Off line help by one person to another in making significant transitions in knowledge, work or thinking' (Clutterbuck, 1998: 87). Here, 'significant transitions' suggest a transformative learning outcome, but the definition does not address whose goals are addressed in the mentoring activity and says nothing about the relationship.

Morton-Cooper and Palmer classify mentor types (see Table 5.2), showing true mentoring as 'Classical mentoring, a naturally chosen, personal and emotional enabling relationship in an organisational and professional context' (2000: 46).

We identify classical mentoring as evolutionary, as the 'naturally chosen' implies clients will generate their own goals, the relationship suggests a person-centred approach and the learning outcome has the potential for transformation. However, the organizational and professional context may influence ownership of goals. For readers seeking to launch a contract mentoring programme, Morton-Cooper and Palmer (2000) offer a clear continuum from formal through semi-formal to informal, so that practitioners can be aware of the type of mentor they will end up with (see Figure 5.1).

Contract mentoring programmes that aim to stimulate true evolutionary mentoring rarely address the issue of whose purpose is being served and hence may regress into functionalist or engagement mentoring mode. Where contract mentors insist on clients generating their own goals the evolutionary quality is preserved. Clutterbuck supplies a list of 'must-haves' for a successful contract programme (1998: 102), which includes training for everyone concerned, ie mentor, mentee and line manager, as well as ongoing support for mentors, an identified need

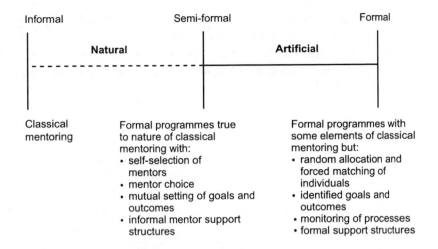

Informal	Semi-formal	Formal
Natural		**Artificial**

| Classical mentoring | Formal programmes true to nature of classical mentoring with:
• self-selection of mentors
• mentor choice
• mutual setting of goals and outcomes
• informal mentor support structures | Formal programmes with some elements of classical mentoring but:
• random allocation and forced matching of individuals
• identified goals and outcomes
• monitoring of processes
• formal support structures |

Source: Morton-Cooper and Palmer (2000: 69)

Figure 5.1 *Mentoring: the continuum of informality and formality*

in mentor research (Brockbank, 1994). We discuss the training and development of mentors and coaches in Chapter 12.

Darling's (1984) typology uses three components, attraction, action and affect:

1. Attraction means admiration and/or a desire to emulate the mentor.
2. Action means that the mentor invests time and energy for and on behalf of the protégé.
3. Affect means that the relationship has an emotional component, ie the couple respect and like each other, and the mentor offers encouragement and support as well as challenge.

A major mentor is defined as having all three necessary components, and this (see Darling, 1984) suggests that major mentors have the potential to be placed in the evolutionary quadrant, because the relationship enables the purpose and learning outcome to be agreed collaboratively between the mentor and the client. Similar findings exist in education and business where Carruthers (1993) suggests that mentoring relationships are evolutionary in intent if they can be described as those that address the owned professional and personal development of the client, and an emotional bond exists between the mentoring pair.

Julie Hay (1995) has done a thorough job of untangling the variety of mentoring meanings and formats available, and she recommends using the term 'developmental alliance' rather than the more confusing term 'mentor'. Hay defines 'developmental alliance' as follows: 'A relationship between equals in which one or more of those involved is enabled to: increase awareness, identify alternatives, initiate action, and develop themselves' (1995: 3).

How evolutionary is this kind of mentoring? The client here is enabled to generate his or her own goals, the relationship suggests a person-centred approach, and the 'develop themselves' indicates the learning outcome as transformation. Hay's definition of evolutionary mentoring echoes Clutterbuck's description of a developmental mentor (1998), particularly the propensity of developmental alliances to benefit both parties, and the realization of learning as tacit knowledge is made explicit.

Hay (1995) makes a sharp distinction between developmental alliances and a typically functionalist mentoring scheme in business where the mentor is a senior manager who is expected to develop protégés within corporate norms or functions, and whose career prospects will depend on how successful he or she is. In a mentoring scheme that promotes developmental alliances, on the other hand, the organization trusts the mentor (who may not be senior) to develop staff for their own benefit and that of the organization. The difference in values here can be seen in the respect for the individual shown in the latter, whilst also promoting organizational goals. Because such a scheme offers a larger list of potential mentors, an adaptation of the Clutterbuck quote 'Everyone can be a mentor' can be realized, 'provided that they are willing to apply skills of listening rather than telling' (Hay, 1998: 23). Hay's approach emphasizes the quality of a relationship that recognizes and values the subjective, adopts humanistic values and, because of its person-centred approach, promotes transformation. A developmental alliance depends on genuine connection, and she asserts that it 'will not work properly unless those involved believe that it is normal for people to want a close connection with each other' (Hay, 1995: 47).

The range of learning outcomes in mentoring is identified by Hay as traditional, transitional and transformational, and these are defined as follows:

- Traditional learning is learning how to do things, by being taught or observing.
- Transitional learning is learning how to do things differently, ie improvement.
- Transformational learning is a complete change of perspective, altering the client's world-view and including an understanding of how to learn.

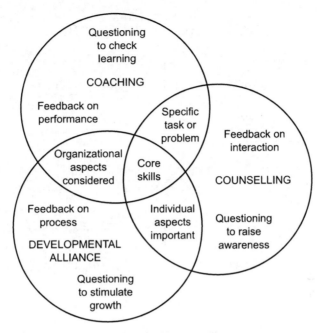

Source: Hay (1995: 60)

Figure 5.2   *Overlaps in mentoring, coaching and counselling*

These learning outcomes are equivalent to traditional rote learning; being coached for improvement – functionalist single loop learning; and challenging the tfgs for transformation – evolutionary double loop learning.

The Hay approach (1995) also establishes the skill set needed for transformational mentoring, and is not afraid to admit that the skills are common to other activities like coaching and counselling. This is illustrated in Figure 5.2.

The long-term focus of Hay's definition includes a process she calls 'bonding' to differentiate it from coaching, counselling and traditional mentoring (see Figure 5.3). We discuss the boundary between mentoring and counselling in Chapter 13.

Andy Roberts of the Birmingham College of Food Technology and Catering Science reviewed the mentoring literature from 1978 to 1999 across a variety of disciplines (Roberts, 2000) in order to uncover its essential attributes. His motive can be summed up in his comment that 'if no definitional agreement exists [about mentoring] how do we know we are talking about the same thing?' (Roberts, 2000: 150). The result of his findings revealed that the essential attributes of mentoring (ie those without which mentoring is not mentoring) were identified as:

Source: Hay (1995: 62)

Figure 5.3   *Different perspectives*

- a process;
- an active relationship;
- a helping process;
- a teaching–learning process;
- reflective practice;
- a career and personal development process;
- a formalized process;
- a role constructed by or for a mentor.

And the contingent attributes of mentoring (without which mentoring can still be seen as mentoring) were identified as:

- role modelling;
- sponsoring;
- coaching.

On the basis of these findings, Roberts offers a definition of mentoring as 'A formalised process whereby a more knowledgeable and experienced person actuates a supportive role of overseeing and encouraging reflection and learning within a less experienced and knowledgeable person, so as to facilitate that person's career and personal development' (2000: 162).

Is this a definition of functionalist or evolutionary mentoring? We place this definition within the evolutionary quadrant, as the potential for transformation is present with its suggestion of reflective dialogue, but it may also support a functionalist or engagement equilibrium outcome. Many definitions cover the possibility of both.

Sue Cross (1999) summarizes the variety of purposes to which mentoring is put in the modern 'learning organization', and this includes:

- counteracting the stress of restructuring (engagement);
- initiating new staff (functionalist);
- enhancing performance (functionalist);
- developing new skills (functionalist);
- refreshing motivation (engagement);
- exploring potential (evolutionary);
- changing direction (evolutionary);
- breaking new ground for under-represented groups (evolutionary).

This list covers mentoring in all of our three quadrants, the functionalist, engagement and evolutionary. Cross is adamant that mentoring is different from being a friend or colleague because 'mentoring is neither mutual nor spontaneous. It is planned, contrived and one-way' (1999: 230), echoing our requirements for reflective learning in Chapter 3. She does not exclude the possibility of peer or co-mentoring but does emphasize that, 'during the actual process, the roles of mentor and mentee are clearly defined and mutually exclusive' (Cross, 1999: 230).

RELATIONSHIPS AT WORK

Clarkson and Shaw (1992) have identified five aspects of relationships at work: the unfinished relationship; the working alliance; the development relationship; the personal relationship; and the transpersonal relationship. How do these relationships affect employees and any mentoring activity in the organization?

As its name suggests, the unfinished relationship is historical, left over from childhood, and projections or transferences enter the working environment, getting in the way of all the others. An understanding of the nature of unfinished relationships will enable organizations to deal with them appropriately, usually by referral. Mentors are normally not trained to deal with such unfinished material in people's lives and should not be expected to 'counsel' the situation better. We discuss this further in Chapter 13.

The working alliance relates to shared tasks where the sharers generate the energy and will to complete the task together, without being driven or supported by the organization. Such alliances are the key to modern 'flat' structures with less bureaucratic control, and though largely self-facilitated they may benefit from mentoring support. This relationship can be seriously interfered with by unfinished relationships.

The developmental relationship appears when adult (not unfinished) needs for growth are met, by mentoring (or coaching) for the benefit of colleagues and the organization. The most likely models utilized will be evolutionary, as the individual identifies his or her own development needs, the process is humanistic or person-centred and the learning outcome is transformation.

The personal relationship is based on the trust and authenticity that develops between colleagues who respect each other and who, over time, become close and affectionate friends. The provision of company support groups or mentoring can optimize such relationships for the benefit of the organization.

The transpersonal relationship is that connection between parts of an organization that combine energy towards a corporate vision or mission. Like the working alliance, this relationship is self-facilitating but may benefit from evolutionary mentoring. Each of the relationships above can become distorted and dysfunctional, and these have been discussed elsewhere (Clarkson and Shaw, 1992).

This view of organizational life suggests that healthy work relationships hold the key to productive endeavours, confirming the link between learning and relationship. The potential for psychosocial functions to trigger feelings, fantasies and memories or experiences from the past may take the mentoring relationship into the realms of therapy and the 'unfinished relationship', a relationship likely to obstruct the contractual work relationship as it transfers elements of past relationships into the present (Clarkson and Shaw, 1992). We discuss the boundary between mentoring and therapy in Chapter 13. The projective fantasies that characterize such an unfinished relationship, whilst part of everyday life, can lead to inappropriate or exaggerated behaviour and so can be dysfunctional. Psychosocial functions in evolutionary mentoring, such as acceptance and confirmation or affirmation, are likely to enhance a 'developmental' relationship that provides the individual with the information, support and challenge needed to meet his or her development needs (Clarkson and Shaw, 1992). The

description of such a developmental al? still present in today's
tionary mentoring relationship, namel
sciously chosen contractual arrangemercurrent (in 1988) myths of
(Clarkson and Shaw, 1992). Active learms:
to emerge from developmental mentori
cur, as such relationships foster autonotégé, as the mentor gains
than passivity and dependence. Positiv does the mentor often bask
career advancement and satisfaction anuccess, but the mentor may
toring have been reported (Dreher and d may be gently challenged

When we review how definitions 'five refer to such an outcome
toring, the focus of business in functioi
is the focus of the helping professions i positive experience for both
mentoring. In addition, where externalik, 1994; Beech and Brock-
rate contexts there is the possibility of parties to feel disappointed

BARRIERS, OBSTACLES AND
ne in all work settings. Our
ng varies depending on the
Morton-Cooper and Palmer (2000) havised, even if this is not made
abling traits, based on what are called
Farrell, 1986). They describe three suchvailable to those who want
typical mind with set values and ideaentoring for the purposes of
zations, so a danger in the public servis otherwise, and there is ev-
self interested and self important, urpportunities for mentoring,
trepreneurial so a danger in busineson.
mind, devious and calculating, obsesdividual growth and career
danger anywhere'. he effect of having a mentor,

Morton-Cooper and Palmer have ssed this above.
in two axes: enabling/disabling and
Figure 5.4). n mentoring couples include

The destructive minds mentioned ahese in the following section.
as they can 'infect' their protégés. Darliative consequences of func-
identifies a gallery of 'toxic' mentorri effects. The Matthew effect
nurses. These include avoiders, dumpts get mentors, but the less
icizers, and their related behaviours g the gap between them and
undermining and withholding. eri phenomenon is based on

Are toxic mentors a fact of life? Dard (without success) to keep
mentors as follows: nized (Carruthers, 1993: 19).
ve consequences in dysfunc-

■ avoiders who are neither availableoring, as was established by
■ dumpers who place protégés into ne
  abandon them; in mentoring that is believed
  or both mentor and client, the

significance in mentoring relationships of diversity in terms of race, gender, age, class etc.

Diversity in mentoring

By diversity in mentoring we are referring to relationships between mentors and clients who differ in gender, race, ethnicity, sexual orientation, class, religion, disability and any other groups associated with power in organizations. For example, a mentor may be a white male and the client may be a black woman of African-Caribbean origin, or a white female mentor may be working with a white gay male client. In referring to power in organizations we are recognizing the varying degrees of power and influence that groups may have in organizations, deriving from access to resources and roles that exist over time. For example, organizations in the City of London are still dominated by white males over their female counterparts and people who belong to ethnic minorities. Moreover when mentor relationships are created, the group memberships to which each belongs will be brought into the relationship. Indeed group membership may well influence the creation of the mentor relationship as well as what it brings to the relationship, for example senior women acting as mentors to junior women managers, and mentors chosen from the same ethnic group as their clients.

Thus mentoring relationships have a political dimension, in that they represent interpersonally the sense of power and powerlessness that is found in any group or organization. Individuals can feel a sense of power or powerlessness vis-à-vis others. This power can be described as 'innocent' in the sense that an individual may not be aware of his or her position or role but nevertheless live it. Issues of power can be implicit in the mentoring relationship so mentors and clients will need to work explicitly with these politics to promote learning. Where the relationship denies or avoids these politics it will discourage learning, and we discuss this in Chapter 2.

Let us examine briefly the term 'innocence' used above. There is still a tendency to make assumptions in organizations about 'the way things are done around here'. Managers and staff fit into implicit norms of behaviour that actually represent and reflect the power dynamics within organizations. Our society is still in transition in this respect – some organizations are endeavouring to acknowledge and work with difference to the benefit of the previously disadvantaged, whilst other organizations are still living innocently with the assumptions of the past. This has been referred to as 'the power of innocence' (James and Baddeley, 1991: 115):

People's personal positions are arrived at and sustained by being in a group of people whose understanding of the world is similar to their own. Thus their position is both sustained by other group members ('That's the way the world is') or even attributed to the group ('If you're a manager this is what you think'). The last thing the fish discovers is water. Innocence derives its power through being comfortably and unreflectively surrounded by others of like mind. From this stance individuals cannot see themselves colluding with the larger flow of institutional direction and its consequences.

'This is the way things are done around here' is being replaced by the acknowledgement that those who created the world in which such a condition could prevail are having to reflect upon those norms and share power with those who previously did not share power with them. An obvious example is where women are increasingly finding but challenging the 'glass ceiling' above them and white men are discovering the 'innocent' power they have held as being untenable. That ceiling is, for some men, unwittingly applied at the personal level but is also institutionally discriminatory. A similar position applies in respect of race and disability as well as age and sexual orientation.

Evolutionary mentoring and life coaching offers the opportunity to overcome the discriminatory practices without resorting to scapegoating or blame of those who have held power traditionally, as well as enabling opportunity for those who have not shared power. For both groups the result can be empowering and create a necessary pluralism. 'As the cloak of hegemony is discarded the individual can re-centre, rediscover themselves and build their own connections, relationships and identity. This may involve a personal crisis but losing one's innocence need not entail an enduring loss of personal power' (James and Baddeley, 1991: 117).

This re-centring is further enhanced by the explicit recognition of the emotional and political aspects of learning and development in organizations. Where mentoring and coaching relationships recognize such power relations, through recognition of the discursive context, this may enable clients to transform the dominant paradigm, the tfgs, in which they are embedded. Clients may set a political agenda for change if that is what they desire. We note here our use of the term 'political', often perceived as negative, and consciously wish to draw attention to the way that discourse itself promotes particular power relations, by naming and then silencing unwelcome voices as 'political'. Where the client becomes aware of the reality of such discourse and identifies practices that dominate relationships in the workplace, through mentoring or coaching, there is hope of personal and organizational transformation.

The importance of a learning context that addresses the power of an embedded discourse has been recognized by others (Reynolds, 1997), and evolutionary mentoring and coaching is one way of enabling the critical approach needed to realize its existence.

Recent findings suggest that in company headquarters and executive suites the people will be 'overwhelmingly white, male, able-bodied and of a certain age' (Arkin, 2005: 26). Although there is increasing awareness of the business advantage of recruiting from a wider base that reflects the ultimate customer or end user, the fact is that 'in reality we are terrible at it' (Arkin, 2005: 26). Now that there are more women and ethnic minorities in senior positions they are often recruited as traditional mentors for the next generation and, if such role models cannot be found, forward-looking businesses will seek external mentors to give high-flying potential managers from outside the traditional talent pool the confidence to reach for the very top. Programmes that seek to encourage greater racial diversity are typically functionalist in that the objective is explicit and while benefiting the client they aim to bring business benefits to the organizations concerned. Examples of engagement mentoring to improve the school performance of particular racial groups have all the characteristics identified by Colley (2003), including payment of student mentors, disenchantment of participants, as well as an opportunity to discuss what issues were having a detrimental effect on them (Clutterbuck and Ragins, 2002: 241).

Whether your race or gender affects your chances of being a client was explored by a wide range of researchers, and the results suggest that your gender does not mean you are less likely to get a mentor but your ethnic background may do (Clutterbuck and Ragins, 2002). So much for getting a mentor. What happens within the diverse mentoring relationship?

How diversity impacts on mentoring functions

Research has provided inconsistent results in finding out about how diversity influences the type of mentoring received, and the reason for this may be the typical use of protégés' reports, which are considered unreliable (Clutterbuck and Ragins, 2002). Some gender studies show that women favour psychosocial help while men prefer instrumental, and this affects them as mentors as well. Other studies have shown equal amounts of both, and this inconsistency is replicated in race studies. When mentoring outcomes or benefits (such as income) are examined, the gender or race of the protégé has little effect, but mentors who are non-white or female do not generate significant benefits. There is evidence that, in mentoring pairs of the same gender and race, protégés receive more instrumental help but not more psychosocial help, and these differences are thought to relate to differences in rank (McGuire, 1999). Andy Roberts of the Birmingham College of Food Technology and Catering Science has explored mentoring in terms of two psychological dimensions, instrumentality and expressiveness. These two traits have been stereotypically associated with the male and female genders respectively. However, experienced and successful mentors were found to demonstrate both traits, and were dubbed 'androgynous' mentors (Roberts, 1998). The research findings alert us to possible barriers that may exist in diverse mentoring and suggest a careful examination of the factors that might influence mentoring in diverse couples.

Stereotyping

Stereotyping is a basic human tendency that we resort to in order to help us to process information, by fitting people into easily defined groups. The process is an oversimplified mental image of some category of person, based on the perceiver's knowledge, beliefs and expectations. Stereotypes often lead to distortions in our assessment of others and this is a serious matter for mentors and their clients who may hold gendered or racially biased views about each other's competence. Mentors are advised to test their responding to clients in an out-group in terms of three levels:

■ category-based responding where the out-group are viewed as different from the in-group but similar to each other;
■ differentiated responding where the out-group are still viewed as different from the in-group but are perceived as different from each other;
■ personalized responding where each member of the out-group is perceived as distinct and the interaction is with the individual rather than with the group.

(Clutterbuck and Ragins, 2002)

Mentors in the Western world may need to bear in mind that they live in a society with a range of mechanisms that exist, consciously or unconsciously, to perpetuate systems of disadvantage for persons whose race, gender, sexual orientation and capability are not white, able-bodied, heterosexual male. Many of the latter group find themselves unable to cope with black people's pain and anger, with a realization that gender equality means giving up their power, and that ability/disability and sexual orientation are individual characteristics of a human being. Because of the emotional content of stereotyping, diversity training should form part of mentor training, and we offer some ideas for this in Chapter 12.

We complete this chapter with a case study of diverse mentoring from Canada.

CASE STUDY

First Nation mentoring in Canada

The term 'First Nation' came into common use in the 1970s to replace 'Indian', which some people found offensive. The term 'First Nations' collectively describes all the indigenous people of Canada who are not Inuit or Metis. 'Aboriginal peoples' is the collective term for all the original peoples of Canada and their descendants, who consist of the three groups mentioned, namely First Nations, Inuit and Metis. First Nations have unique heritages, languages, cultural practices and spiritual beliefs. The Indian Act of 1876, revised in 1985, sets out the obligations of federal government and regulates the management of Indian reserve lands. The Indian Act describes a reserve as lands that have been set apart for the use and benefit of a particular group of Indians. The legal title of reserves rests with the Crown in right of Canada, and the federal government has primary jurisdiction over those lands and the people living in them.

Our mentor is a mature white Canadian woman, J, who is well educated, with a thriving business of her own and lots of experience of setting up and running small and medium enterprises. Her client is an Indian man, Les, an Ojibway, from the Rainy River First Nation, one of the 633 First Nation communities in Canada, within which 700,000 citizens live on reserves. Les was adopted and brought up in a white family with four of his siblings who had been found without their parents in their reserve home. He was 10 years old when his white parents adopted him.

One day when J was driving to her business, she saw a white limousine cruising up the circular drive in front of an expensive home along one of the prestigious streets in her neighbourhood. In the front yard were a number of teenage boys in tuxedos and several teenage girls in expensive prom dresses. J realized that the graduation party was the one her son was attending, and it occurred to her that the only reason those young people were there was because of an accident of fate. She decided to try to give someone who hadn't had one the opportunity to better his or her life.

J had become interested in aboriginal people and decided that she would start an aboriginal business group, hoping that, through changing their status to business person from unemployed person on the margins of society, it would increase their self-esteem and allow them to try things they normally wouldn't feel they could do. A social worker offered her space in his drop-in centre and selected four aboriginal people he thought might benefit from the group. Les was the only one of the four who attended all the meetings and did whatever was required to get the Indian products developed and marketed.

When it became apparent that the business would only provide a summer income, Les decided that he wanted to go to university. Since there was no provision for someone on social assistance to be able to take a correspondence course at a university, most of the profit from the sales of products went to pay for three distance education courses at Laurentian University, Sudbury, Ontario. J, a former teacher, helped Les to set up a programme where he would study at a set time every day. When he passed three courses with the appropriate marks, Les was able to attend full time on a student loan. J believes that part of the reason that she and Les got along so well is that he was adopted by white people and they shared many white values. However, she believed that the only way he could proceed forward was to find out about his Ojibway culture. At first he was very uncomfortable with his people since he didn't know how to talk to them. Eventually, he became familiar with them and felt quite comfortable and is now quite proud of his culture.

When Les met J, he was planning to make a change in his life, and it seemed like 'perfect timing'. Les was feeling frustrated about his lack of a home and meaningful work. In addition, Les did not know how to interact with a female in a mature way. He was never taught how to do this and rarely had female friends as he was growing up, preferring his own company. Sometimes he would say the wrong thing, like making a comment about a woman in a movie or TV show that they happened to be watching. J would correct Les and he reports that he 'would get upset and go somewhere and pout for a while. J has taught me much about life and myself.' In the 12 years since Les met J, he considers he has had opportunities he never had before, a university degree, a home and the choice to be alone or not as he pleases. He says he is 'happy and comfortable with what these changes have provided me'.

The relationship is described by both mentor and client as a warm and respectful friendship, and Les comments: 'I consider her above all other people and will drop whatever I am doing for her.' Les was aware of her experience and expertise, and knew that 'she had quite a bit of knowledge and knew what she was doing. I trusted her in her decisions and direction.' In addition, J helped Les by offering him accommodation in her home – not a usual mentoring arrangement but deemed necessary for this homeless and low-income client. They would go out for meals and each pay for their own. Les says that J taught him the value of money and today their friendship 'rivals no other... we have a meaningful and mature, long-lasting friendship'.

J considered that Les, having been brought up as a white person, needed to find out who he was, and this was achieved by Les setting up, with J's help, an Indian business, selling Indian-specific products at Indian functions that were held on Indian reserves. In addition the business supplied gift stores at the National Art Gallery of Canada, Toronto Art Gallery, and London and Hamilton Art Galleries. In doing this Les found his place in life, as an Indian man, working with his own people as well as white people, and he also discovered what he wanted to do with his life. Les has graduated with a degree in social work from Laurentian University in Sudbury, Ontario, and plans to continue his studies to Master's level. He is presently employed in the social work field in Toronto and hopes eventually to teach at an Indian college or school.

The diversity of their mentoring relationship did present some difficulties, not when they were alone, but when they were in public. Initially they had experience of disapproval from Native people who did not like them being together, although after 12 years their association has become accepted. Some people just do not like interracial couples and said so. However, they were never in danger of being hurt as Les is '280 pounds and solid'. Their colleagues and J's family and friends accepted Les fully with J's father attending his graduation. Les describes his situation in this way: 'As a First Nation person I feel quite ordinary... even though I am a Native person I have been raised within the white world. Today I know much about the Native traditional ways but do not interact with Native people. I neither feel Native nor do I feel not Native.'

The First Nation mentoring relationship appears traditional, with an experienced, powerful and older mentor guiding a younger, less experienced protégé. The duration of the relationship, 12 years, and its continuation identify it as true classical mentoring as described on page 257. There is warmth and affection between J and Les as well as respect and recognition of each other. The mentoring was productive because Les was focused on what he wanted to do and J offered him the core conditions we describe in Chapter 6. Les's ownership of his goals, the nature of this relationship and the transformational outcome of the mentoring place it in the evolutionary quadrant. If such mentoring was commonplace and offered to all First Nations, the result could be revolutionary with far-reaching consequences for Canadian life.

Acknowledgement: Les MacDonald Ojibwe and J

This completes our review of mentoring definitions.

NOTE

1   TAANA – the acronym means 'There Are Always Numerous Alternatives'. It arose as a reaction to the Thatcherite expression TINA – 'There Is No Alternative' (Halfpenny, 1985).

6 What is coaching?

The confusion about naming a coaching activity replicates the difficulty with the term 'mentoring' discussed in the last chapter. We seek to clear up some of the confusion about the term by categorizing coaching as functionalist, engagement or evolutionary, depending on the purpose, the process or method used, and the learning outcome that is implied in the definition.

We begin with how coaching is generally defined and described. The dictionary definitions of 'coach' include the terms 'instructor', 'teacher', 'trainer', 'giving instructions' as well as 'professional adviser'. A typical internet site suggests that 'the name allegedly recalls the multi-tasking skills associated with controlling the team of a horse-drawn stagecoach' (Wikipedia, 2005). US college sports teams have always had their own coaches and, more recently, coaches emerged who were non-experts in the specific technical skills of their clients but who nevertheless ventured to offer inspiration to their clients. Current practice in performance coaching focuses on non-directive questioning and helping clients to analyse and address their own challenges rather than offering advice or direction.

Whose purpose is served by coaching? A typical question when managers are offered coaching training is 'Why do coaching? Can't we just tell them what to do?' The definitions above seem to suggest that the purpose of coaching is learning by the client, but what kind of learning? We refer readers to Chapter 3 where we discuss the different kinds of learning. Let us take a simple example of learning how to make tea.

As learners we remember:

20% of what we read	It's on the packet
30% of what we hear	Being told to do it
40% of what we see	Shown how to do it
50% of what we say	Saying you'll do it

60% of what we do   All of the above
90% of what we see, hear, say and do   Doing it

(from Rose and Nicholl, 1997: 142)

How long do learners remember what they have read, seen, heard, said or done? And what does this mean for the coaching process?

We refer to further research about learner recall in Table 6.1.

Table 6.1   Learner recall

	Told	Told and shown	Told, shown and experienced
Recall after three weeks	70%	72%	85%
Recall after three months	10%	32%	65%

Source: Whitmore (1996: 18)

Clearly being told or shown does not enable learning in terms of recall, and Whitmore (1996) recommends actually doing the activity in question. So effective coaching will need to do more than tell and show. At this point it would be useful to identify what sort of learning is being sought here. Is the desired learning the sort that is memorable or recallable? What learning outcome is intended with coaching? Improvement or transformation? We recall the three coaching approaches under examination in this book:

▪ functionalist coaching, where the intended learning outcome is single loop or improvement with no alteration to the status quo and the method is didactic and advice-driven;
▪ engagement coaching, where the intended learning outcome is also single loop or improvement but the method is humanistic and relationship-driven;
▪ evolutionary coaching, where the intended learning outcome is double loop or transformational and the method is humanistic and relationship-driven.

With this in mind, we can identify how the available definitions have implicit philosophies within them that reveal their purpose, whose purpose, the process involved and the desired learning outcome. How do the available definitions of 'coaching' fit into these four approaches? The answer will depend on whose purpose is being served, and we discuss below the purpose of coaching for an organization and for an individual, including the intended learning outcome. Clearly there may be an alternative outcome but this cannot be known in advance. We also discuss the process of coaching in each case.

FUNCTIONALIST COACHING

When factual learning, which can be recalled at will, is the organization's purpose, a teaching approach is sufficient, with instructing and training as the process with the learning outcome single loop, a classic case of learning for improvement (Brockbank, McGill and Beech, 2002). We have identified this as functionalist coaching, with equilibrium as the aim and an objective goal to be achieved, with little or no exploration of the client's personal world. The model of reality is rational, objective and instrumental, with the status quo maintaining an equilibrium and the relationship often a line relationship; the process has been described as follows: 'a structured two-way process in which individuals develop skills and achieve defined competencies through assessment, guided practical experience, and regular feedback' (Parsloe, 1995: 1).

Coaching programmes in organizations that aim to support staff to achieve a minimal qualification or competence level are functionalist in that their purpose is an increase in qualified staff, the process is didactive, directive and rather like teaching, and the learning outcome is improvement. Problems arise where staff as clients have expectations of coaching that go beyond these and expect personal, even emotional, support in their endeavours. We recommend that these points are clarified to the coaching clients at the start, so that there is clarity of intent, agreement about process, and realistic expectations about outcomes. Michael Carroll (2004) refers to such coaches as 'first-generation coaches', and they are represented by the statement 'I have been there – I can help you get there.'

Here the earlier dictionary definition of 'teaching, tutoring, instructing' is valid, as the purpose is transfer of factual material. The first-generation coach is the expert who can advise others and give direction to the client. As Gore Vidal said, 'there is no human problem which could not be solved if people would simply do as I advise' (cited in Carroll, 2004). So for functionalist coaching the purpose is transmission, the process is teaching or telling, and the learning outcome is single loop and limited to improvement.

What happens if the 'telling strategy' used by the functionalist coach fails? The coach, if line manager, may move on to the 'forcing strategy' where authority and sanctions are employed, the two-step process typically adopted by change agents (Quinn, 2000: 11). The telling strategy assumes people are rational, whilst the forcing strategy using coercion is likely to generate anger and resistance, and the coaching project may lead to disappointment when it fails to achieve its aims.

The psychological approach here is behaviourist, and Peltier (2001) recommends conducting a behavioural audit, based on a shadowing programme, followed by a functionalist analysis in order to effect behavioural modification through reinforcement. Despite the negative connotations of behaviourism, the method is useful for measuring and evaluating the coaching process. The benefits of behaviourism in combination with a recognition of the cognitive elements in a client's behaviour can lead to coaching that is problem-solving and solution-focused. The cognitive-behavioural approach declares that clients' beliefs and thinking are linked to how they feel about events and therefore influences their behaviour, an idea that is used by neurolinguistic programming (NLP) coaches (Neenan and Dryden, 2002). We explain and discuss NLP further on page 106.

We note that coaching initiatives that are functionalist in intent may be presented differently to potential staff clients, with the functionalist intent masked, when resistance is likely or there is tension between organizational goals and individual goals. Such coaching we term 'engagement coaching'.

ENGAGEMENT COACHING

When there is a desire in the organization to improve performance in an unpopular activity, a teaching or telling approach is unlikely to be successful, which is why humanistic approaches have been popularized. Colley's (2003) work informs us here as she highlights how such approaches are used to mask the functionalist agenda at work. Engagement coaching seeks to persuade the client to adopt the learning objectives of the organization or system. The method is used for downsizing, culture change and restructuring programmes where the coaching purpose is not owned by the individual and there is likely to be resistance to change. No wonder such coaching is described as an 'art': 'coaching is the art of facilitating the performance, learning and development of another' (Downey, 1999: 15).

What is missing from the definition is the desired learning outcome. Does the coaching aim to develop the client to the point of transformation? In engagement coaching, the hidden agenda is maintenance of the status quo. The engagement coaching approach where the model of reality tends to value the subjective, and is also concerned with maintaining the status quo, is a process that recognizes the value of relationship in learning and change. The method has been described as 'participative' (Quinn, 2000: 14), as the coach invites the client to explore a limited range of potential choices within his or her subjective world. Engagement coaching includes Carroll's second-generation coach, who is characterized by the statement 'I may or may not have been there – I create the learning environment' (Carroll, 2004). Here the coach has begun to step away from the action, and is quizzing the client about his or her learning needs. Modern sports coaches work away from the pitch rather than on it. The purpose is established in advance, by the team's trainer, even if the goals are shared. So the purpose is improvement without altering the status quo, the process is humanistic, and the learning outcome is single loop with the potential for the kind of reflection illustrated in the Kolb cycle (Kolb, 1984). The ultimate purpose here is engagement with the organization's mission, rather than individually transformational, and hence we identify such coaching as 'engagement coaching'.

The participative strategy commits to a 'win–win' outcome and is equivalent to the sports analogy of Carroll's (2004) second-generation coach, the sports coach being a favourite metaphor in the literature (Whitmore, 1996; Gallwey, 1974; Parsloe and Wray, 2000). The importance of relationship in such coaching suggests a humanistic orientation and, when underlying values and systems remain unchanged, we have called this 'engagement coaching', also discussed in Chapter 2. The support and encouragement in some programmes of engagement coaching mask its hidden functionalist purpose and may lead clients to have unrealistic expectations about potential learning outcomes.

Engagement coaching can be seen as a response to the flatter management structures in modern technology-driven organizations. It is an integral part of a properly defined human resource strategy, which must be concerned with the development of people in the most effective manner (Keep, 1992). Formal and informal coaching using a humanistic approach have increasingly been seen as part of a human resource strategy in which public and private organizations seek to develop their human resources in a way that leads to competitive success (Warren, 2005; Cluttterbuck and Megginson, 2005). The recent coaching guide published by the Chartered Institute of Personnel and Development notes that line managers are most likely to deliver coaching, and includes among the core characteristics of non-executive coaching:

- short-term;
- individual and organizational goals;
- time bounded;
- provides feedback;
- non-directive.

(Jarvis, 2004: 17)

The non-directive style of engagement coaching is evident in this fuller description, where both purpose and process are declared: 'Coaching is unlocking a person's potential to maximise their own performance. It is helping them to learn rather than teaching them' (Whitmore, 1996: 8). This understanding is associated with a 'soft' human resource strategy and management style, which are concerned to develop abilities, competencies and concepts in people, and to facilitate and encourage their use, rather than creating a functionalist system of control and extrinsic motivation, the latter being seen as a 'hard' human resource strategy. However, engagement coaching sustains a state of equilibrium and maintains the status quo, suppressing the possibility of transformative learning for the individual and the organization. The tension between individual and organizational goals because of the legal rights of proprietors in preference to those of employees, in private sector organizations, has been noted by Coopey (1995), and the nature of engagement coaching where the organizational goals are promoted using humanistic methods resolves some of that tension.

The humanistic approach utilized by non-directive coaches is almost always based on the ideas of Carl Rogers. His name however is notably absent from the coaching literature, and coaches may not even be aware that they are using his core conditions in their work. In spite of his rigorous research into personal change and learning, he is seen as being a 'touchy-feely' therapist, out of touch with the hard realities of business. The so-called 'soft skills' needed for this approach are not much in evidence (perhaps they are hard?), although they are known to be associated with individual and organizational learning and improvement (Cooper, 1997).

We draw on the work of Rogers to identify the necessary and sufficient conditions for enabling learning, and they can be applied to the context, the coach and the individual client concerned (Rogers, 1983):

1. Learning is affected by the context in which it occurs, ie the vision and values of a company or organization will influence the learning process.

2. Learning is affected by the stance of the individual learner and his or her dispositions.
3. Learning is affected by the stance of those who seek to facilitate learning and their dispositions.

We discuss these conditions in more detail below:

1. The context affects learning, so mission statements reveal the value that an organization places on learning and development. In practice, the organization can prescribe learning as functionalist by limiting coaching to identified improvements or offer a broader canvas through executive coaching.
2. The stance of the individual affects his or her learning. Where there is a history of fear and mistrust, learning is unlikely to happen (this is all too common in the workplace where memories of school experiences may be negative). Where individuals are unwilling to take risks their development is unlikely to be transformational, whereas openness and disclosure will enable the paradigm shift described in Chapter 3.
3. The stance of the coach as a facilitator of learning has been researched by learning theorists. For deep, holistic and intrinsic learning that results in worthwhile and significant change, a humanistic, person-centred approach is recommended (see Brockbank and McGill, 1998).

Rogers (1983) offered some principles of learning that guide the potential coach:

▪ Human beings have a natural potentiality for learning and a natural curiosity, and they also experience the ambivalence associated with the accompanying pain of any significant learning.
▪ People learn when the subject has relevance and meaning for them. More relevance also affects speed of learning.
▪ Learning that involves change in self-perception is threatening and tends to be resisted. Such learning is more easily achieved when external threats are minimized.
▪ Significant learning is achieved by doing and action. Learning is facilitated when the learner participates in the learning process.
▪ Self-initiated learning that involves the whole person, feelings as well as intellect, is most lasting and pervasive.
▪ Independence, creativity and self-reliance are facilitated when self-evaluation is primary and evaluation by others is secondary.

■ The most useful learning in the modern world is learning about the process of learning itself (Brockbank, McGill and Beech, 2002).

Rogers insists that the key to effective learning is the relationship between the coach as facilitator of learning and the client, as 'the facilitation of significant learning rests upon... qualities that exist in the personal relationship between the facilitator [ie the coach] and learner' (Rogers, 1983: 121).

What are these qualities?

■ Acceptance and trust of the learner, ie a belief that the other person is fundamentally trustworthy, which means living with uncertainty as that person might make a mistake.
■ Congruence, ie self-disclosure, a willingness to be a person rather than a role, to be and live the feelings and thoughts of the moment.
■ Empathic understanding of the learner's world, which must be communicated (silent or invisible empathy isn't much use).

We discuss these qualities in more detail in Chapter 11. When a coach holds such attitudes and qualities, they revolutionize learning, 'giving freedom and life and the opportunity to learn' (Rogers, 1983: 133), although Rogers recognizes the difficulties here: 'the person-centred way... is something that one grows into. It is a set of values, not easy to achieve, placing emphasis on the dignity of the individual, the importance of personal choice, the significance of responsibility, the joy of creativity. It is a philosophy, built on the foundation of the democratic way, empowering each individual' (1983: 95).

The primacy of a person-centred approach in any coaching that recognizes the subjective world of the client is confirmed by a useful statement of criteria for coaching given by Flaherty: 'coaching must allow for people to change, to become more competent, and to become excellent at performance' (1999: 21). Hence approaches that suggest that people have fixed attributes deriving from personality tests or learning styles would make engagement coaching impossible. This is confirmed by others who suggest that 'coaching... can properly be viewed as the preferred option for developing personal skills and self-managed learning' (Parsloe and Wray, 2000: 7).

An example of engagement coaching that used the person-centred approach to achieve a functionalist objective is presented in the Addaction case study below.

CASE STUDY

Addaction: project managers becoming coaches

Addaction is a drug and alcohol charity whose mission, 'Reducing both the use of and the harm caused by drugs and alcohol' (Corporate Plan 2005), includes a vision of first-class leadership, a national reputation for clinical excellence, a leading authority on the issue of drugs and alcohol, as well as a reputation in local communities as an organization equipped to meet the challenges of the future.

As part of this mission and in response to the National Treatment Agency's quality initiatives, Addaction identified the need for a core competencies framework. The framework was created, accredited and launched in March 2002 with the aim of enabling front-line project workers to demonstrate knowledge, skills and values, in nine key areas of service delivery, considered essential for good practice.

Project workers in Addaction are managed by project managers and team leaders who would be responsible for guiding and supporting their staff through the framework. In order to facilitate such guidance and support, all project managers in Addaction were offered coach training over a period of two years.

The training, entitled 'Introduction to coaching', for up to 18 managers at a time consisted of two days initially and, a week later, a follow-up review day where participants would reflect on their coaching practice. The workshop was highly participative and experiential with the aim that on completion project managers would:

1. understand coaching models;

2. identify coaching skills;

3. practise coaching skills;

4. reflect on their coaching practice as managers.

(A pre-questionnaire alerted participants to their existing coaching ability.)

Three coaching models were presented: GROW; the skilled helper; and a model designed specially for Addaction, the SOS model (see Chapter 8). A booklet was provided that included brief and accessible notes about reflective learning and coaching skills, as well as pro formas to enhance practice.

The first two days were intensely practical with project managers engaging in experiential exercises and live coaching sessions with their colleagues. Addaction's project managers were revealed as deeply committed individuals, with a passion for the organization's purpose. They were almost without exception working up to their limits, as project support appointments usually followed their own. Whilst they fully supported the core competencies programme they were anxious to avoid pressurizing their staff, and these concerns formed the basis of several of their live coaching sessions. The experiential nature of the training was appreciated by participants, who identified the following as effective:

- role plays and practice;
- discussion and feedback;
- presentation of models;
- reflection on third day;
- differences and overlap with supervision and counselling.

Additional comments, apart from complaints about the venue and the food(!), included:

- 'Made us think.'
- 'Clear, easily digested.'
- 'Gave me a lot of confidence.'
- 'One of the best courses.'
- 'Hope to attend advanced coaching course.'

(Attendance at 'Introduction to coaching' was a requirement for attendance at a further training course, 'Advanced coaching'.)

Outcomes for Addaction

The functional purpose of the coaching programme was to equip project managers with the skills and confidence to guide and support their staff through the core competencies framework. A degree of persuasion was required as not all project workers were enthusiastic about the core competencies framework, and managers needed a broad range of skills to achieve the organization's objectives and ensure that the outcome was positive for the organization.

The Addaction project managers were invited to engage in their development as coaches without generating that goal for themselves and to invite their staff to engage in acquiring their core competencies qualifications, again without generating that goal for themselves. The recommended approach for their coaching activities was person-centred, and the learning outcome was improvement. Hence the coaching programme was engagement coaching leading to single loop learning for both managers and staff.

We argue in Chapter 3 that truly significant and transformative learning demands that there is client ownership of goals and that the process is characterized by a humanistic stance that recognizes both the subjective world of the learner and the social context, and we have called this 'evolutionary coaching', to which we now turn.

EVOLUTIONARY COACHING

Evolutionary coaching adopts a subjectivist view of reality, and works with clients to define their own goals, whilst offering the potential for challenge and transformation. An evolutionary coach may work at all levels, from improvement through engagement to transformation. Carroll (2004) identifies such a coach as third-generation, and he defines evolutionary coaches as 'professional facilitators of learning at different levels'. Coaching becomes evolutionary when the relationship supports trust, the focus is decided by the client, who becomes responsible for his or her own learning and development, and the process recognizes the client's world and leads to potential transformation. The learning may include factual material and improving performance, as for functional coaching or engagement coaching, as above, but the characteristic of evolutionary coaches is their ability to support the client through double loop learning to transformation. Evolutionary coaches are able, when and where appropriate, to adopt the processes of functionalist and engagement coaching as part of their approach. However, the evolutionary purpose is personal and professional development, promoting the client's own desires, the evolutionary process is humanistic and the learning outcome is transformation. Because the purpose is owned by the client, the process is humanistic and the outcome has been identified as transformational, this coaching approach is identified as evolutionary. Evolutionary coaching can last a lifetime: 'Coaching is a powerful alliance designed to forward and enhance the lifelong process of human learning, effectiveness, and fulfilment' (Whitworth, Kimsey-House and Sandhal, 1998: 202).

A very clear statement of the principles of evolutionary coaching is given by Jenny Rogers (2004), who offers six principles that follow the humanistic philosophy almost exactly and echo the core conditions of Carl Rogers, her namesake, as follows:

■ The client is resourceful.
■ The coach's role is to spring loose the client's resourcefulness.
■ Coaching addresses the whole person – past, present and future.
■ The client sets the agenda.
■ The coach and client are equals.
■ Coaching is about change and action.

(Rogers, 2004: 7–8)

Indeed, at its most effective, 'Coaching is an art in the sense that when practised with excellence, there is no attention on the technique but instead the coach is fully engaged with the coachee and the process of coaching becomes a dance between two people moving in harmony and partnership' (Downey, 1999).

One crucial component of coaching that is evolutionary is the ability of the coach to conduct a reflective dialogue with the client, as this offers the potential for double loop learning and transformation. We discuss the conditions for reflective dialogue in Chapter 3 and we discuss the skills needed in Chapters 10 and 11.

EXECUTIVE COACHING

Where the organization is able to offer coaching to staff in order to promote their own development and this is believed by both parties to be for the benefit of the organization, then evolutionary coaching may happen. However, the usual coach-and-line manager arrangement is unlikely to promote evolutionary coaching because the relationship is hierarchical, and clients may not disclose what their development needs are within a power relationship with their senior who can 'hire and fire'. For evolutionary work, the coach will need to be outside the remit of the line, and ideally outside the organization itself, and these are known as 'executive coaches'. The risk for the organization is that support is being provided without control, so that executive coaching may prepare a client to leave the organization rather than benefiting it.

Further risks in executive coaching have been identified by Berglas (2002) and Williams and Irving (2001). For CEOs, executive coaching offers quick and easy solutions, and the number of executive coaches working for business is expected to reach 50,000 in the UK by 2007. However, Berglas believes that, 'in an alarming number of situations, executive coaches who lack rigorous psychological training do more harm than good' (2002: 87). He mentions the propensity for 'unschooled' coaches to exploit the powerful hold they develop over their clients. Indeed the practice of executive coaching has been described as 'an un-regulated, unstructured and (potentially) unethical process' (Williams and Irving, 2001). Typically, practitioners with a business background focus on the business context and are unaware of the psychological state of their client. Alternatively, coaches with a background in psychology tend to focus on the inner life of their client and forget the business context. The consequence of such unbalanced work is not likely to be beneficial to the client or sponsor. We discuss the guidelines for regulated coaches in Chapter 12.

Peltier (2001) confirms that executive coaching uses Rogerian princi-ples without necessarily recognizing them, emphasizing the importance of relationship and the core conditions given above. Where it is accepted that unconscious factors influence behaviour, as established recently (Cramer, 2000), the evolutionary coach is able to consider the effect on the client's learning of defence mechanisms, without of course pathologizing him or her. Such an approach to coaching includes recognition of anxiety and defensiveness, and the toleration of conflict, whilst promoting choice and authenticity for the client.

LIFE COACHING

The life coaching movement starts from the client's own desires and adopts a largely humanistic stance to clients. Because of this, together with its focus on transformation, we identify life coaching as within the evolutionary quadrant. We note here that the term is used by many to describe functionalist or engagement coaching, as above, with advice giving within a directive process. The dangers of dabbling in 'life' issues using directive methods have been noted by clients who have reported putting 'your life in their hands', who recommend that potential clients should 'proceed, if at all, with extreme caution' (Burt, 2005). At the other extreme, caution is recommended by the British Association for Counselling and Psychotherapy's head of media Philip Hodson: 'Problems may arise if the distinction between counselling and coaching is lost' (Pointon, 2003: 21). We discuss the boundary between counselling and coaching in Chapter 13.

(Life) coaching has been described as answering 'the needs of a growing number of people for personal development, however different their initial drives – psychological pain or the desire to become more successful professionally' (Bachkirova and Cox, 2004). They suggest that with the advent of the internet people have become aware that 'there are certain types of relationships that provide not only relief from pain and problems, but sometimes bring about satisfaction with work and are beneficial for confidence and various skills and competences' (Bachkirova and Cox, 2004).

These comments mirror the definition offered by the International Coaching Federation (2005):

Professional coaches provide an ongoing partnership designed to help clients produce fulfilling results in their personal and professional lives. Coaches help people improve their performances and enhance the quality of their lives. Coaches are trained to listen, to observe and to customize their approach to individual client needs. They seek to elicit solutions and strategies from the client; they believe the client is naturally creative and resourceful. The coach's job is to provide support to enhance the skills, resources, and creativity that the client already has.

Neurolinguistic programming (NLP) and life coaching

The NLP coaching approach is based on the original work of Richard Bandler and John Grinder (1979), which combined concepts about neurology with linguistics to produce a collection of ideas for training and development. The models in NLP include:

- the link between body and mind (eye patterns and imagery);
- the language people use (deep and surface structures);
- mirroring (symmetry in posture, gesture and movement).

The principles of NLP coaching are not unlike those of cognitive psychology, as they assume that 'people can learn to notice and change their own thoughts with powerful emotional and behavioural benefits' (Peltier, 2001: 82), and we outline some NLP ideas below. We do not intend an exhaustive treatment of NLP; interested readers may like to explore further elsewhere. NLP begins from a series of principles known as presuppositions. They are:

- Respect another person's model of the world.
- The meaning of communication is the response you get.
- The mind and the body affect each other.
- The words we use are *not* the event or the item they represent (the map is not the territory).
- The most important information about a person is that person's behaviour.
- All behaviour has a positive intention.
- Behaviour is geared for adaptation, and present behaviour is the best choice available.
- A person's behaviour is not who they are (accept the person, change the behaviour).
- People have all the abilities they need to succeed (there are no unresourceful people, only unresourceful states).
- You are in charge of your mind and therefore your results.
- The system (person) with the most flexibility of behaviour will control the system.
- There is no failure, only feedback.

- Resistance in a client is a sign of a lack of rapport (this can be said for relationships).
- There are no resistant clients, only inflexible communicators.
- All procedures should increase choice.
- Behaviour and change are to be evaluated in terms of context and ecology.
- All procedures should increase wholeness.
- All meaning is context-dependent.
- If it ain't broke don't fix it!
- All people are magnificent.

(JS International, 2005)

These presuppositions are broadly humanistic in content and, as mentioned above, conform to cognitive theory. A particular idea used by NLP practitioners, which is useful for all levels of coaching, is the idea of deep structures and surface structures in language. Surface words and sentences are incomplete or distorted versions of deep statements, and the coach may offer the client the opportunity to recover the deep structure in order to communicate more effectively. An example is given below:

Surface structure 'It's not fair – nobody ever tells me anything.'
Deep structure   'I have not been informed about the work rota.'
          'X has not informed me.'
          'This happened last month.'
          'I feel unjustly treated.'

Before leaving the subject of NLP we refer briefly to the coach's use of eye patterns as a method of understanding messages from their clients. Basically the NLP imagery systems assert that when clients communicate they do so using systems of representation that are aural, visual or kinaesthetic (touch or feeling). The eyes of clients communicating in visual mode will drift up to the left (if they are right-handed) and in aural mode to the side (either right or left), while clients believed to be communicating in kinaesthetic mode will tend to look down often to the right (McCann, 1988). The method appears cumbersome to aspiring coaches, but may well be acquired with practice.

DIVERSITY IN COACHING

Coaching across cultures, global coaching, has been described as a more creative form of coaching because it 'challenges your cultural assumptions and propels you beyond your previous limitations to dis-cover creative solutions that lie outside the box' (Rosinski, 2003: xix). Traditional coaching can fall into the trap of ethnocentrism, ie the assumption that one's own culture is a true representation of reality. Coaching in an ethno-relative way, on the other hand, recognizes and accepts difference, adapts and integrates by accepting different frames of reference simultaneously and moving outside the coach's comfort zone (Rosinski, 2003: 30). Using a cultural orientations framework, Rosinski offers global coaches a model for practice that attends to the following dimensions:

- Sense of power and responsibility, which can be based on control, harmony or humility.
- Time management, which can be based on an idea of time as scarce or plentiful; be one at a time or multi-task; and focus on the past, the present or the future.
- Identity and purpose an important dimension, which can be indi-vidualistic or collectivist, and focused on being or doing.
- Territories or boundaries can be either protective or shared.
- Organizational arrangements that encompass hierarchy or equality; are universalist or particularist; seek for stability or change; and are competitive or collaborative in style.
- Communication patterns that may be formal or informal; affective or emotionally neutral; direct or indirect; and coded or explicit.
- Modes of thinking that may be deductive or inductive; and analytic or systemic.

Perusing these dimensions brings into question some of the coaching definitions given above, as they may appear unilaterally Eurocentric or Western in their approach. Global coaching is defined as 'the art of facilitating the unleashing of people's potential to reach meaningful, important objectives' (Rosinski, 2003: 4), which neatly sidesteps the issues of whose purpose or objective is met by the coaching, whose potential is in question, and how 'meaningful' and 'important' are to be understood. Without such information the intended learning outcome remains a mystery.

Where coaching is an intercultural encounter, there are likely to be barriers to effective communication between coach and client. The coach carries responsibility for ensuring that these barriers are minimized. Barna has identified six such barriers, and we list them below:

- anxiety due to feeling like a stranger or outsider in a different culture;
- assuming similarity instead of difference;
- ethnocentrism – negatively judging aspects of another culture by the standards of one's own;
- stereotypes and prejudice – judgements made about others on the basis of their ethnic or gender membership;
- non-verbal misinterpretations, as non-verbal expressions vary from culture to culture and can easily be misunderstood;
- language – the Sapir–Whorf hypothesis that culture is controlled by *and* controls language.

(Barna, 1997: 50)

In Table 6.2, we give some dos and don'ts in cross-cultural communication for coaches who may find themselves giving offence without meaning to and perhaps not realizing what has given the offence.

Table 6.2 Dos and don'ts in cross-cultural communication

Do	Don't
Do be aware that in some communities it may not be the custom to shake hands, especially for a woman.	Don't underestimate the influence of your own cultural background in your perceptions and the way you behave.
Do avoid use of racial and ethnic terms like 'coloured', 'Afro-Caribbean' and 'half-caste', as they are liable to give offence. Alternatives may include 'black', 'African-Caribbean' and 'mixed race'.	Don't ask what someone's 'Christian' name or 'surname' is but do ask what his or her 'personal' or 'family' name is.
Do appreciate how cultural differences in body language can cause misunderstanding and conflicts, eg touching or putting an arm around someone may cause offence.	Don't assume that breaking eye contact is a sign of dishonesty or disrespect. In some communities it may be the opposite.
Do be sensitive to using terms of endearment that may cause offence to some individuals from minority ethnic communities, eg 'love' or 'dear'.	Don't assume that when members of an ethnic minority raise their voices they are losing control or becoming aggressive.

We refer the reader to our discussion of diversity in Chapter 5.

Thus the purpose of coaching is declared in general terms but the all-important ownership of that purpose is often unstated. We have clarified that functionalist coaching has its place, but clients should be made aware of its limitations. We have categorized engagement coaching as often functionalist coaching in disguise, using a humanistic approach to achieve a 'don't rock the boat' purpose. Again we recommend that such programmes come clean about their intended outcomes in order to minimize disappointment. Executive coaching and life coaching are identified as evolutionary, with their clearly defined transformational purpose and their humanistic person-centred methods. However, we have noted the need for clients to check the purpose and approach of potential providers, as many functionalist advice givers masquerade dangerously as life coaches. We recommend that clients or contractors ensure that coaches are properly trained and accredited if possible, and we discuss these matters in Chapters 12 and 14.

7 Mentoring models

In this chapter we review existing and well-tried mentoring models before recommending a cyclical model that can be used for all types of mentoring, from functionalist to evolutionary. The traditional developmental mentoring model maps against the passage of time and charts changes or stages in the relationship from its beginning to its end, but tends to be silent on how to structure each session. These are represented by Kathy Kram, David Clutterbuck, John Carruthers, Lois Zachary and Julie Hay.

Our recommended cyclical model is holographic in that it offers mentors a plan for a single session or a programme to be used over a long time period. We conclude with a description of an additional in-depth mentoring model for evolutionary mentors, the double matrix model.

TRADITIONAL STAGE MODELS AND THEIR IMPLICATIONS

Kathy Kram conducted research in a US business context and identified four stages of mentoring, which replicated the stages found by Levinson et al 10 years before. The phases of a mentoring relationship were identified as: initiation, cultivation, separation and redefinition (Kram, 1988; Levinson *et al*, 1978). We show the stages in Table 7.1.

Table 7.1 Kram's stages of the mentoring relationship

Phase	Definition	Turning points*
Initiation	A period of six months to a year when the relationship begins and becomes	– Fantasies become concrete expectations. – Expectations are met; senior manager provides

Phase	Definition	Turning points*
	important to both managers.	coaching, challenging work, visibility; junior manager provides technical assistance, respect and desire to be coached.
		– There are opportunities for interaction around work tasks.
Cultivation	A period of two to five years when the maximum range of career and psychosocial functions are provided.	– Both individuals continue to benefit from the relationship.
		– Opportunities for meaningful and more frequent interaction increase.
		– Emotional bond deepens and intimacy increases.
Separation	A period of six months to two years after a significant change in the structural role relationship and/or in the emotional experience of the relationship.	– Junior manager no longer wants guidance but rather the opportunity to work more autonomously.
		– Senior manager faces midlife crisis and is less available to provide mentoring functions.
		– Job rotation or promotion limits opportunities for continued interaction; career and psychosocial functions can no longer be provided.
		– Blocked opportunity creates resentment and hostility that disrupt positive interaction.
Redefinition	An indefinite period after the separation phase	– Stresses of separation diminish, and new relationships are formed.

Phase	Definition	Turning points*
	when the relationship ends or takes on	–
		– The mentor relationship is no longer needed in its previous form.
	significantly different characteristics, making it a more peerlike friendship.	– Resentment and anger diminish; gratitude and appreciation increase.
		– Peer status is achieved.

*examples of the most frequently observed psychological and organizational factors that cause movement into the current phase
Source: Kram (1988: 49)

The parallel with biological phases of development and mating behaviour has been noted, as well as the status and dependency implicit in the mentoring relationship (Bushardt, Fretwell and Holdnak, 1991). All relationships carry an unconscious element, the deep energy in each partner that can fuel creativity and transformation as well as potential problems. The unconscious fantasies that each partner brings to the mentoring relationship can feed hopes and dreams as well as collusion and defensiveness. Researchers have shown that the anxieties and defences in such situations are powerful echoes of early life experiences (Lapierre, 1989; Clarkson and Shaw, 1992). Clients in mentoring relationships may relive emotional experiences that they had with their parents as young children and if these are painful they can lead to behaviours that relate to 'projective identification'. Here both parties in the relationship may defend against inner pain by projecting troublesome aspects of themselves on to the other. A typical consequence of such projection is the taking on of these aspects by the receiver who feels and enacts them as if they were his or her own. Hence the projector is able to disapprove of the troublesome quality when portrayed so exactly by another (Krantz, 1989).

The parent/child analogy, noted by Levinson *et al* (1978) and others (Kates, 1985; Kahn, 1981), and psychoanalytic analyses of mentoring have concentrated on the early life stages (including the Oedipal stage) with all the anger and aggression this implies (Baum, 1992). The power of unconscious expectations within mentoring pairs has been explored, and findings reveal that effective mentor relationships incorporate an intensity of emotion not unlike parenting or falling in love (Phillips-Jones, 1982).

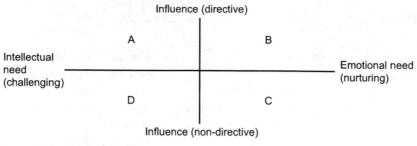

Source: Clutterbuck (1998: 8)

Figure 7.1 *Dimensions of mentoring*

What do the observations above mean for the traditional stage mentoring model?

If we relate the stages to the early stages of life, initiation is the stage where we are helpless and vulnerable so mentoring needs to support the fledgling nature of client learning. Cultivation is the 'getting-to-know-you' stage of childhood where congruence and honesty will nurture a robust relationship for learning. Separation is the inevitable stage of moving away to independence, so painful for parents, but essential for growing up. This may take the form of the client taking more responsibility and being proactive in the relationship, while the mentor needs to take a back seat. This can be a tricky time for mentors in senior positions who feel 'cast off' by the client, but acceptance of the inevitable leads to a healthy redefinition where both parties respect each other as equals in terms of learning outcomes. Most models ignore the unconscious processes and intimacy that occur in a mentoring relationship, and our recommended models address these invisible but powerful factors in mentoring couples.

Clutterbuck (1998) draws on two dimensions for his model, the directive/non-directive axis and the need axis that runs from intellectual to emotional, a truly Cartesian measure separating as it does the mind from the body (Ryle, 1983). In Figure 7.1, four sectors correspond to four roles in assisting learning: the coach in quadrant A, the guardian in quadrant B, the counsellor in quadrant C and the facilitator in quadrant D. The European mentoring model draws on all four of these roles, giving a rich picture of the developmental alliance Clutterbuck recommends for mentoring. He suggests that the most effective developmental mentors will be able to adopt whatever role is necessary using coaching and counselling behaviours when needed and alerts practitioners to the spectrum of directiveness in the guardian role, and the role of broker to expand the client's network.

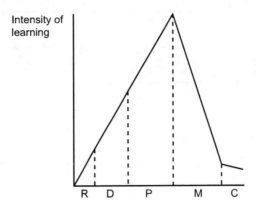

Source: Clutterbuck (1998: 95)

Figure 7.2 *Evolution of the mentoring relationship*

In addition, Clutterbuck's model mirrors the stages of mentoring described above with:

R = rapport building;
D = direction setting;
P = progress making;
M = maturation;
C = close-down.

The stages are shown in Figure 7.2 alongside the intensity of learning at each stage.

The relationship begins with rapport building and low learning intensity, moving towards direction setting and progress-making with high learning intensity. As the client becomes self-reliant, the mature relationship moves towards its close with reduced learning intensity. We differ from this idea. The intensity is one of intimacy rather than learning, as we would want the learning to reach its peak with completion of the relationship as intimacy is reduced.

A well-known mentoring model (see Figure 7.3) shows the stages through which both mentor and client pass, as the mentor's influence wanes and the protégé's personal power increases (see Carruthers, 1993), with the power balance moving gradually from the mentor to become wholly with an autonomous protégé. This mirrors the parent/child analogy and comes with all the unconscious elements described above that are largely ignored (or denied) by clients and practitioners alike.

Key:
M = mentor
m = mentor influence wanes
p = protégé dependent
P = protégé going through stages to autonomy

Source: Carruthers (1993: 21)

Figure 7.3   *Stages in a well-known mentoring model*

This mirrors another model offered by Carruthers that identifies stages in the mentoring relationship and hints at some of the unconscious elements within it, as:

- formal, where a protégé is dependent on the mentor's guidance;
- cautious, where a protégé is likely to begin to feel confident in completing tasks alone;
- sharing, where the protégé's opinion is respected as much as the mentor's;
- open, where both recognize the expertise of the other and this is openly acknowledged;
- beyond, where the relationship evolves into a friendship of equals.

(Carruthers, 1993: 82)

Zachary (2000) offers another phase model with four stages: preparing; negotiating; enabling; closing. She analyses a mentor story in terms of these stages. In *Tuesdays with Morrie* (Albom, 1997), the mentoring relationship follows the four stages as Morrie and his client (Albom) journey from their initial meeting as teacher and student (preparation), through agreeing how they will work together (negotiating) and Albom becoming a reflective learner (enabling), to the last months of Morrie's life as he moves towards his death (closing). The model includes high levels of mentor disclosure and a focus on values in Western culture, and a description of Morrie as a charismatic learner-centred teacher. The Morrie mentoring fits our description of evolutionary mentoring based on the author's own account of his transformation.

Julie Hay's (1995) transformational mentoring model of seven stages emphasizes the quality of a relationship that recognizes and values the subjective, adopts humanistic principles and, because of its person-centred approach, promotes transformation. The relationship is defined as a developmental alliance, and the holographic model (for one session or the entire relationship) is in seven A stages:

- Alliance – getting to know each other and establishing a contract, the all-important building of a relationship within agreed boundaries.
- Assessment – a reminder of Dickens's character Fagin, who 'assessed the situation', including the context and the 'dream'. This is the story.
- Analysis – a chance to see things differently and become aware of potential opportunities and problems.
- Alternatives – exploring options, even silly ones, and challenging or confronting.
- Action planning – what each option means and selecting.
- Application – how to proceed.
- Appraisal – review the actions from last session.

We would want to include a closing for each session as well as an ending for the relationship itself, and we discuss this in our recommended cyclical model below.

We offer now two alternative models drawn from the helping professions, the cyclical model and the matrix model. We recommend the cyclical model for all types of mentoring from functional to evolutionary. The matrix model is appropriate for evolutionary mentoring but is unlikely to be used by functionalist mentors as the approach is likely to be in-depth and deals with strongly emotional material.

THE CYCLICAL MENTORING MODEL

The cyclical mentoring model is adapted from the cyclical model of supervision developed by Steve Page and Val Wosket (1994) for counsellors. The model has its roots in Gerard Egan's models of helping, which can be found in *The Skilled Helper* and other publications that are not counselling-specific (Egan, 1990; Carkuff, 1969).

Traditional developmental models offer a view of the relationship over time but tend to leave the detail of individual sessions alone. In addition, developmental models fail to address variable rates of transitions, and may overemphasize stages, taking less account of individual needs. The development of the relationship itself is not addressed in developmental models except in the rather simplistic observation that the client becomes less dependent over time. Our recommended model as its name suggests can be used over the entire cycle of mentoring

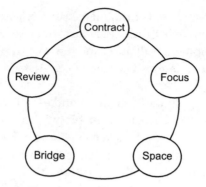

Source: Adapted from Page and Wosket (1994: 34)

Figure 7.4 *Overview of cyclical mentoring model*

meetings as well as providing a model for each mentoring session. The adapted model is shown in Figure 7.4.

There are five stages in our adaptation of the original model:

1. contract – and possibly re-contracting, which can occur at any session;
2. focus – the subject or material under consideration to be decided by the client;
3. space – 'holding' the client with a mixture of support and challenge described in Chapter 11;
4. bridge – agreeing what to do;
5. review – evaluating the session.

We review each stage now in more detail, bearing in mind that each stage can be visited in each and every session, so that the contract may be checked for suitability if things have changed, the focus may alter from session to session etc.

1 Contract

The contract should cover the detail of ground rules, boundaries, accountability, expectations and the nature of the relationship, as shown in Figure 7.5.

Ground rules

These are the rules by which the relationship will operate and should be part of the contract agreed between mentor and client. Examples of ground rules include who contacts whom, confidentiality, duration, timing and frequency, code of ethics, cancellation and fees, and

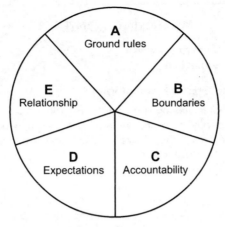

Source: Adapted from Page and Wosket (1994: 44)

Figure 7.5 *Cyclical mentoring model, stage 1: contract*

re-contracting. An example of ground rules agreed in one of our mentoring contracts appears below and applies to both mentor and client, eg time keeping and disclosure refer to the mentor as well as the client.

1. Review the ground rules together.
2. Confidentiality is total.
3. Time keeping.
4. Regular attendance.
5. Questions for clarification are OK from either party.
6. Tolerance: both have the right to disagree and have a different opinion.
7. Listening to each other.
8. Both parties to be prepared to disclose.
9. Both parties have a choice of whether to disclose or not.
10. Respecting diversity and learning from diversity.
11. Client to take responsibility for him- or herself and his or her learning.
12. Use of 'I' statements in mentoring sessions.
13. Right to say 'no-go' area.
14. We agree to reflect periodically on the relationship itself.

An example of a mentoring contract is given below. This is an adaptation of Michael Carroll's life coaching contract (2004).

MENTORING CONTRACT

This is a mentoring contract between _____ and _____ from _____ until its review (or ending) on _____.

What do we understand by mentoring?

We are agreed that mentoring is a contracted forum used by clients (ie those being mentored) to reflect on aspects of their life and work, and where they learn from their reflection how to maximize their potential and consider alternative ways of achieving their aspirations.

Practicalities

We will meet for _____ hours every _____ in room _____ at _____ at a time to be arranged at the end of each mentoring session. Ours is a non-smoking environment and we have agreed that each of us will ensure that there are no unnecessary interruptions (mobiles, phone, people). We have agreed on a fee of _____ payable at each session.

Procedures

We have agreed that the following arrangements will take place in the following situations:

1. Cancellation of session _____

2. Non-attendance at coaching session _____

3. Where there are disagreements, disputes, conflict areas between mentor and client _____

4. If there is need or desire for extra mentoring sessions _____

5. Contracts with others, eg an organization or a training course _____

6. Keeping of notes _____

7. Emergencies (you are free to phone me if there is an emergency on the following number _____). What will you (client) do if I (the mentor) am not available?

Guidelines

The following guidelines/ground rules will guide our time together:

1. Confidentiality (what we mean by confidentiality is _____).

2. Openness/honesty (about work done, the relationship etc).

3. Challenge is part of the agreement.

4. Gossip is not part of the mentoring relationship.

5. The relationship allows both parties to use feedback to learn.

Roles and responsibilities

We have agreed that as mentor I will take responsibility for:

- Time keeping
- Managing the overall agenda of sessions
- Giving feedback
- Monitoring the mentoring relationship
- Creating a safe place
- Monitoring ethical and professional issues
- Keeping notes of sessions
- Drawing up a final report (if requested)

We have agreed that as client you will be responsible for:

- Preparing for the mentoring session
- Presenting in the mentoring session
- Your learning (objectives)
- Applying learning from the mentoring session
- Feedback to yourself and to me
- Keeping notes of sessions

Evaluation and review

We have agreed that informal evaluation of:

- client
- mentor
- the relationship

will take place every sixth session. Formal evaluations will take place every year or as requested by either of us. The criteria against which evaluation of clients will take place are given below.

Renegotiation of contract

At any time either party (mentor and/or client) can initiate discussion around renegotiation of the contract or any part of it. This will be done in advance so that there is preparatory time available.

Signed: _____ (Mentor)

Signed: _____ (Client/s)

Signed: _____ (Others, eg organization or pay sponsor)

Criteria for evaluation of the mentoring relationship should be agreed at the outset by both parties and included in the contract.

Mentoring contracts will usually refer to a code of practice, and we recommend that provided by the European Mentoring and Coaching Council (EMCC).

MENTORING CODE OF PRACTICE BASED ON THE EMCC PUBLISHED CODE

1. Mentoring is a confidential activity, in which both parties have a duty of care towards each other.

2. Both mentor and protégé should be volunteers; either may dissolve the relationship if they feel it is not working. However, they have a responsibility for discussing the matter together and coming to a mutual agreement about the ending.

3. The mentor's role is to respond to the protégé's developmental needs and agenda; it is not to impose his or her own agenda.

4. Mentor and protégé should respect each other's time and other responsibilities, ensuring they do not impose beyond what is reasonable.

5. Mentor and protégé should also respect the position of third parties, other members and colleagues.

6. The mentor should not intrude into areas that the protégé wishes to keep off-limits, unless invited to do so. Mentors should check this out with protégés and, where appropriate, suggest that protégés seek counselling.

7. Mentor and protégé should be open and truthful to each other about the relationship itself, reviewing from time to time how it might be more effective.

8. Mentor and protégé share responsibility for the smooth winding down and proper ending of their relationship, when it has achieved its purpose, or renegotiating a future relationship.

Boundaries

These are defined by what the relationship is and is not, ie it is not therapy or teaching, and should include clarification of any role overlap, eg with line manager or friendships. Boundaries should be discussed and agreed at the beginning of the relationship and any slippage addressed without delay. Both parties should agree to refer when issues arise that are on the verge of therapeutic material. Unqualified mentors are in danger of harming clients if they try to 'therapize' them and should have a list of suitably qualified psychotherapists or accredited counsellors to hand to their client. We discuss the boundary between mentoring and therapy in Chapter 13.

Accountability

This is the accountability of professionals to monitor each other. Every profession has its code of conduct, and mentors will need to alert clients to their (the mentor's) role here. For instance, where clients are making racist or sexist statements, their mentor has an ethical duty to call attention to them. Where the client confesses to wrongdoing or unprofessional or illegal acts, the mentor has a duty to negotiate a way of making this known to the relevant authorities. The mentor should not have to become an accessory to illegal or unprofessional behaviour.

Expectations

As part of our work training mentors, we have experienced the discrepancy in expectations when mentors and their clients are consulted on the subject in preparing mentors and clients (separately) for their role. Clients imagine a saint-like character (idealized parent), and mentors imagine an autonomous client who will take responsibility for him- or herself. The expectations of each party can be identified at the beginning, and fantasy images of magic mentors can be adjusted to more realistic ordinariness. Mentors may find it tempting to retain the adoration of a client who sees them as all-powerful, all-knowing and all-caring, but if they don't confess their ordinariness there will be trouble ahead. This is part of being congruent, discussed in Chapters 9 and 11, which is the key to building rapport in the mentoring relationship. As well as expectations about the other party, mentors are known to carry expectations about how they feel they are expected to behave, and this departs from their actual behaviour (Roberts, 1999a, 1999b). Two aspects of behaviour, instrumentality and expressiveness, were studied in an educational context, and mentors were found to favour expressive behaviour over the expected instrumentality. We would argue that expected instrumentality signifies a functionalist purpose, which when the mentoring actually happens is masked by a humanistic nurturing expressivism, placing such mentoring in the engagement quadrant.

Relationship

The quality of relationship is the major element influencing the outcome of the mentoring project, so bonding and rapport are the most important task for the mentoring couple. Both will need to be prepared to disclose and accept each other, when they have only just met. We discuss some of the skills needed to do this in Chapter 11. We noted above the propensity for such pairings to liberate archaic feelings in both parties, and how

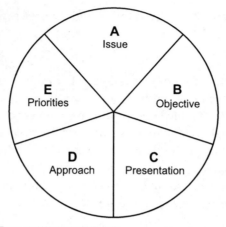

Source: Adapted from Page and Wosket (1994: 69)

Figure 7.6   *Cyclical mentoring model, stage 2: focus*

the relationship is defined will accommodate some of these. Rogerian core conditions of respect, empathy and congruence are recommended, and if the intention to work in such a way is voiced this will enable the relationship to inspect itself using the skill of immediacy, which we discuss in Chapter 11. Initial agreements should accommodate the possibility of the relationship failing and how this should be handled.

2 Focus

The focus stage incorporates the issue, objectives, presentation, approach and priorities, as shown in Figure 7.6.

The focus of a mentoring session may be prescribed, as in functionalist mentoring, prescribed but undeclared, as in engagement mentoring or, as in evolutionary mentoring, left open for the client to explore. So the question of whose issue is on the table is an important one. Functionalist mentors may be working with organizational objectives, and so are engagement mentors. Evolutionary mentoring enables the client to decide on the issue and, although the mentoring relationship is not strictly a therapeutic one, personal issues may be affecting the client's work, so these are legitimate concerns for the relationship (Clarkson and Shaw, 1992). We discuss the management of emotional material in Chapter 11. It is the mentor's responsibility to ensure that, whether the mentoring is functionalist, engagement or evolutionary, the client is enabled to assent to whatever he or she is working to achieve.

Objectives

These emerge from the discussion about the issue and for all mentoring will need to be assented to by the client. Agreeing objectives gives both parties a structure for review and evaluation later. The use of mnemonics is popular here, and we explain them below:

■ R A W:
  - Realistic
  - Attainable
  - Worthwhile

■ S M A R T:
  - Specific
  - Measurable
  - Achievable
  - Realistic
  - Time-bounded

■ MMM (Hay, 1995):
  - Measurable
  - Manageable
  - Motivational

A more thorough approach to objectives can be found in Egan's (1990) seven-point goal-setting checklist:

1. Objectives should be stated as outcomes using the 'past participle' method. For instance, the statement 'I want to lose weight' is a description of an aim. To become a goal it needs to be phrased differently, eg 'Within six months I will have lost half a stone', the past participle being 'lost'. So goals need to be described as something that is 'acquired' or 'achieved' or 'decreased' as the case may be.
2. Objectives should be clear and specific using the verbal techniques we discuss in Chapter 11 to recover deep structures. For instance, 'I want to be a better negotiator' can be made more specific by unpacking what 'better' means and establishing 'better than what?' If the goal is clear and specific it will define what better means, eg 'I will have achieved 90 per cent of my negotiating objectives this month.'
3. Objectives should be measurable and verifiable using the clear and specific statement of the goal as above as a basis. Any defined outcome can be verified, either by counting or at least by its presence or absence, eg a promotion achieved or not.

4. Realistic goals are dependent on the necessary resources being available, external factors not militating against it, the goal being controllable by the client, and the cost not being too high. If any one of these is questionable the goal may be unrealistic.
5. A substantive goal will be stretching for the client but not to breaking point. An inadequate goal will be set too low for the client concerned. The goal of an appraisal that is 'good enough' may not represent a substantive goal for a client who aspires to promotion and needs to achieve an 'excellent' appraisal.
6. Goals that are inconsistent with a client's values are unlikely to be achieved, as the client experiences dissonance and even distress. For instance, the bankers in the Sterling case study in Chapter 10 were unhappy about being asked to 'hard-sell' financial services to their customers, as their value system was based on serving their customers, not taking advantage of them.
7. A goal to be achieved 'sometime' is unlikely to see the light of day. Mentors are responsible for persisting in the question 'When?' so that clients can set their goals in exact terms, eg 'I will have qualified in accounting by the end of the year' or 'I will have completed my report by Monday next.'

Presentation

This refers to how the client lays out his or her situation in detail with context, other issues and any relevant materials, reports or documents, eg organizational maps, former appraisals, evaluations, customer complaints or comments, or even a video recording for a client who seeks to address his or her public-speaking capabilities.

Approach

This is the mentor's response to what the client has presented. A non-punitive approach is recommended for every kind of mentoring. There is evidence that mentors' approaches may not be what their protégés want or need, eg mentors may be over-intrusive and over-involved with their clients (Beech and Brockbank, 1999). Part of the contracting may include elicitation of the client's preferences in this regard. For example, Socratic questioning, whilst highly effective, may put off more reserved clients who prefer to talk problems through and find the solution themselves.

Priorities

The decision about what is important or urgent is made by the client in an evolutionary relationship but may be prescribed in functionalist or

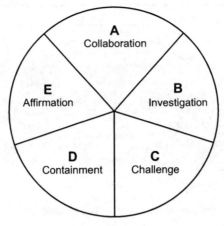

Source: Adapted from Page and Wosket (1994: 98)

Figure 7.7   *Cyclical mentoring model, stage 3: space*

engagement situations. When issues are addressed and in what order will normally be decided by clients except when the mentor is calling attention to avoidance or relevant personal matters that are not being raised by clients themselves, eg consistent complaints at work that a client is dismissing as being 'picked on' may alert the mentor to matters that need to be addressed.

3 Space

This stage includes collaboration, investigation, challenge, containment and affirmation, as shown in Figure 7.7.

Collaboration

This refers to the reflective alliance forged within the initial contract to keep a watching brief on what is happening beneath the surface of the relationship. We illustrate this in Figure 7.8.

The unconscious material can manifest itself in the mentoring relationship, as it does in other pairings of this kind, as transference, counter-transference or parallel process. Transference is a particular kind of projection, which we discussed above on page 113, where the projector is the client, who may idealize or demonize the mentor, and the receiver is the mentor, and the positive or negative feelings are historical, ie from relationships in the past. Counter-transference is the other way round so that the mentor will respond as if he or she is part of the past relationship, either wanting to look after the client or being impatient with the client. Skilled mentors are aware of these projections

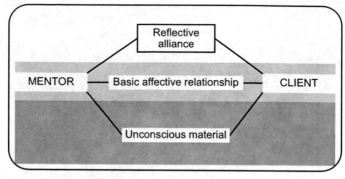

Source: Adapted from Page and Wosket (1994: 100)

Figure 7.8   *Components of the mentoring relationship*

in order to limit their effects on the relationship. Another unconscious element that may occur in mentoring is parallel process, where the mentoring relationship experiences in parallel some of the feelings occurring in the client's own world, perhaps with the client's manager or staff. Hence the mentor may be irritated by the client being unusually scatty, a behaviour that characterizes one of the client's staff who is a problem for the client in his or her work. An example of this kind of projection is given in the case study below, 'Emotions in evolutionary coaching'.

Investigation

Here the mentoring couple explore the unconscious sources, using the reflective alliance mentioned above, insofar as they are affecting the relationship and potentially the client's work.

Challenge

We discuss challenge in detail in Chapter 11. The discomfort with challenging experienced by mentors is described by Heron as follows: 'A confronting intervention unequivocally tells an uncomfortable truth, but does so with love, in order that the one concerned may see it and fully acknowledge it' (1991: 43). The success of a challenge depends on the skilled feedback given by the mentor, and we discuss feedback in Chapters 10 and 11.

Containment

Although containment, that is, the security of working within solid boundaries, should already have been achieved, the mentoring session may have generated discomfort or disorientation in the client, as he or she considers alternative scenarios or experiences archaic feelings, eg transference. The mentor is able to contain emotional material by

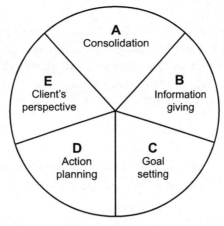

Source: Adapted from Page and Wosket (1994: 119)

Figure 7.9   *Cyclical mentoring model, stage 4: bridge*

acknowledging it and articulating its impact on the mentoring pair. We discuss the management of emotional material in Chapter 11.

Affirmation

In a mentoring relationship clients are seeking to learn, at least to improve and at best to transform themselves. The process takes its toll on clients and in the mentoring relationship they can be refreshed by affirmation, a pleasant duty that is often forgotten. We mention affirmation in the NCH case study on page 208.

4 Bridge

At this stage the mentoring couple may consolidate their work, exchange information if relevant, revisit goals, engage in an action plan and review the potential consequences of the action plan, as shown in Figure 7.9.

Consolidation

This is the gathering together of what has gone before. Here the restatement skills of mentors will pay off as they will find that they are able to summarize accurately what has been discussed in the session.

Information giving

This is relevant for functionalist and engagement mentors but inappropriate for evolutionary mentors, and the preferred method for evolutionary mentors is to direct the client to an appropriate source or reference.

Goal setting

This entails checking out ownership of goals, with functionalist and engagement mentors ensuring that organizational goals are articulated clearly whilst evolutionary mentors reiterate declared goals owned by their client. In addition, evolutionary mentors are likely to encourage their client to articulate learning goals, which can be addressed at the review stage.

Action planning

The most common mistake here is to go linear too soon, neglecting to inspect all possible ways of achieving a given objective. Egan (1990: 46) warns:

> one reason people fail to achieve goals is that they do not explore the different ways in which the goal can be reached. They choose one means or strategy without a great deal of exploration or reflection, try it, and when it fails conclude that they just can't achieve that particular goal. Coming up with as many ways of achieving a goal as possible increases the probability that one of them or a combination of several will suit the resources of a particular client.

Client's perspective

This is the moment to create the bridge back to the client's own work environment by checking out with the client how he or she foresees the effect of the actions that have been agreed. For example, how will the client's boss receive his or her intention to work towards qualification and promotion?

5 Review

Here both parties give feedback, reground, evaluate, assess and, if necessary, re-contract with each other, as shown in Figure 7.10.

Feedback

The focus of this feedback is the relationship itself, and the exchange aims to improve the quality of the mentoring relationship. The two-way mutual interaction may include dynamics in the relationship, eg dependency, and skills used by both parties, as well as styles and approaches, eg questioning and empathy. We discuss the process of giving and receiving feedback in Chapters 10 and 11.

Grounding

This is a moment of pause before moving on to evaluation and may be silent or comprise general comments about the session, eg 'Have

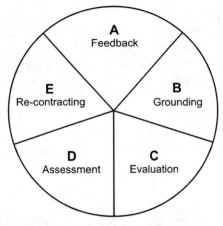

Source: Adapted from Page and Wosket (1994: 130)

Figure 7.10   *Cyclical mentoring model, stage 5: review*

we covered everything you wanted to talk about?' or 'We seem to be spending a lot of our time on the difficulties with x – have we forgotten anything important?'

Evaluation

The purpose here is to consider the value of the session and note any changes that need to be made to the process, eg allocating a minimum length of time to particular issues. For mentors who are serious about their development, the IPR (interpersonal process recall) method (Kagan, 1980) offers both mentor and client the opportunity to analyse their sessions in detail. For many mentoring couples this will be a step too far as it involves audio-taping a session and then analysing it. However, if the mentoring relationship forms part of a continuing professional development (CPD) programme, the recording of such analysis is valuable and important evidence. For professions that are self-monitored, the method may be a useful tool.

Assessment

This is an activity for functionalist mentors only, who have already agreed at the outset with their clients to breach confidentiality for the purpose of conveying information to relevant parties in the organization, eg the client's line manager. Engagement mentors may also be required to assess, in order to meet hidden functionalist purposes, and this is likely to distort the mentoring relationship, as discussed in Chapter 2. We do not expect this activity to occur in evolutionary mentoring relationships except in the form of self-assessment.

Re-contracting

Both parties review their contract with each other, check whether it is still appropriate, revisit and renew their initial agreement. If re-contracting is part of the original contract this can be done at any session, as the relationship develops, taking account of some of the changes discussed above.

We include here a case study of executive coaching, which illustrates how projections, tranference, and soon, can emerge in both coaching and mentoring contexts.

CASE STUDY

Emotions in evolutionary coaching

'In the coaching relationship, whether short-term or long-term, the significance of observing the emotional atmosphere has often been useful in assisting me ask questions that lead to significant thinking for the client. I think that this operates at a number of levels.

'A client I had not seen for some time booked herself in for some additional sessions. The initial hour was taken up with a narrative of how well things had been going, how significant the earlier coaching sessions had been in assisting her through a very difficult year and how much progress she had made. I noticed that I was feeling very tense and anxious, to a greater extent than was warranted by the situation, and felt that the anxiety was the client's. So there was a significant disjuncture between what she was saying and the feelings in the session. I said that there seemed to be some anxieties and asked what was really concerning her now. This helped to open up a discussion about her deep anxieties about an impending reorganization and her own future. Without noticing the atmosphere we might have remained on the surface and dealt only with smaller issues of current work rather than exploring the major issue and how she would manage herself and her team through that period of time.

'Another example was working with a very experienced and long-standing client. The client uses the sessions in different ways, sometimes exploring situations with difficult elected members, sometimes relationships with partners, sometimes work–life balance. I realized part-way through one of the sessions that I was feeling really bored, which was unusual as this client is interesting and very pleasurable to work with, and I wondered what was the cause of this feeling. I commented that it was beginning to sound as if he was bored with his current role. We then went on to discuss this and whether it was time for him to move on or how he could find more challenge and stimulus in the current situation.

'Perhaps the biggest challenge I faced was when a client was in the process of applying for a different senior job (after not being successful in a recent application) and, during a session, blamed me (and his wife) for having encouraged the application, in a very angry and aggressive way. This was not the case. If anything I had explored carefully with the client at the previous session all the reasons why the application might not be the right thing. Because I had been aware of his angry feelings in relation to his wife wanting him to apply for the post, and the fear of not getting it, I managed *not* to respond and say 'Well, actually, that is not true', in a possibly equally angry way, but moved on to explore how he could approach the interview in a positive way. With hindsight, I might have commented on the amount of anger. However, this might have been moving into territory that could be more appropriate to therapy.

'I choose to have supervision for my executive coaching work, and my supervisor frequently asks me what my feelings were during a session and what insight it gave me for what was of real concern to the client. These are useful questions that enable me to think more about the emotional atmosphere and how my questioning and comment can be of most value to the client. This also has facilitated discussions on issues that were not consciously top of the client's agenda, but important issues, often emotion-laden ones, that were there, hovering in the unconscious or not wanting to be thought about because of the emotions involved.'

Here the skilled executive coach is using the relationship to enable the client by attending to the emotional atmosphere. In addition, this example illustrates the importance of supervision for evolutionary mentors or life coaches.

We look now at an alternative model, the matrix mentoring model.

THE DOUBLE MATRIX MENTORING MODEL

Unlike the cyclical model, which can be mapped on to a single session or a whole programme, the matrix/process model adapted from Hawkins and Shohet (1989) is a snapshot model, with no perspective over time. Hence the model allows for inspection and analysis of one meeting between mentor and client, with depth and detail. The model is particularly good for mentoring that supports clients with managerial responsibilities, ie they lead or manage teams of people with whom they have ongoing working relationships.

The double matrix model seeks to 'turn the focus away from the context and the wider organisational issues to look more closely at the process' (Hawkins and Shohet, 1989: 55).

At any time there are four elements to consider (shown in Figure 7.11):

- the mentor;
- the client;
- the staff or colleagues with whom the client works;
- the work context.

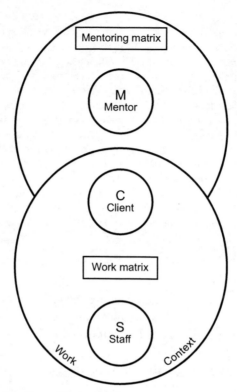

Source: Adapted from Hawkins and Shohet (1989)

Figure 7.11   *The double matrix model for evolutionary mentoring*

There are two interlocking systems that connect these four elements. First, the work matrix is where the relationship between the client and the client's staff is reported and *reflected upon* in the mentoring relationship. We discuss reflective dialogue in Chapter 4, and this is an example of it. Here the mentoring pair pay direct attention to the work relationships, by reflecting together on the reported accounts given by the client or supplied by others to the client. Second, the mentoring matrix is where the work matrix is *reflected in* the mentoring process itself. Here the mentoring pair pay attention to the work matrix through how that system is reflected in the here-and-now experience of both.

Each interlocking system can be subdivided into three categories, giving six modes of mentoring.

The six modes of mentoring

The work matrix:

1. The mentoring pair will attend to reports of the client's interaction with staff, reflecting upon events or previewing potential scenarios. An example of this is a recounting of recent staff issues, the client's actions and the actual or potential consequences.
2. The mentoring pair will explore strategies and interventions, reviewing and evaluating previous actions and considering future developments. An example of this is the analysis of a committee meeting, chaired by the client, where strategies and interactions were (un)successful, so that plans can be made for a future rerun.
3. Here the mentor (mainly) will attend to what seems to be happening between the client and the client's staff, either consciously or unconsciously, patterns and images that have emerged from the first two modes. The purpose here is to understand better the dynamics of the client's relationships within the work matrix. An example here is a discussion about the consistent difficulty that emerges with a particular individual or group and some reflections about what may be happening between them.

The mentoring matrix:

4. The mentoring pair attend to what the client is experiencing within the work matrix, particularly counter- transference, the response to unconscious material from staff members being projected on to the client. An example of this is the annoyance felt by a client who experiences a fussy member of staff who is just like her 'fussy' mother. We discuss projection, transference and counter- transference earlier in this chapter.
5. The here-and-now process within the mentoring pair can hold up a mirror to the parallel process occurring between the client and the client's staff. The mentor is a potentially powerful source of information about hidden dynamics between the client and the client's team. The mentor may note a change in attitude or behaviour in the client, like faster speech, uncharacteristic terms or style, perhaps more typical of the person(s) concerned, ie the client momentarily behaves like his or her staff member, in the phenomenon known as 'parallel process'.
6. The mentor may experience counter-transference as a consequence of unconscious projection from the client, and this is a valuable

source of information for both. For example, the mentor may detect in him- or herself perhaps a feeling of impatience with the client, in response to the client's dithering and indecisiveness, and the mentor must decide if this information may be relevant for the client or should be handled by the mentor.

The double matrix model is not suitable for functionalist or engagement mentoring. It is particularly suited to evolutionary mentoring relationships where there is a strong and trusting relationship, where the client's work is primarily with people and where the client is likely to find the interventions acceptable. Because it is based on a supervision model, it concentrates on the unconscious but powerful aspects of the client's work relationships (in the work matrix) and the relevant aspects of the mentor–client relationship (the mentoring matrix), on the grounds that all six modes hold valuable messages for the client's continuing development.

Most models are time-line driven, indicating how the mentoring relationship alters over time, rather than focusing on what happens in a mentoring session. We have offered the cyclical model, which can be used for both purposes, and a further model, the double matrix model, that takes the focus even deeper for interested readers.

8 Coaching models

Traditional coaching models start with a definable goal, which may or may not be owned by the client, and proceed to methods of achieving that goal. Such models are likely to be used for basic or functionalist coaching, and we review the GROW, FLOW and SOS models for this purpose. For evolutionary coaching, that is, executive coaching or life coaching, we recommend Rogers's approach and the Egan model because they enable clients to generate their own goals as well as their own methods of achieving them.

THE GROW MODEL

The GROW model developed by John Whitmore starts from his definition of coaching as 'unlocking a person's potential to maximize their performance. It is helping them to learn rather than teaching them' (Whitmore, 1996: 8). The purpose is declared as improvement and the process as humanistic or person-centred so the model fits into the engagement quadrant. Whitmore is clearly seeking to promote coaching using humanistic values, as he suggests that 'To use coaching successfully we have to adopt a far more optimistic view than usual of the dormant capability of people, all people', indicating a person-centred or humanistic value, discussed in Chapter 2. To move the model into the evolutionary quadrant, the goals would need to be generated by the client and there would need to be access to emotional material in the coaching process.

Let us examine the method in more detail. First, we unpack the acronym to reveal the meanings behind the word 'GROW' as follows:

- **G** – establish the goal
- **R** – examine the reality

- **O** – consider all options
- **W** – confirm the will to act

In a purely functionalist context the GROW model enables the coach to check out that the client agrees to the organization goals, to examine the current situation for the client, to discuss possible options and, finally, establish what action will be taken, when and by whom. However, Whitmore recommends that before embarking on the model proper the coach explores the client's levels of awareness and responsibility. Awareness includes self-awareness, and this is described as 'recognising when and how emotions or desires distort one's own perception' (Whitmore, 1996: 28). In addition, in his exploration of responsibility Whitmore suggests that when a client is given choice then responsibility and improved performance follow. The addition of choice moves the model at least into the engagement quadrant. To move the coaching into the evolutionary quadrant there would need to be total choice of objectives for the client, as is the case in executive coaching or life coaching, as well as high levels of skill in the coach, particularly dealing with emotional material.

So the model can work at several levels, functionalist, engagement and possibly evolutionary. However, the prime positioning of goal setting suggests that the subjective world of the client is less important than the objectives of the coaching, making client generation of goals unlikely. In functionalist mode there may not even be any attempt to gain assent to the prescribed goals, and this limits learning to single loop improvement. We explore how to use the model below.

Goal setting

G is for goal setting, and this will differentiate functionalist activity from evolutionary. For functionalist or engagement coaching the client is invited or persuaded to align personal goals with organizational objectives. For evolutionary coaching, ie executive or life coaching, clients generate their own goals. For either purpose, goal setting can be done using a choice of acronyms, SMART, MMM or RAW, and we adapt their meaning for coaches below:

- SMART:
  - **S** means that the goal should be specific and concrete, not vague and undefined, eg 'I will have completed this 5,000-word report by [a specified date]' rather than 'I must finish this report soon.'

- **M** means that the goal should be measurable, even if the measure is just a presence or absence of something, eg the report is complete or it isn't.
- **A** means the goal is achievable, and here the coach may help by checking out with the client how likely it is that the report can be completed by the specific date.
- **R** means the goal should be realistic, and this refers to the ability of the client to achieve the goal, eg is the report within the capability of your client?
- **T** means the goal should be time-bounded, and so it should be achieved by the specific date given.

■ MMM:

- **M** means that the goal should be measurable, eg 'I am going to get better at using the spreadsheet' is not measurable whereas 'I will have completed a spreadsheet for the departmental budget by [a specific date]' is.
- **M** means that the goal is manageable, so the coach checks out with the client whether the date is realistic and whether the client has the skill required to complete the goal.
- **M** means that the goal is motivational for the client, as otherwise it is unlikely to happen. An exploration of WIIFM? is useful here. The answer to 'What's in it for me?' will reveal what the client hopes to gain from achieving this particular goal. If the outcome is more unpaid overtime doing the company accounts then your client may decide this goal is not motivational, but if the use of the spreadsheet will release the client's time or staff then it may well be.

■ RAW:

- **R** means the goal should be realistic, so the coach, after listening and restatement, uses open questions as above to check this out with the client, eg 'You say you must complete the competency programme this year – what has to happen to do that?'
- **A** means attainable, and this entails further listening, restatement and questioning, eg 'How will you complete the programme in time?'
- **W** means worthwhile, and this may be difficult for the functionalist or engagement coach, as it's the client who must believe the goal to be worthwhile, not the coach. This time it is summarizing that enables the coach to check out the client's attitude. For example, 'You say you must complete the programme – what's in

it for you?' and, for evolutionary coaches, 'You don't sound too keen.'

Reality

R stands for reality testing, and this can be done by Socratic questioning, which we discuss in detail in Chapters 10 and 11. Open questions are the key to this part of the model, so the coach uses 'What?', 'Why?', 'When?', 'Where?', 'Who?' and, most important, 'How?' For instance, our report-writing client above might be asked 'How will you complete a 5,000-word report in two days?' In order to be able to deploy open questions effectively, the coach will need to have some knowledge about the client's situation and this means listening first, restatement for checking and then being in a position to offer open questions that will test the reality of the given goal. We discuss listening and restatement in Chapters 10 and 11.

Options

O stands for exploring options, and this can be done using the key skills for basic coaching: first listen and then restate, question and summarize. For instance, with the report client above, 'You were saying that you have been given too much work. Is that right?' and 'How are you going to manage the report?' and 'What other options are there?' If the coaching is evolutionary, an empathic exploration is appropriate where the client's frustration and anger about being overworked may surface, with the coach recognizing this, eg 'You sound a bit annoyed about this', and the coaching moves into a different purpose, ie the client's handling of his or her manager.

Will

W stands for verifying the client's will to act, and this is achieved by restatement and summary. In functionalist and engagement coaching the client may be assenting to an outcome that is outside his or her dispositions. For instance, a coach may summarize 'So you have agreed to do three hours' overtime to deliver the 5,000-word report by [date]' although the client likes to work a nine-to-five day. In evolutionary coaching the coach should ensure that the summarized outcome is within the client's dispositions, and this can be ensured by the coach asking the client to summarize, eg 'What have you decided to do then?' Where the coach is summarizing, he or she might like to be aware of

Clutterbuck's wonderful list of the different meanings of the answer 'yes', which we replicate in the box below.

The meaning of 'yes'

7	Yes	I'll dedicate myself to seeing this through
		↓
6	Yes	I'm committed to following this up
		↓
5	Yes	I'm willing to help follow that up
		↓
4	Yes	There's something in this
		↓
3	Yes	This is exciting and engaging
		↓
2	Yes	It's quite interesting
		↓
1	Yes	I'll go along with it
		↓
0	Yes	Over my dead body

Source: Clutterbuck (1998: 61)

The GROW model is recommended for clients who are willing and cooperative, and is especially suited for functionalist or engagement coaching. The structure ensures that clients are informed about the functionalist purpose of the coaching programme, and there is less potential for disappointment. The model may unearth a functionalist purpose within an engagement programme, and coaches may need to deal with this outcome. However, with the addition of key factors like choice, responsibility and empathy, the model may be used for evolutionary purposes by executive coaches or life coaches. The GROW process may take six months to achieve or one session, and may be repeated for different projects.

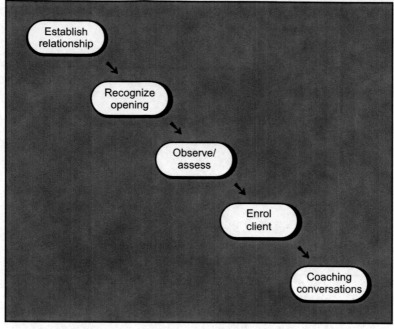

Source: Flaherty (1999: 38)

Figure 8.1   *The flow of coaching*

THE FLOW MODEL

This five-stage model was developed by James Flaherty (1999), and is illustrated in Figure 8.1.

Flaherty (1999) states very clearly the criteria for coaching to occur. Coaching must allow for people to change, to become competent and to become excellent. The psychometric testing that 'fixes' people in predefined categories denies the possibility of coaching and has no place in it. We refer to this issue again below. His five stages are:

1. Establish relationship.
2. Recognize opening.
3. Observe/assess.
4. Enrol client.
5. Coaching conversations.

The first stage, establishing the relationship, is equivalent to a contracting stage, which we discuss in Chapter 10, with the emphasis on shared commitment, mutual trust, mutual respect and freedom of expression.

It has even been declared that if there is no shared commitment there can be no coaching. Where there is an existing relationship, the task at this first stage is to establish how it can be used as the basis of a coaching relationship. Functionalist and engagement coaching may need to develop coaching relationships within historical, and not always comfortable, company relationships. Evolutionary coaching almost always starts from a new beginning in that the coach/client relationship can be defined by both parties from the start. Hence executive coaches and life coaches discuss and agree with clients exactly how their relationship will work for the duration of the coaching project.

The second stage, recognizing openings, relates very much to functionalist and engagement coaching, as it is designed to find a time when the client is approachable for coaching. The idea of openings is to be ready to take advantage of a moment when the client is experiencing difficulties or having his or her habitual identity questioned and to offer coaching then. The advice for coaches when the client declines coaching is to revert to traditional management techniques of command and control. For evolutionary, executive or life coaches, the relationship supports an egalitarian connection where the idea of an 'opening' does not occur.

The third stage of observation and assessment also seems to relate very much to functionalist or engagement coaching, and we note again here that the concept of personality inventories and learning styles is inconsistent with coaching, as they present individuals as collections of fixed properties that cannot be changed. However, the interpretation of assessment in this model aims to explore with clients their concerns, their history, their desires and their satisfactions as well as their qualities, skills and commitment to their declared goals and is clearly aimed at evolutionary coaching. There are three assessment models on offer. The first, with five elements, covers the client's immediate concerns, commitments, future possibilities, history and mood. The second explores the client's domains of competence as follows: the 'I' domain or self-management; the 'we' domain or relationships with others; and the 'it' domain where the client seeks to understand technical matters, systems and mechanisms. The third assessment model identifies the necessary sources of satisfaction and effectiveness as intellect, emotion, will, context and soul. These three assessment models are coaching models in themselves. The first, based on taking stock and looking to the future, is similar to Rogers's (2004) model discussed below; the second, based on a focus on 'I', 'we' and 'them', is similar to the SOS model discussed below; and the third mirrors the Egan model, which is our recommended model for evolutionary coaching.

The fourth stage of enrolment is the moment when the client 'buys into' the coaching project, and this again has echoes of functionalist or engagement coaching. The necessity to 'buy in' does not arise in evolutionary coaching, as clients generate their own objectives and the executive or life coaching process addresses them.

In the fifth stage, coaching conversations, Flaherty offers us three types of conversation, which correspond approximately to functionalist, engagement and evolutionary coaching. An example of the trigger for the first, functionalist, type of conversation is 'clarifying standard for performance', which sets the scene for a dialogue aiming at improvement. The second, engagement, type of conversation takes place over time and its purpose is to address a client who is, for example, 'not being open to the input of others', which suggests some overcoming of resistance, a characteristic of hidden functionalist objectives to which the client may not have assented. The final type of conversation is clearly evolutionary, being described as 'more profound'; 'it will bring about deeper change' and 'in most business situations there is not very much of an opening' for it (Flaherty, 1999: 107). This confirms our recommendation that evolutionary coaching approaches work best as external coaches or life coaches.

The excellence model described above, although utilizing many valuable evolutionary approaches and methods, does not present itself in evolutionary mode, where clients hold ownership of their objectives, and restricts itself to functionalist and engagement mode, where clients are invited to align themselves with organizational or societal objectives.

THE SOS MODEL

We turn now to another model, adapted from Parsloe and Wray (2000), designed for a corporate client, which enables the coaching pair to identify the focus of a coaching session and whether that focus lies in the past, in the future or both. The SOS model suggests that coaching should focus on:

■ **S** The situation, issue, task or project
■ **O** How others feature in the situation
■ **S** How self can act to progress the issue

In addition, the coaching may focus on the past, called 'review' mode, or the future, called 'preview'[1] mode. We show the options in Figure 8.2.

Mode / Focus	**S** Situation	**O** Others	**S** Self
REVIEW			
PREVIEW			

Figure 8.2 *Coaching focus*

Let us examine the model in more detail and explore how to use it in practice:

- **S** stands for the situation in which clients find themselves or the context in which the coaching is taking place, such as clients who seek an additional qualification in their work. For functionalist or engagement coaches, this may seem obvious, as they understand what is required to gain the qualification. However, what they have not heard is the client's own 'take' on that situation, ie the client's power horizon (see Chapter 2), to which the executive or life coach will attend, eg the client may be a single mother who is not able to find time to study.
- **O** stands for others who feature or act in the client's world and these may be colleagues, staff, senior managers, family or friends. The open question starting with 'Who?' is relevant here and can be followed up by other open questions. For instance, the coach will try to focus on the client's sources of support and how colleagues and managers view the client's situation as well as the significance of studies in the workplace.
- **S** stands for self and this is where the functionalist coach is clearly differentiated from the engagement or evolutionary coach. There is a temptation to identify the failings of clients, highlighting their faults or shortcomings, and this is typical functionalist behaviour. Engagement coaches seek to encourage their clients and celebrate their attributes, while still seeking to persuade them to adopt the required dispositions. Executive or life coaches will seek to connect with their

clients, offering an empathic understanding, thereby providing the potential for a transformative learning outcome.

Alongside the three points of focus given above, the coach will find that the discussion deals with either the past or the future, and this indicates either review coaching or preview coaching. For instance, if the client is discussing his or her performance in the previous week and trying to work out what went wrong, the process is review coaching, and is important for laying the basis for the next stage, ie preview coaching. Here the process aims to prepare the client for a future event, often drawing on what has been discovered and realized in the review mode part of the coaching.

Some typical questions for review coaching are:

1. What were you trying to achieve?
2. What were the facts? What happened exactly?
3. Was the performance better than, worse than, or equal to the objective agreed?
4. What were the reasons for your level of performance?
   - Clarity.
   - Competence.
   - Environment.
5. What is the improvement plan?

Some typical questions for preview coaching are:

1. What are you trying to achieve?
2. How will you know if you are successful?
3. How will you handle it?
4. What might get in the way or affect your performance?
   - Clarity of objectives.
   - Competences (skills, knowledge, behaviours).
   - Environment.
5. Can we confirm your action plan now?

The SOS model is popular with managers taking on a coaching role with their staff, as it is simple, easy to remember and can be used in review or preview mode. The power of the model depends (as they all do) on the skills of the coach, and even SOS could be used to effect by an executive or life coach.

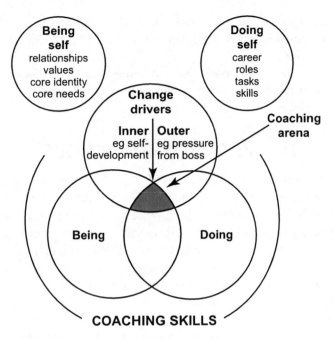

Figure 8.3 *Jenny Rogers's model of coaching*

JENNY ROGERS'S MODEL

Jenny Rogers's (2004) model for evolutionary coaching, which she describes as 'creating trust, taking stock and choosing the future', offers a clear process for evolutionary coaching, ie executive or life coaching, and includes all the skills needed. Her model, firmly based on the quality of the coaching relationship, draws on the 'being self' and the 'doing self', and the coaching arena is where they intersect. This is shown in Figure 8.3.

Rogers is quite clear that 'you cannot coach a client who does not want to change' (2004: 8), placing her approach firmly in the evolutionary quadrant. Her six principles are descriptive of client ownership of goals, and humanistic values within a holistic approach. The principles are:

- The client is resourceful.
- The coach's role is to spring loose the client's resourcefulness.
- Coaching is holistic and addresses the whole person.
- The client sets the agenda.
- The coach and the client are equals.
- Coaching is about change and action.

In addition, Rogers offers some helpful guidance on how to avoid giving advice and resisting over-disclosure by spotting the statements embedded in questions.

We move now to the model we recommend for evolutionary coaching, ie executive or life coaching, based on Gerard Egan's publication *The Skilled Helper*.

EGAN'S SKILLED HELPER MODEL

Although we recommend this model for evolutionary coaching, it can also be used for functionalist coaching, but would need to be adapted to work with the alignment of client objectives to predetermined goals. It is suitable where there are generous time resources available, coach and client can take their time, and there is a clear beginning and end to the work. In particular, the model assumes that clients have freedom to choose their own objectives and work towards them in their own way, both characteristics of evolutionary approaches in executive coaching or life coaching.

The model provides a structure to maintain focus and enable appropriate use of skills. The structure is linear, and tends to hold the coach in each stage until the client is ready to move to the next stage. However, the model can be repeated as often as necessary for different objectives.

The model is a three-stage one, shown in Figure 8.4.

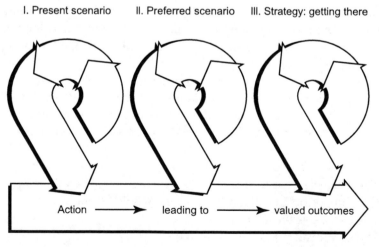

Source: Adapted from Egan (1990: 30)

Figure 8.4 *The skilled helper mentoring model*

The model proceeds in three stages:

1. the present scenario where the coach helps the client to clarify the existing situation;
2. the preferred scenario where the coach helps the client to develop goals and objectives based on an understanding of the situation;
3. action strategies where the coach helps the client to develop strategies for accomplishing goals, ie getting from the present scenario to the preferred one.

Each stage has within itself three stages as follows:

1. The present scenario: identifying and clarifying problem situations and unused opportunities (see Figure 8.5).

   A = Telling the story, as the client sees it. This may be incoherent or told in terms of other people. The coach is challenged at once to connect with the client, offering empathy as described in Chapters 3 and 10, so that the client's world is unconditionally accepted and the coach is mentally noting issues that strike him or her as crucial.

   B = Recognizing unawareness, and gently easing the client, through restatement, empathy and questioning, towards a more

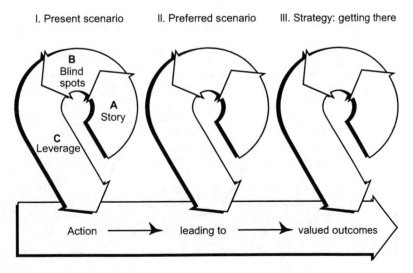

Source: Adapted from Egan (1990: 36)

Figure 8.5   *Stage 1: the present scenario*

complete picture without judgement and without being directive. This process should continue throughout the model.

C = The search for what will make a difference where the coach is in Socratic questioning mode, helping the client to prioritize, and thereafter enabling a focus on the chosen issue for the client's attention.

2. Developing a preferred scenario (see Figure 8.6).

A = Exploring a range of possibilities, which is typically where the coach may be seduced into a linear process, following the client down one line of enquiry without consideration of alternatives. Lateral enquiry demands that the coach stops the process, repeats the client's own words and may say 'How would having a qualification change your life?', possibly using 'clean language', which we describe in Chapter 11.

B = Creating viable agendas, ie the coach helps the client to identify which ideas are capable of being put into action. This stage uses some of the techniques for recovering deep structures described in Chapter 11.

C = Making a choice and commitment to one preferred agenda and investigating incentives, particularly if the choice is a tough one. The WIIFM? ('What's in it for me?') technique is simple and useful here.

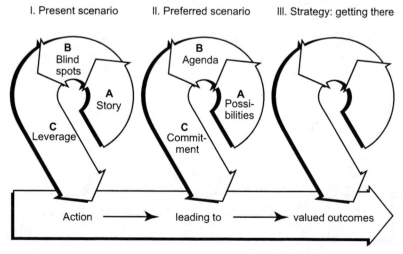

Source: Egan (1990: 43)

Figure 8.6   *Stage 2: a preferred scenario*

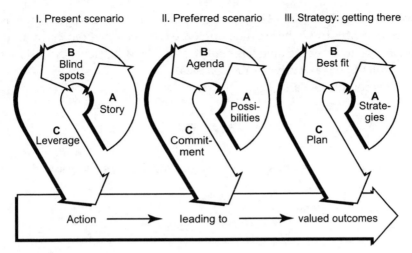

Source: Egan (1990: 48)

Figure 8.7   *Stage 3: Action strategies and plans*

3. Action strategies and plans (see Figure 8.7).

A = Brainstorming strategies, where the coach enables the client to consider a wide range of possibilities rather than going with the first thing that comes to mind. As many strategies as possible should be considered, as even seemingly outlandish strategies can provide clues for realistic action plans. Repeated questioning and acceptance of any ideas, however crazy, will result in a variety of strategies to choose from, and strategies are known to be more effective when chosen from a number of options.

B = Choosing the best strategy, where the client finds the 'best fit' for his or her needs, preferences and resources, and the one that is least likely to be blocked by factors in the client's environment.

C = Turning the strategy into an action plan is the final stage of the model, where the client is enabled to formulate a plan, a step-by-step process that will achieve the desired goal. Techniques for goal setting discussed on page 125 are useful here, as an action plan includes steps and realistic timing.

The model has power in direct proportion to the skills of the coach using it. For executive or life coaches, using the model ensures that clients explore their world in detail before addressing their desires in the second stage. Hence when goals are agreed (having been generated by the client) they have the seven characteristics needed for success, which we described earlier. The model encourages a dialogue that is person-centred, and the learning outcome is potentially transformation. So the ideal use of the model is evolutionary, and it is used extensively by professional executive or life coaches.

This completes Part II.

NOTE

1   We acknowledge this idea as originating from our work with The Oxford Group.

Part III
PRACTICE SKILLS

9 Being a client

The purpose of this chapter is to illuminate the enhancement of an evolutionary mentoring or coaching relationship by focusing on the client's skills, although it is not essential that clients should be skilled, the responsibility for the relationship being with the mentor or life coach. For functionalist mentoring or coaching, clients may choose to limit their use of these skills, especially in a situation where their coach has the power to 'hire and fire'.

Being effective as a client has four interpersonal aspects, namely congruence, self-disclosure, managing emotion and receiving feedback. We use a diagram known as the 'Johari window' to illustrate the effect of disclosure; a scale of emotional expression from easy to difficult; and make the assumption here that you and your mentor have agreed on a contract with ground rules including confidentiality and that this is recorded by both parties (see Chapters 7 and 10).

CONGRUENCE

When speaking as a client you may ramble, repeat yourself, get mixed up or just pause to consider what to say next. In mentoring sessions you may tell your story in your own way and in your own time. As the relationship develops, you will become aware of the importance of congruence.

When taking the role of client, for mentoring to be most effective, congruence is a key skill attribute, and we define 'congruence' as a way of being genuine, being real, sharing feelings and attitudes as well as opinions and beliefs or judgements. Egan (1973) has defined this kind of congruent speech as 'story' and the less congruent version as 'history'. We will identify the characteristics of both here.

Telling it like a story

'Story' is involvement. It is authentic self-disclosure – an attempt to re-veal the self as a person and to reach the listener. Story involves emotion. Story is a signal of invitation – you as client are opening the door to your self. It is a story if it is a description by you about yourself expressed, for example, as 'I felt thoroughly undervalued by my manager when my administrative assistant was transferred without consulting me.' The defining characteristic of story mode is the use of 'I' statements rather than 'we', 'one' or 'it'.

'History', on the other hand, is non-involvement. History is a state-ment or message that is analytical, factual – it ticks off the facts of experience and even interpretation of these facts but leaves the person who is making the statement untouched, relatively unknown, eg as client you might say 'The management takes decisions without consul-tation.' You may go into unnecessary detail and become boring. You are detached and uninvolved, taking no risks, treating yourself as object who is 'there and then' rather than subject who is 'here and now'. Gen-eralities may be disguised by the use of words like 'we', 'one' or 'it'. History does not reach or engage the listener. It is flat or boring because it is divorced from the person. It is not really disclosing of the person.

Story	History
I	Them, it, people
Feeling, affect	Fact
Actual	Abstract
Real	Abstract, detached
Interesting	Boring, a turn-off

In other words, when you are expressing feelings (the emotive or affec-tive part of the self) as well as the knowing (cognitive) and doing (conative) part you are likely to be in story mode and disclosing some-thing about yourself that has the basis in a real meaning that will make connections with your mentor.

Story is selective in detail – not necessarily complete in communicat-ing fact, but complete in communicating self. The storyteller is taking a risk and knows it. By so doing the storyteller is requesting support from the mentor. In a mentoring relationship, self-disclosure is a leap of trust – and demands dialogue 'here and now'. It is unusual not to be engaged when someone is telling his or her story. It is almost always interesting. Storytellers may have taken a risk and made themselves vulnerable in the process, but they will not lose the attention of their mentor, as he or she will seldom be bored by a story that includes sincere self-disclosure. However, the mentor may be embarrassed! This embarrassment can be a cultural bias against self-disclosure and the expression of emotion – seen in some contexts as a weakness at one extreme or exhibitionism at the other. Self-disclosure peaks in childhood and is seen as a passing phase that disappears with oncoming maturity. In the fullness of time we become fully locked-in mature adults! However, as human beings we do not lose our emotions; they remain in us and can be a barrier to our development or can enhance that development. Self-disclosure is often associated with the psychiatrist's couch – we must be weak and in need of 'treatment'.

Fortunately, this model (a medical model) is becoming outmoded with our increasing understanding of ourselves as having feelings that impinge on our everyday lives. For example, earlier in this chapter the client expressed the feeling of being undervalued by the manager, although the client might appear super-confident to colleagues at work. The mentoring relationship is a safe place to explore 'undervalued' feelings and decide what to do about them.

Thus telling it like a story is more likely to convey congruence between what we are saying and what we are feeling or thinking. It is more likely to create bridges of understanding than history, which takes no risk and may lead to misinterpretation.

What happens when you are unable to be congruent in the relationship?

When you communicate in 'history' mode, with a great deal of factual material and opinion about other people, situations and events but lacking feeling or real issues, your mentor may challenge your incongruence, and we deal with this process in Chapter 11. What happens if your mentor does not challenge you? The relationship becomes a problem-solving exercise, with the focus on a factual issue, distant from you and for which you are not responsible. The mentoring relationship is working 'at one remove', and personal commitment to action is unlikely.

What happens when you are able to be congruent?

Our mentor can work with you immediately, responding to the 'story' (eg the account of your difficulty with your manager) in both supportive and challenging ways, and we describe these in Chapter 11. A useful way of seeing what is happening when you are congruent in a mentoring session is the model known as the 'Johari window'.

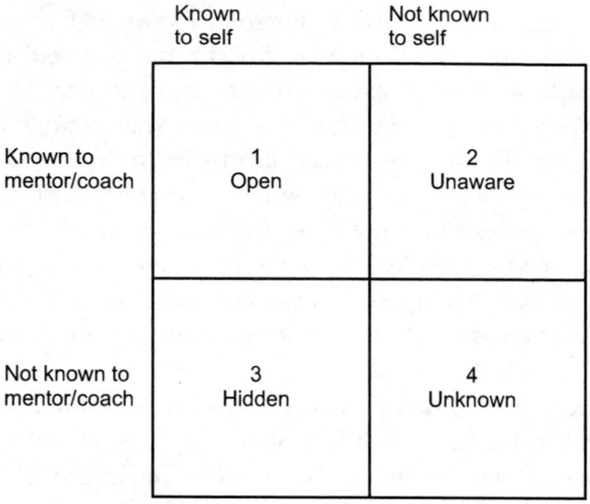

Source: McGill and Brockbank (2004: 151)

Figure 9.1 *The Johari window*

The Johari window

How we may relate to people is seen in the diagrammatic representation known as the 'Johari awareness model' or 'Johari's window' (the name being coined from the joint authors' names (see Luft, 1984). The model, shown in Figure 9.1, rests on humanistic, holistic and psychodynamic assumptions as follows:

- Subjective factors dictate our impressions of each other.
- Emotions influence behaviour more than rational reason or logic.
- Human beings have limited awareness of self, and benefit from information from other sources.
- Change promotes the possibility of learning and development.
- Experience is fluid and ever changing.

Interaction between you and your mentor depends on the extent of openness between you. The square or window describes the possible forms of awareness of behaviour and feelings, and the window represents your relationship with your mentor:

- Quadrant 1. The open quadrant refers to those behaviours, feelings and motivations that you know about yourself, and your mentor also knows these, having seen or been told about them. This is the window that you lay open to the world. It is the basis of most interaction that is willingly displayed.

■ Quadrant 2. The unaware quadrant is that which refers to those behaviours, feelings and motivations that your mentor sees but that you do not. This is the window you may display to your mentor without being aware that you are displaying it. Your mentor sees the public self in quadrant 1, but may also get an insight into quadrant 2, where you are unaware. For example, you may comment in a sexist way, without realizing it. Only if your mentor points out the remark will you become aware of it. How such feedback is conveyed to you and how you react to it will influence whether you get to know that particular aspect of yourself. We deal with the skill of giving feedback in Chapters 10 and 11.

■ Quadrant 3. The hidden area is the window that refers to those behaviours, feelings and motivations that you know about but, currently, are unwilling to convey to your mentor. For example, you may be unwilling to disclose what you feel is a weakness, eg the feelings noted earlier about being undervalued by the manager were within this hidden quadrant. When you choose to disclose information about yourself, that information is transferred from quadrant 3 to quadrant 1 and your relationship with your mentor becomes more open.

■ Quadrant 4. The unknown area is the behaviour, feelings and motivations of which you and everyone are unaware. Access to this area can be found through our dreams when we sleep or even in the occasional daydream. This quadrant will contribute to your behaviour but you do not, as others do not, normally see that part of yourself and hence working in this quadrant is not appropriate for a mentoring or coaching relationship. It is possible to gain insight into this part of the self through therapy, and that is the place for it.

The total window is drawn to scale for ease of representation, although Luft (1984) suggests that quadrant 4 is much larger than displayed. Using the Johari window, we can see in Figure 9.2 how disclosure works in a mentoring or coaching relationship.

In window a, we have a starting point, say in a new relationship. In window b, you begin to disclose some of quadrant 3, ie that which is hidden from the view of your mentor. The result is an enlargement of the open quadrant, quadrant 1, as the material is now shared with your mentor, and this is represented by window c in Figure 9.3. This enlargement is likely to apply only within the mentoring relationship. Outside

	Known to self	Not known to self
Known to others	1	2
Not known to others	3	4

Window a: unchanged

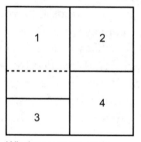

Window b: disclosing

Source: McGill and Brockbank (2004: 152)

Figure 9.2   *Johari window: disclosing*

1	2
3	4

Window c: more open

Source: McGill and Brockbank (2004: 153)

Figure 9.3   *Johari window after disclosure*

the relationship, in interaction with other people and groups, you may choose to return to the original window a, shown by the broken line.

Clearly such a transfer is managed as a choice by the discloser and is relevant to the context. For instance, disclosure in a family situation differs from disclosure at work or with friends. In mentoring, the context is reflective dialogue, discussed in Chapter 4, with the purpose of enabling connected learning. We discuss connected learning below.

Belenky *et al* (1986) have identified connected learning as very different from the separated learning that maintains a distance from the issues concerned. Belenky and her colleagues described 'really talking' as characteristic of constructivist learners (described in Chapter 4). The constructivist approach to learning is one of sharing, as, if learners 'do not articulate what they've learned, then that renders their knowledge useless if they can't share it with other people' (Belenky *et al*, 1986: 144). In addition to sharing what they know, constructivist learners also have a willingness to describe how they got there. They differentiate 'really talking' from the holding-forth style of communication, where there is no intention to share ideas, only to transmit them one-way. Really talking enables learners to engage in reflection through reflective dialogue. We shall explore below what 'really talking' means in terms of the skill of self-disclosure, as it is a key dialoguing skill.

We know that reflective dialogue involves disclosure, as the client as learner seeks clarification of his or her learning processes through sharing them with others. This sharing builds the structure for connected knowing, which enables you as learner to allow yourself to be 'known' by your mentor. If this seems too 'personal' we need only look at the separate knowing that results from impersonal, objective approaches to learning, which we discussed in Chapter 4. In sharing the personal components of your learning in reflective dialogue you take the opportunity for deep and significant reflection. The kind of reflection that challenges assumptions hitherto held firmly and questions the taken-for-granteds (tfgs), the 'givens' that we never think to question because they are there, has the potential to construct a new view of the world. In order to maximize deep and significant reflection, you will be asked to self-disclose to your mentor and vice versa, as appropriate. As your mentor is a role model here, we therefore recommend that mentors acquire the skill of appropriate self-disclosure, so that you as a client are given an idea of how to proceed.

SELF-DISCLOSURE

In order to convey your genuine and real issue you will need to engage in self-disclosure. In operational terms this means that you will tend to make 'I' statements, owning your statements, rather than using 'you', 'they', 'one', 'we' or 'it', all of which have a tendency to distance the speaker from ownership of what is being said.

Although the term 'self-disclosure' may put people off, as it sounds exposing and like being stripped naked, in reality in all our relationships we self-disclose, and we control how much we reveal of what we are thinking and especially feeling. How much we disclose is likely to be related to differences in culture, gender, class, race, sexual orientation and disability. It will also relate to the nature of the relationship concerned, eg:

■ a loving partnership;
■ a working relationship as:

- colleagues;
- manager and managed;
- doctor and patient;
■ woman to woman;
■ man to man.

Any disclosure you make will be transmitted through messages between yourself and your mentor, and may be subject to some loss and potential misinterpretation. We discuss this under 'Listening' in Chapters 10 and 11. As a client you may also disclose intentionally or unintentionally. The messages you express that carry disclosure may be conveyed via:

■ the body – face and parts of the body;
■ the voice – our tone of voice, ie how we talk;
■ touch – physical contact with another;
■ verbal – what we say;
■ actions – what we do as a contrast to or confirmation of what we say and how we say it.

Appropriateness of disclosure

Too much self-disclosure is embarrassing. Too little and we may find we do not relate to others and reduce our capacity to reflect upon ourselves in the mentoring relationship. Quadrant 3 in the Johari window is hidden from our mentor. How far we disclose depends in part upon our values and the norms of the mentoring relationship. Some people value openness, others privacy. Over-disclosure occurs when the disclosure is inappropriate to the context.

The level of disclosure that is suitable to the context can be called 'appropriate' self-disclosure. 'Appropriate' is defined by:

■ amount (how much);
■ depth (how deep);
■ duration (how long);
■ the target (to whom);
■ the situation (time and place).

We all have experience of a myriad of versions of the above combinations. For example, someone who insists on talking in detail about him- or herself constantly and at length (duration) is deemed inappropriate, as is the over-discloser who reveals intimate details (depth) to almost anyone (target) on any occasion (situation). So we have a true sense of appropriate self-disclosure, and moderately well-adjusted persons disclose appropriately for human contact and social intercourse. In addition to the above, the literature on self-disclosure reveals that women are higher disclosers than men, and that disclosure is reciprocal in effect, ie where high disclosers are present this increases disclosure by everyone (Cozby, 1973).

There may be strong cultural imperatives against self-disclosure, and this may inhibit your behaviour, especially in conditions where you perceive yourself to be under test. For many people, self-disclosure implies weakness and supports the reverse halo effect (where a weakness in one area is presumed to exist in other areas), and fear of shame and rejection is a strong inhibitor, especially in a relationship where no trust has been established. And here we have the conundrum. A sure way to establish trust is some self-disclosure, and on the other hand you may fear self-disclosure until you are confident of trust in the relationship. How can this loop be breached?

The first person to take a risk is the mentor, who, we recommend, discloses first, and we discuss this further in Chapter 11.

Our experience of mentoring relationships is that clients do engage in self-disclosure as the atmosphere of trust develops between the couple. We have seen earlier that the development of that trust depends on the mentoring relationship adhering to the ground rule of confidentiality. Knowing that what is said in a mentoring session will not be repeated to anyone outside the relationship is crucial. Mentoring relationships can provide for a degree of self-disclosure that may not be available elsewhere. Consequently, this provides a means of finding out things about ourselves of which we may not be aware. If 'I' am able to be open with my mentor, 'I' am conveying something of myself that may be crucial to my development.

MANAGING EMOTION AS A CLIENT

Emotion plays a key role in reflective dialogue, double loop learning and connected or constructivist learning. The expression of emotion is socialized on cultural and gender lines, eg privileging particular emotional expression to females but not to males, such as weeping. Some emotions are more acceptable in particular cultures than others, and this is inculcated very early in life. There is no further training in the handling of emotions (Skynner and Cleese, 1983), leading to the inadequacy of emotional matters in the wider (Western) society (Orbach, 1994).

People who declare that they feel no emotion have just got the lid on tighter than the rest of us and will reveal 'leakages' in some way. Emotion in itself is a fact. We are living human beings for whom emotion is an integral part of ourselves. A confidential relationship offers us the chance to express feelings safely.

Being socialized to discourage the expression of some of our emotions is partially useful. I may be angry with someone. That does not mean I can hit out physically or abuse the person emotionally. That is useful socialization. However, some forms of socialization may result in inhibiting the display of emotions so that we may become 'locked in' emotionally as adults.

Jourard (1971) suggests that people who are 'known' by others are healthier and happier than those who are not. The suppression of emotion in Jourard's view is a major component of stress in modern society. In our role as mentors we have often heard a client say that being able to give voice and express emotions has been a major breakthrough in tackling a major task in work or in life, confirming expert findings on stress management (Cooper, 1983).

As we have observed, if people do not express their emotions verbally there will be a tendency to 'leakage' – the expression non-verbally of the emotions. Both channels can of course be used together, and when they match this is known as 'congruent' behaviour. Non-verbal expression of emotion may include tone of voice, gesture and body language. Verbally, emotions may also be expressed inadvertently when the words belie the stated intention, as in Freudian slips!

The root of the verb 'emovere' suggests movement, and it doesn't take a lot of thought to recognize that emotion is a strong motivator. Given our Western cultural heritage that leans towards not revealing our emotions, how can we deal with expression of emotion and what is its value in a mentoring relationship?

Expression of emotion

First, emotions are part of being human, in themselves neither right nor wrong, and though we can suppress or even repress 'unacceptable' emotions they are not so easily controlled and may be released verbally and/or non-verbally. Second, the motivating power of emotion provides the 'fuel' for the adventure of double loop learning (see Chapter 3). Emotion is an important source of energy to support and sustain the learner through the 'dip' of the learning curve. In addition, an ability to deal with emotional material is necessary if we wish to 'unpack' the blocks to learning that emerge in reflective dialogue.

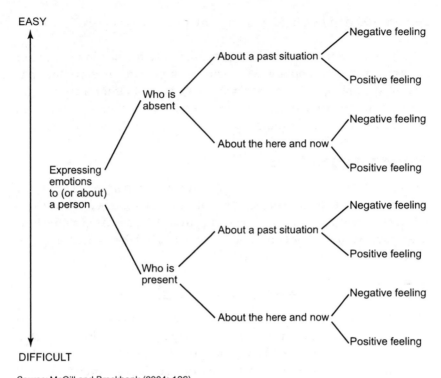

EASY

Expressing emotions to (or about) a person

Who is absent

About a past situation
Negative feeling
Positive feeling

About the here and now
Negative feeling
Positive feeling

Who is present

About a past situation
Negative feeling
Positive feeling

About the here and now
Negative feeling
Positive feeling

DIFFICULT

Source: McGill and Brockbank (2004: 196)

Figure 9.4 *Expressing emotion: the difficult-easy continuum*

We recognize our heritage and seek to identify where our difficulties may lie. The difficult–easy continuum, based on the work of Egan (1977) and shown in Figure 9.4, indicates how awkward or easy we find emotional expression under a variety of circumstances.

Figure 9.4 suggests that we find it easier to express negative emotion, and this is borne out by our lop-sided emotional vocabularies, which incorporate more negative feelings than positive ones. Further, we are able to express emotions about people in their absence more easily than to their face, what we call the 'gossip syndrome'. In the light of this for you as the client, how might you express your emotions appropriately?

Responsibility for emotion: owning it

We are each responsible for our emotions. If, say, a mentor seems dismissive of your issue, you may feel angry and disappointed. What do you do with this anger? You could respond with either 'You are making me feel angry' (which may be received as an accusation) or 'I feel angry because you don't seem to be taking my problem seriously. I'm disappointed.'

With the latter you are taking responsibility for dealing with your own anger and disappointment. This is important. If you make the former statement, your mentor, who isn't perfect either, may feel accused, threatened and defensive, whilst if you make the latter statement you are speaking about yourself and this cannot be gainsaid.

Storing up emotions

Saving or storing up emotions is not helpful for when they eventually erupt they may explode. Subject to social situations, it is better to express feelings as they arise even if they are negative. We may need a little time to identify what the emotion is and how we feel but that is different from putting the emotion into storage.

Knowing your own emotional states

Awareness of our emotional states enables us to express clearly in words what it is we are feeling and why. You may have difficulty expressing some emotions or express them indirectly. For example, you may feel anxious or inadequate, while your mentor may feel frustrated or impatient. The first is likely to be revealed by lack of eye contact and drooping body language, and the second may be leaked in the tone of voice used by your mentor.

Parking it

You may decide, having identified your feelings about an issue or person, to 'park' the feeling until the situation arises where it can be dealt with. The person concerned may not be available or the time may not be right, and emotional intelligence means judging when to deal with and when to 'park' emotion.

As noted above, feelings and emotions are basic human characteristics. They are neither good nor bad, right nor wrong. However, we may seek to control the expression of our emotions even though we may feel them. In fact, how we handle our emotions is a learnt style of behaviour. We may be socialized not to show some of our emotions, eg hurt or anger. As a consequence we may not be able to handle them in ourselves or in others. An example of the first is a reluctance to cry if another person makes 'me' feel angry or hurt because it may be seen as a sign of weakness. An example of the second is that, if another person is in tears, 'I' might feel embarrassed and avoid the situation.

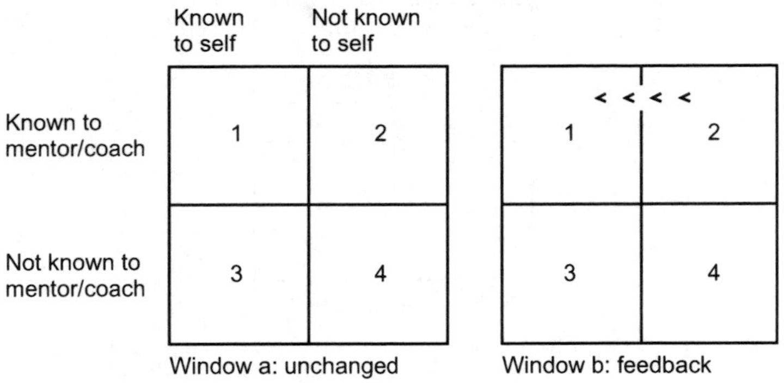

	Known to self	Not known to self
Known to mentor/coach	1	2
Not known to mentor/coach	3	4

Window a: unchanged

< < < <

	1	2
	3	4

Window b: feedback

Source: McGill and Brockbank (2004: 159)

Figure 9.5   *Johari window showing feedback*

A mentoring relationship is conducive to the couple expressing their feelings in a safe environment where the usual sanctions against displaying emotion are less powerful. Hence, as a client, you may express anger or weakness within the mentoring relationship that you would never dare to show in the workplace. The mentoring process is designed to give you the opportunity to express your needs, wants, opinions, beliefs and feelings in direct, honest and appropriate ways. This is most effective when you have an awareness of what is happening in yourself and the ability to convey that message appropriately to your mentor.

RECEIVING FEEDBACK

For a mentor who will be engaging in reflective dialogue, an important skill to develop is that of giving feedback, and we discuss this in detail in Chapters 10 and 11. As a client you will need to receive feedback in a way that will enable you to achieve connected and constructive learning. To understand the role of feedback in reflective learning we look again at the Johari window (see Figure 9.5), the details of which were introduced in Figure 9.1.

This time we are considering movement of information from quadrant 2 to quadrant 1, after you have received feedback from your mentor. If there is trust in the relationship, you will receive information about yourself from quadrant 2, which you are unable to know without the insight of others. The result may be that you discover a new, more informed self, represented by the enlargement of quadrant 1 as shown in Figure 9.6.

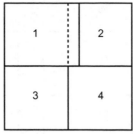

Window c: more open

Source: McGill and Brockbank (2004: 159)

Figure 9.6 *Johari window: the client's window after feedback from mentor or coach*

The concept of feedback comes from systems theory and the idea that systems, which include individuals, can be self-correcting as a consequence of information from inside or outside the system. Mentoring is an example of the latter. In a mentoring relationship, effective feedback on our actions and behaviours is a way of learning more about ourselves and the effect our behaviour has on others. Research suggests that constructive feedback increases our self-awareness, offers us more options to how we can act, relate to others and take the opportunity to change our behaviour (London, 1997). An example of such an outcome is presented in the case study below.

CASE STUDY

A client's tale

'I have been working with a professional mentor/executive coach, Janet, for about two years. Her approach is very "client-centred" and responds to what I need at the time rather than an inflexible "this is what I do" approach, and I really appreciate this.

'Over the past few months, I have been trying to plan my future. I have been in my current non-executive leadership role for about 11 years and feel that I want to move on. In future my aim is to give up this role, work less, do more of the things I enjoy and to focus on my consultancy work. What I enjoy, and am told I am good at, is executive coaching and mentoring, facilitating learning sets and conflict resolution with individuals, teams and whole organizations. However, like many consultants, I have worries about whether the work will keep coming in, despite the fact that it always has. My response to this is always to take work even if it isn't what I ideally want and will enjoy.

'Working with Janet I have come to understand that my anxieties reveal a deep-seated insecurity that is partly based on background and class and some more recent baggage around "rejection" and fear of rejection when bidding for work. On a particular day, she gave me very positive feedback around how I am perceived, and asked me to focus on what I know is a very sound reputation, acceptance of my skills and experience and what she had heard me say I wanted in my life. She then invited me to consider other options and another vision of the future, born out of deep listening to my concerns. She said "Let me paint you another scenario and tell me how you would feel about it." The scenario was that I may not plan at all, that I could take a "mini-sabbatical", let people know my change of direction and signal what I will be doing (the things I enjoy and am good at) and see what happens… and that I could think about moving in environments that would provide "succour" for my new life. Considering this new scenario changed my outlook. As I "tried this on for size", I warmed to the idea, and as the days have gone on I have become positively enthusiastic and energized.

'A remarkable thing then happened, which reinforced and reaffirmed this approach. I had been asked to undertake a piece of work that I really didn't want to do, partly because I felt strongly that it wasn't what the organization really needed. I spoke to my contact in the organization and said "I don't do this sort of work – just dropping into the organization and running an away day that won't get to the heart of what you are telling me is needed. What I would like to do is work with you and your chief executive to help you get the best out of your partnership and look at how you can really lead together."

'To my amazement, this was accepted, and we moved to focusing on her underlying concerns and issues in a way that hadn't been there before. My analysis of this was that my "authenticity" and directness touched the heart of the matter and revealed a truth that often we don't "sense" in organizational life. It felt quite profound and has affirmed the rightness of the way forward for the work that I am beginning to craft.

'My reflection is that a wise mentor can help not just with day-to-day issues and tasks, but knows when a critical point is reached, when to work on a deeper emotional plane, with a deeper responsiveness to the client. I can honestly say that it has been life-changing and opens up for me more complex and subtle consideration of the relationship between work, self, values and "passion".'

Here the quality of relationship enabled the client to hear the feedback she received from her mentor. Effective feedback can lead to double loop learning and transformation, as elicited here, providing the client is able to receive it.

In order to maximize the benefits of feedback we describe here how to receive it effectively:

1. The LAW rule: listen and wait. Listen to the feedback rather than immediately rejecting or arguing with it. Feedback may be uncomfortable to hear but we may be poorer without it. People do have their opinions about us and will have perceptions of our behaviour, and it can help to be aware of these. However, having listened

carefully it is important to clarify your understanding of what you have heard.

2. Clarify. Be clear that you understand what has been said without jumping to conclusions or being defensive before responding. A useful device is to restate what it is you think you have heard to check for accuracy. This also gives you time to consider how you will respond. A useful discipline is writing the feedback down and reading it slowly before responding or even opting to take it away and consider it at leisure. There is no rule that says the receiver of feedback must respond.

3. Consider whether you agree or disagree. If you agree, you may like to accept the feedback and you may also wish to comment on its significance for you. Again there is no rule about this. You are free simply to accept the feedback and say nothing more. Alternatively, you may disagree and choose not to accept the feedback as it stands. Here you may choose to consider checking out the feedback with another, ie get a second opinion.

4. Check out with others where possible rather than relying on one source. In a mentoring relationship it may be part of the ground rules that you as a client can seek a second opinion, as others may give another view.

5. Ask for the feedback you want but don't receive if it does not occur naturally. Feedback is an important part of learning for you and you should ask to receive feedback from your mentor when you need it.

6. Decide what you will do because of the feedback. 'It takes two to know one' is the meaning of the Johari window. Rather than relying only on our own view of ourselves, this offers instead an alternative view for our consideration.

7. You may like to recover the deep structures within the feedback. When you receive feedback you may like to consider what is hidden beneath the surface. This is known as 'recovering' the deep structures that are in many surface structure statements (see Table 9.1).

Table 9.1   Recovering the deep structures

Surface structure	Deep structure	Recovering question
'You are always late.'	'You were late on X and Y occasions.'	'Always? When was I late?'
'You are too slow on reception.'	'I believe you are too slow in comparison to me/the previous receptionist.'	'Slow compared to whom?'

Surface structure	Deep structure	Recovering question
'You will have to do better.'	'I need you to answer the phone after two rings.'	'What do you mean by better?'
'This report is too long.'	'This report is too long in comparison with other reports I have read.'	'Too long in comparison with what?'
'You should see someone.'	'I believe you need to see a counsellor/therapist.'	'You think I need to see a counsellor?'

Surface structures and deep structures are based on Chomsky (1957, 1969) and we discuss then fully on pages 211 and 216.

We now examine the skills needed by mentors and coaches working in the functionalist or engagement quadrant.

10 Being a functionalist mentor or coach

In this chapter, for ease of reading, we use the term 'coach' throughout to mean functionalist mentor or coach.

Why are special skills necessary for coaching? There is general agreement that coaches are not born – they are made by a combination of experience and development of people skills. For many the skills come naturally, so this chapter will put names to what you are doing already. For others there will be difficult areas, like how to agree a contract and ground rules with your client, or trying to limit how many times you interrupt or talk over your client. Most of us are poor listeners and it is possible to make improvements in how we listen to clients. The ability to restate clients' sentences enables you to build rapport with them. Questioning is a key skill for coaching, as are summarizing and feedback. We make the assumption that all our readers know how to give advice and that developing that skill is not a priority.

So if it isn't giving advice, what does 'being a coach' entail? 'Coaching is a process that enables learning and development to occur and thus performance to improve. To be a successful coach requires a knowledge and understanding of the process as well as the variety of styles, skills and techniques that are appropriate to the context in which the coaching takes place' (Parsloe and Wray, 2000: 42).

The coaching process is described below in terms of the following skill areas:

- contracting and ground rules;
- listening;
- restatement;
- empathy;

- questioning;
- summarizing; and
- giving feedback.

CONTRACTING

No coaching should begin without an agreed contract. If you are also the line manager then coaching will form part of the working alliance between yourself and the staff member concerned. Ground rules will also be dictated by the line relationship or the nature of the relationship. For example, you may be asked to coach a staff member whom you do not line-manage and convey that person's progress to his or her manager. This breach in confidentiality should be clear from the start, as otherwise the coaching partnership is doomed. Issues of confidentiality within organizations tend to make the coaching role a managerial responsibility and functionalist mentoring an off-line activity. In both cases, for a healthy partnership we recommend contracting at the start. A sample contract is given below, based on an original idea by Michael Carroll (2004).

COACHING CONTRACT

This is a coaching contract between _____ and _____ from _____ until its review (or ending) on _____.

What is coaching?

We are agreed that coaching is a contracted forum used by clients (those being coached) to reflect on aspects of their life and work, where they receive formal and informal feedback on that work and where they learn from their reflection how to maximize their potential.

Practicalities

We will meet for _____ hours every _____ at _____ at a time to be arranged at the end of each coaching session. Ours is a non-smoking environment and we have agreed that each of us will ensure that there are no unnecessary interruptions (mobiles, phone, people). (Add here anything about groups if group coaching, or fees if necessary, or equipment, eg flip charts, overhead projectors, video, audio etc.)

Procedures

We have agreed that the following arrangements will take place in the following situations:

---

1. Cancellation of session _____

2. Non-attendance at coaching session _____

3. Where there are disagreements, disputes, conflict areas between coach and client (coachee) _____

4. If there is need for extra coaching sessions _____

5. Contracts with others, eg an organization or a training course _____

6. For appeals _____

7. Keeping of notes _____

8. Emergencies (you are free to phone me if there is an emergency on the following number _____). What will you (client) do if I (the coach) am not available?

Guidelines

The following guidelines/ground rules will guide our time together:

1. Confidentiality (what we mean by confidentiality is _____)

2. Openness/honesty (about work done, the relationship, reports etc)

3. Line management issues that may pertain (especially if the coach is also the line manager)

4. Gossip (any leakage of information in the systems)

5. Using feedback to learn

Roles and responsibilities

We have agreed that as coach I will take responsibility for:

- Time keeping
- Managing the overall agenda of sessions
- Giving feedback
- Monitoring the coaching relationship
- Creating a safe place
- Monitoring ethical and professional issues
- Keeping notes of sessions
- Drawing up the final reports (if needed)

We have agreed that as client you will be responsible for:

- Preparing for the coaching session
- Presenting in coaching
- Your learning (objectives)

- Applying learning from coaching
- Feedback to self and to me
- Keeping notes of sessions

Evaluation and review

We have agreed that informal evaluation of:

- client
- coach
- coaching

will take place every sixth session. Formal evaluations will take place every year or as requested by either of us. The criteria against which evaluation of clients will take place may be arranged with an organization or solely with the client and will include criteria or competencies against which the client wishes to be appraised, or competencies given by his or her organization. Formal reports will be sent to _____ and can be viewed by _____. They will be kept at _____.

The process for formal evaluation of clients (written) will be:

1. self-evaluation

2. evaluation by coach

3. initial report by coach to be seen and commented on by client

4. final report written by coach with space for comments by client

5. report sent to agreed personnel (above)

Renegotiation of contract

At any time either party (coach and/or client) can initiate discussion around renegotiation of the contract or any part of it. This will be done in advance so that there is preparatory time available.

Signed: _____ (Coach)

Signed: _____ (Client/s)

Signed: _____ (Others, eg organization or training institute)

Further examples of ground rules can be found in Appendix 3.

LISTENING

When a coaching relationship is working effectively, the coach is *really* listening. We regard this as one of the most important skills brought to coaching, because although it is a basic skill the remainder of the skills we address in this chapter and the next depend on it. By 'listening', we mean the ability of the coach to 'Capture and understand the messages [communicated by the client], whether these messages are transmitted verbally or nonverbally, clearly or vaguely' (Egan, 1990: 108).

People spend much of their lives listening, unless they have an impediment in their hearing. It is a very familiar activity. However, despite the significance of listening, people experience *not* being listened to. It seems that listening is not as easy as it sounds! The difficulty and rarity of real listening was noted by one of the founders of humanistic psychology, Abraham Maslow, and his comments are still relevant today: 'To be able to listen… really wholly, passively, self-effacingly listen – without presupposing, classifying, improving, controverting, evaluating, approving or disapproving, without duelling with what is being said, without rehearsing the rebuttal in advance, without free-associating to portions of what is being said so that succeeding portions are not heard at all – such listening is rare' (1969: 96).

It is easy to state the above but there is a significant tendency for us to lose some of what a person has said because we are human. We may lose a significant part of what is being said simply because the act of verbal communication is itself complex even though we take it for granted. We illustrate what happens when A communicates with B in Figure 10.1. When A communicates with B in five stages, accuracy may be compromised and the message reduced or distorted at every stage in the process:

1. A formulates an idea and creates a message that may or may not signify exactly the original idea.
2. A transmits a message. The message in the form of sounds and visual signals travels through space and time to B and may be distorted by external factors like noise, light and wind.
3. B hears approximately 50 per cent of the message, as B may make judgements or create arguments, perhaps while A is still speaking, and may miss part of the message.
4. B decodes the message, and may decode incorrectly for all sorts of reasons, including lack of understanding through different forms of discourse, which can be influenced by, for example, class, gender or culture. B may also be confused by conflict between verbal and non-verbal information.

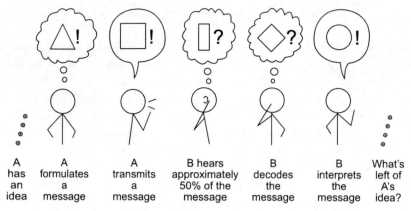

| A has an idea | A formulates a message | A transmits a message | B hears approximately 50% of the message | B decodes the message | B interprets the message | What's left of A's idea? |

Source: McGill and Brockbank (2004: 166)

Figure 10.1 *A communicates with B in five stages*

5. B interprets the message to fit his or her cognitive map, ie B may have a negative or positive 'fix'. By the word 'fix' we mean the tendency for selective listening – only hearing what we want to hear. We often evaluate people as they are speaking, eg when a politician of a different persuasion to ourselves speaks we may 'switch off' and only hear what we want to hear. Conversely, with a politician of our own persuasion we accept the speaker's message without question. An effective coach evaluates the message as it is transmitted, judges it and rejects (or accepts) it without critical analysis.

After the five stages of communication, how much is left of A's message? How can we reduce this loss of what is transmitted? The largest loss occurs at the point where B receives or 'hears' A's message, and this is where training and practice can improve the situation. There are records of 25 per cent improvement in the accuracy of coaches after training. But surely listening is a 'natural 'skill? Weren't we born knowing how to listen? Burley-Allen suggests the reason for our poor showing on listening lies in its absence from our education (see Table 10.1).

Table 10.1 The absence of listening from education

Mode of communication	Years of formal training	Estimated percentage of time used
Writing	12	9
Reading	6–8	16
Speaking	1–2	35
Listening	0–½	40

Source: Burley-Allen (1995: 39)

So how can we ensure accurate listening? How can we reduce this loss of what is transmitted? We can reduce the loss by *attending* to our client, suspending our responses to enable us to reflect on the client's message, and checking internally that we are with him or her in a non-judgemental way.

Attending to your client

In order to listen it is necessary that you first attend to your client. The reinforcement power of attending means that attending can alter another's behaviour (quoted in Egan, 1976: 96). Indeed the withdrawal of attention has been described as psychological punishment (Nelson-Jones, 1986) and likely to damage development (Bowlby, 1969). Certainly the effects of never being listened to have been summarized in the statement: 'A riot is at bottom the language of the unheard' (Martin Luther King, 1968).

Attending refers to the way in which you can be *with* your client both physically and psychologically. Attending is how you as a coach are personally present, physically receptive, calm and grounded, without anxiety, ready to tune in to verbal and non-verbal messages. You can gauge your listening as a coach by checking out the sense your client has of being attended to. By this is meant the quality of the attention you are giving to your client. Your body stance and orientation will influence the quality of your listening, and Egan (1990) has characterized this with the SOLER mnemonic to assist you in adopting an attentive posture in order to convey the minimum requirements for attending to your client:

■ S – Face your client Squarely, that is with a posture (usually seated) that conveys involvement, reflects the client in a positive manner and indicates that you wish to be with him or her. This is in contrast to a posture that turns away from the client or appears disinterested. The square posture shows that you are not distracted and ensures stereophonic reception.
■ O – Adopt an Open posture to signify 'receive' mode. Crossed arms and legs may convey a closed stance towards your client. Such a posture may not necessarily mean that you are closed toward him or her, but it may convey it non-verbally. The key question to ask is: 'To what extent is my physical posture conveying an openness and availability to my client?'
■ L – At times it is possible to Lean toward your client in a way that suggests engagement. We can see this when viewing people in pubs and restaurants by observing how people lean forward, lean back or lean away.

- ■ **E** – Maintain **E**ye contact with your client. This is a useful indicator of involvement, which does not have to be continual to be effective. It does not mean 'eyeball to eyeball' either!
- ■ **R** – Be relatively **R**elaxed in your behaviour. This means not being physically distracting or fidgety. It also means being comfortable with your client so that your body can convey non-verbal expression.

A commitment to listening to your client, utilizing SOLER, ensures authenticity. Artificially contriving a physical stance will convey messages that are counter-productive for your client. Negative or uncomfortable messages might include staring, getting too squared up where it becomes threatening, looking out of a window continuously or tapping a pencil on a table! Being aware of the effect of your physical and emotional presence is the key. SOLER is useful to convey the basic features of attending. To the reader unfamiliar with the approach it may appear that to adopt the features could suggest a lack of genuineness or manipulation. It is designed merely to highlight what we all do naturally when we are authentically attending. We consider now hearing and active and passive listening.

Hearing and active and passive listening

Contrast the distinction between hearing, active listening and passive listening. If you close your eyes you can hear what is going on around you (unless you have a hearing impediment) as well as inner sounds inside you. As you hear you are likely to be interpreting what you are hearing – we place meaning on the sounds we hear quite automatically. Alternatively you may be passively not trying to grasp meaning from it or not really caring what you hear.

Now with eyes open listen to your client.

Listening actively is not just hearing what the client is saying but is a two-way process involving both sender and receiver skills. Active or effective listening can only be assessed by the speaker, so as your client conveys a message to you, about problems at work perhaps, you as coach need to convey to the client that you have received what he or she has tried to communicate. It is possible at this point for active listening to seem passive and polite, whereas it is a procedure for connection. Anyone who has tried to learn to hear the other in the other's own terms knows how difficult it is to become 'an observer from within' (Schwaber, 1983: 274). This is why active listening is a tough-minded process. We have to really work at it and if we are really listening it shows! Your client is aware of you really listening.

Active listening also involves listening to the whole person, not just the words he or she may be using at the level of intellect. Our culture emphasizes listening to the words people *say*. We tend to listen at the level of words – the verbal channel. But active listening also includes listening to what a person's non-verbal messages are saying: *body* messages and, often forgotten, the messages in the vocal channel — the tone of voice used. As senders of messages we often convey our *feelings* through the vocal channel whilst denying them in the verbal channel, eg when we say in a wobbly voice 'I'll be all right.' Underlying these channels is the spirit of the message, your client's will to act.

Let us take an example of your client talking about a potential promotion. The client is saying that he or she is considering going for the promotion because of being well qualified for the post — the verbal channel. The client's body is sending out messages that convey lack of confidence about the post, as is his or her tone of voice. Underlying these messages is another that is transmitted about the client's will or spirit to go for the promotion. If as coach you passively went by what the client said you would conclude that all he or she needed to do was to get on with the application form. However, by actively listening you are picking up the more complex messages from the other two channels.

Contrast passive listening and the signals that are conveyed between your client and yourself. With passive listening you convey, often non-verbally, that you are not really listening. Consider situations in which you have been on the receiving end of passive listening and identify the signals you picked up. Recall situations where you have given out the signals of passive listening to a person who wanted your attention!

Further aspects of effective listening

There are other ways in which you can impede the effectiveness of your listening. You can evaluate; filter; be distracted; be sympathetic; interrupt; or just be working out your own next response.

Evaluative listening

When you listen evaluatively you may impose your own values upon your client's message. In our example where your client is considering promotion, you may do any of the following whilst apparently listening:

■ think that the client really hasn't a chance (or that it is a walkover);
■ feel jealous ('Why am I not going for it?');
■ think 'Who would want the job anyway?';
■ think that the client should not go for it ('Women are not good managers').

You are judging what you are hearing whilst it is being transmitted instead of putting these thoughts to one side in order to hear what the client is conveying. It is very difficult to put judgements aside entirely. It is important to recognize where they are coming from however. Evaluations of the situation may be helpful at a later stage provided they enable your client.

Filtered listening

This is similar to the above but, more specifically, as coach you are filtering out some of what your client is saying according to your own view of the world so may be missing important parts of the story.

Distracted listening

This occurs when as coach you are distracted by tiredness, your own emotions or your difficulty with differences of culture, gender, race, sexual orientation or disability that 'get in the way' of listening. Anyone can be distracted at any time, and coaches report that listening is an exhausting activity!

Listening with sympathy

This is a common and human response, but sympathy can get in the way for your client. For example, at a later session your client reports that he or she applied for the promotion but was 'pipped' to it by another candidate. As coach you could offer your sympathy and replicate the client's feelings of sorrow and loss at not getting the promotion. By doing this, you could be disabling the client, as he or she is unlikely to move on from there. Being with the client empathically is different, as we shall see below.

Interrupting

Interrupting a person who is conveying his or her thoughts and feelings is a common trait in conversation arising from enthusiasm, boredom, having something to say ourselves, not being able to wait, emotion, or insensitivity toward the person who is speaking.

Silence

At times your client may pause or not want to express words. There may be a tendency for you to fill the silence or space with a question or a response. There is, in fact, no silence – it is just that your client has stopped using words! That 'silence' can be precious for your client, and there are non-verbal cues to observe without words. The session is for your client. It is space for him or her. If that space includes silence, it is to be respected.

How shall I respond?

If you are preoccupied with this question (and it is understandable when we first become conscious of our responses), you may stop listening and therefore stop attending to your client. The key is to forget about a response and just 'be' with your client, using the LAW rule, ie if in doubt, listen and wait.

RESTATEMENT OF CLIENT'S STORY

When you are ready to respond, what will you say? We recommend that, before anything else, you restate your client's words. The representation to clients of their material is both affirming and incredibly useful, laying the basis for a complete summary later. Often clients may not be quite clear about what they want to say. When it is restated for them they can adjust it or agree to it and move on. If responses are critical or questioning too early, the learning may be killed off before it starts, particularly if clients' contributions are attacked or ignored. The skill of 'receiving' contributions from clients without evaluation is the key to building rapport and probably the most valuable skill for coaches to learn. Restatement reflects back to clients key points in what they have said. This enables you to check your understanding and also offers clients an opportunity to revise what they said. This is a valuable tool in enabling clients, as we rarely hear what we are thinking and feeling being articulated.

The technique of 'restating' is a useful way of discovering what you do hear and improving your accuracy, as well as enabling clients to reflect on what *they* have said and critique it themselves: 'one of the most useful tasks we can perform as we seek to develop critical thinking in other people, is to reflect back to them their attitudes, rationalisations, and habitual ways of thinking and acting' (Brookfield, 1987: 75).

Once your client has spoken, as coach you may respond in order to clarify and confirm that what you received is an accurate account of what he or she conveyed. Dialogue is enabled when your client's contribution is affirmed by you and confirmed by him or her. Given that you will wish to restate at least some of what you think you heard, you may wish to start with phrases like: 'What I think you said was that you want to improve your understanding of the job and you are unsure how to start' or 'If I have understood you properly, you want to discuss how to prepare for the regional manager's visit.'

This description may appear simple, obvious or even banal as set on this page. It is stated here because of our social tendency to assess and interpret and think what we are going to say even before the speaker has finished. The purpose here is *accurately* to reflect back to clients what you thought they said. Using some of their exact words in 'reverse' may be helpful if it is unclear, ie changing 'I' to 'you' and changing 'my' to 'your' as above.

An inappropriate response would be to give an interpretation of what was said rather than an accurate response, eg 'You're quite insecure, aren't you?', or to make and convey an assumption beyond what was said, eg 'You want to impress the regional manager.'

Many people find the prospect of restatement or 'reflecting back' embarrassing and are uncomfortable with it, possibly resorting to an inappropriate response because of that discomfort. Clients are unlikely even to notice that you are restating – the luxury of being responded to is so rare and precious that they are likely to move on enthusiastically. The discomfort is in the coach and, with practice, the awkwardness dissolves as the increased potential for understanding the message becomes obvious.

SUMMARIZING

Restatement builds material for a competent summary, which is your responsibility as coach. As a coach who has restated key points, you will be able, with or without notes, to give a résumé of clients' issues for their benefit. Summarizing is a key skill for reflective dialogue and therefore for coaches. Summary relies on the quality of earlier restatement. Identify the key points in what has been said. You will find this easy if you have already done some restatement. Vocal or non-verbal activity suggests a key point for the client. The key points noted by you may not be the ones that are important to your client, so check.

There is one final point about coaches who are non-responsive, preferring to listen in silence. Listening in silence has its place. However, in the initial stages of a relationship your client will be anxiously seeking a response from you, and this is where the 'atmosphere' of the relationship is established. If the first response is silence, which may be perceived as negative or critical, then your client may withdraw. If, on the other hand, a listening response is given, eg a brief restatement, then the climate of support and safety is established from the start.

QUESTIONING

The place for questioning comes after listening to what the client has to say, without judgement, so that some trust and confidence have been established. Questioning too early can be experienced as interrogation, and may halt the process of rapport building. Types of questions include:

- open – questions beginning with 'What', 'Where', 'Why', 'Who', 'How' and 'When';
- closed – questions that can be answered by 'Yes', 'No' or one word or phrase;
- rhetorical – questions that contain their answer;
- probing – questions that go deeper;
- multiple – more than one question at once.

We identify open questions using Kipling's stanza:

I had six honest serving men
They taught me all I knew.
Their names were what and why and when
And how and where and who.

(Rudyard Kipling)

The use of open questions allows clients to develop their own strategies for action. Open questions begin with one of the following: 'What', 'How', 'Why',[1] 'Who', 'Where' or 'When'. On the other hand, closed questions may close down their willingness to speak or speculate, thus limiting opportunities for reflection. In addition, affect questions invite emotional expression, probing questions need to be open to be effective, and reflective questions are challenging. Rhetorical or leading questions may divert clients from their own learning path, and multiple questions just confuse everybody. We give some examples below:

- Open – 'What are the duties in the new post?'
- Closed – 'Have you done anything like this before?'
- Affect – 'How do you like the role?'
- Rhetorical – 'You know you can do it, don't you?'
- Probing – 'What exactly did you do last time you held the position?'
- Checking – 'You said you'd like to do x and y. Is that right?'
- Multiple – 'Which manager did you have and how much of the job did you do? Can you remember what you did?'
- Reflective – 'What would help you to feel confident about the job?'

How can we use questioning to help our clients? By using questioning as part of a dialogue that consists of an iterative process of restatements and questions.

A final point about questioning. You may find yourself, as a coach, asking a question that is really advice in disguise, and you can test this by identifying the statement that is hidden in your question. For instance, 'Have you thought of...?' and 'What about...?' are hidden statements of your opinion. You may like to check your questions for hidden statements. Open questions avoid the problem. When you decide to give advice it is probably best to admit it and then both parties understand what is happening.

EMPATHY

The purpose of this section is to suggest that as a coach you can, with care and respect for clients, receive their story in a helpful way, using primary empathy. For a connected dialogue where as a coach you attempt to 'boldly swing into the life of the other' (Buber, 1965, cited in Kohn, 1990: 112), you are affirming the subjective reality of clients, particularly their emotional world.

A tendency to interpret empathy as 'feeling with' skates rather close to sympathy. When you as a coach start 'feeling with' your client, you exclude the reasoning and inference that are necessary to 'imagine the reality of the other' (Kohn, 1990: 131). For 'without imagining the reality of the other, empathic feeling is ultimately self-oriented and thus unworthy of the name' (Kohn, 1990: 131). On the other hand, a matter-of-fact response that excludes the affective (emotional) part of the client's message will not achieve the 'imagine-other' of empathy. For connected knowing and reflective dialogue, thinking cannot be divorced from feeling. Hence for you to 'truly experience the other as subject... something more than an intellectual apprehension is required... the connection must be felt viscerally' (Kohn, 1990: 150). 'Viscerally' here means that there is a bodily response of some kind, a sense or feeling that connects you to your client.

The Western preoccupation with thinking as superior to feeling ensures that coaches will often feel more comfortable with the cognitive aspects of a client's story whilst the feeling content may be politely ignored (and therefore for them denied). Hence we deal at some length here with the emotive element in the client's world. We make the assumption that coaches are already more than competent with the intellectual content of the client's message. To make a true connection in dialogue demands a marriage of both, and we offer a way of doing this below, using primary empathy.

What exactly is empathy? By 'empathy' we mean an ability to project oneself into another person's experience while remaining unconditionally oneself. Carl Rogers describes empathy as follows: 'Being empathic involves a choice on the part of the *coach* as to what she will pay attention to, namely the... world of the client as that individual perceives it... it assists the client in gaining a clearer understanding of, and hence a greater control over, her own world and her own behaviour' (adapted from Rogers, 1979: 11, our italics).

Others have developed the meaning of 'empathy' as follows:

- a 'bold swinging into the life of another' (Buber, 1965, cited by Kohn, 1990: 1122);
- to 'make the other present' (Buber, 1965, cited by Friedman, 1985: 4);
- 'the imaginative projection of one's own consciousness into another being' (Margulies, 1989: 58; Noddings, 1984: 30);
- to 'receive the other into the self' and 'excluding the intrusive self' (Piaget, 1972, cited by Keller, 1983: 134).

Taking the above into consideration, we define 'empathy' as 'an understanding of the world from the other's point of view, her feelings, experience and behaviour, and *the communication of that understanding in full*' (Brockbank and McGill, 1998: 195, original italics).

So *feeling* and understanding your client's story is fine, but this is not the operational skill in use. For true empathy there needs to be a communication of that understanding from you to your client. The tendency to believe that in order to communicate understanding you must also agree with your client's view of the world may inhibit your use of empathy. To affirm and offer empathy does not mean to agree.

Primary empathy is based on two pieces of information (incorporating the affective and the cognitive domains): 1) what your client is feeling (expressed in words or non-verbal behaviour); 2) the experience and/or behaviour that is the source of that feeling (revealed by what your client has already said).

When these two pieces of information have been identified, the next step is communication of that awareness from you to your client. For example, your client might say 'This job will take over my life — I'm not sure I want to go there.' If empathetic, you may respond with something like 'You feel unsure about this job because you're afraid it might take over your life.' In starting to use empathy it may be helpful to use the form of words given in the box below.

> 'You feel... because...' or
> 'You feel... when... because...'

Using this form of words can be a useful way to get into using the skill, as it reminds us that there are two elements to attend to. First you respond to the feeling and then you communicate the reasoning element in what your client has said. If the feeling element is accurate (or near accurate), your client is likely to be able to work with the cognitive material in his or her story. We give an example below in our words and recognize that coaches will use their own words in their own way.

Let us take the following statement made by your client: 'I see myself as rather ordinary. I'm not sure I'm up to this senior management role. Perhaps I should just not bother and stay where I am. I'm ordinary.'

We discuss below how this statement can be followed by a number of less than appropriate responses including:

- the cliché;
- questioning;
- interpretation;
- inaccuracy;
- response too soon or too late;
- parroting;
- incongruent response;
- giving advice;
- giving an evaluation;
- making a judgement;
- challenging.

We have listed responses above that are not empathic. Each of these responses has its place but none of them is empathic. This is not to say they are not appropriate responses, but we note that they are sometimes believed to be forms of empathy and we simply clarify that *they are not empathy*.

For instance, you may respond with clichés like 'I hear what you say' or 'I understand', which in themselves are of no help to clients. Such statements do not convey to clients that they are understood. They are more likely to convey to clients that they are *not* understood and that you are responding in an automatic and inauthentic manner.

A questioning response to a client's statement might be 'In what ways are you ordinary?' The question does not take account of the fact that the client has taken a risk in disclosing how he or she feels. The question (which may be relevant elsewhere) does not convey empathic support about how and whether you are understanding the client.

Interpreting your client's words occurs when you respond by trying to guess what is implied in the disclosure. An example might be 'This ordinary thing is the outward problem. I bet there's something else behind it that's upsetting you', which might lead to 'You want to get to the top, don't you?'

Your response may just be plainly inaccurate like 'You're not very happy with the way your work is going.' Your client may be taken off-track or stop or hesitate because accurate empathy has not happened and he or she may be blocked by what has been said. You may be listening to your own agenda rather than attending to your client. Giving your client a chance to express him- or herself gives you time to sort out feelings and content.

If you merely repeat to the speaker what has been said you are parroting. You need to 'own' what has been said and then respond. This shows that you have got 'inside' your client in a way that conveys accurate empathy.

You may use language that is incongruent with your client. Using similar language in response to that used by your client encourages rapport, provided the language you use is authentic to you. You can then convey that you are in tune with your client. The use of 'clean language' is discussed in Chapter 11.

An example of giving advice is 'Oh dear, you mustn't worry about promotion – you're all right as you are.' An example of judging what the speaker has said is 'Nonsense, you'll be fine.' And an example of challenging the speaker is 'I bet you can do it if you try.'

When clients express a feeling in their story, it is not necessary for you to treat them as a problem, go into 'rescue' mode or offer advice. The solution may not be appropriate anyway. Understanding of their problem or issue is much more useful – provided you communicate that understanding. We know from the work of Rogers (1992) and Egan (1990) that communication of understanding allows clients to move on to a discovery, in time, of their own solutions and to find ways of handling them, taking with them the knowledge of their own ability to learn and reflect.

We offer now an example of an accurate empathic response (primary) to your client's statement on page 188 about being ordinary (we will use our choice of words here, recognizing that yours might be quite different): 'You say you feel rather ordinary. You are unsure about taking on a senior management role and you are wondering whether to go for it after all'.

Empathy commits you to your client and commits your client to you. That is a sign that your client is valuable and worthwhile and to be respected. The skill of empathy is rather rare in social interaction – few people experience it. When clients experience empathy, they recognize the power of an understanding response that builds trust, establishing the basis for a relationship within which it is safe to engage in reflective dialogue, and thus enables the process of connection and reflective learning.

FEEDBACK

To understand the role of feedback in learning and development, we return to the Johari window shown in Figure 9.5 on page 167.

Window a: unchanged   Window b: feedback

We are considering movement of information from quadrant 2 to quadrant 1, after your client has received feedback from you as the coach. If the window represents your client in interaction with yourself as coach, your client will, if there is trust between you, receive feedback about him- or herself about quadrant 2, which the client is unable to know without the insight of others. The result may be that your client can project a new, more informed self represented by the enlargement of quadrant 1 as shown in Figure 9.6 on page 168.

Effective feedback on our actions and behaviours is a way of learning more about ourselves and the effect our behaviour has on others. Constructive feedback increases our self-awareness and offers us more options to how we can act and relate to others and the opportunity to change our behaviour. We describe the characteristics of effective feedback below.

Window c: more open

Effective feedback does not only mean positive feedback. Negative feedback, given skilfully, is just as important. Destructive feedback is unskilled feedback that leaves the recipient simply feeling bad with little to build on. However, the most commonly voiced complaint is lack of feedback or feedback that can't be used by the recipient.

Feedback is of little value to the recipient unless: 1) the recipient can understand it; and 2) the recipient can use it.

Should we always give feedback? The person offering feedback must make a judgement about appropriateness. This includes when – 'Is this the right time?'; where – 'Is this a good place?'; who – 'Am I the right person to give it?'; and how – 'How can I do it most effectively?'

Feedback principles (adapted from Carroll, 2004)

Rationale:

- There are areas of life we cannot see (see the Johari window in Figure 9.5).
- Feedback enables us to fulfil our potential.
- Feedback can address poor performance.
- Feedback will assist our learning.
- Feedback should be client-focused, not a discharge for the benefit of the coach.
- Giving feedback is a skill and can be learnt.

Purpose of feedback:

- to create awareness;
- to facilitate learning;
- to help change behaviour.

Points to remember:

- You cannot change the behaviour of others.
- Behaviour is difficult to change.
- Intervene as soon as possible.
- Relationships are crucial to feedback.
- Modelling is a powerful method.
- If it's working, continue.
- If it's not working, stop and do something different.

Good feedback is:

- descriptive;
- specific;
- constructive;
- current;
- relevant;
- checked;
- emotionally aware;
- open to discussion;
- owned by the giver (not someone else's opinion);
- limited (three chunks is most people's limit).

Some examples of feedback formulae

1. 'How was it for you?'
2. 'Would you like to know what I see from over here?'
3. Positive/negative/positive sandwich.
4. 'When you... I thought...'
   'When you... I felt...'
   'When you... I noticed...'
5. Recommending:
   'I would like you to do more of... because...'
   'I would like you to do less of... because...'
   'I would like you to continue... because...'
6. What, what and what:
   Tell them what they did.
   Tell them what the effects were.
   Tell them what you'd like them to do.

What if the feedback is negative? How can you give positive feedback without sounding sloppy? We look at some of the difficulties below and identify the skills needed to give feedback properly.

Positive feedback

Often we may not give positive feedback because:

▪ We may forget to do so in taking a person's qualities and skills for granted when something has been done well. We may be more likely to draw attention to those aspects that have not gone well.
▪ We may be embarrassed to say something positive to others for fear that it may be misinterpreted or may not seem genuine or that the receiver may be embarrassed.
▪ We may be brought up to think of self-effacement as better than too much self-confidence.

Some or all of these reasons may inhibit the giving of positive feedback, which is an important part of learning. Staff need to know what was effective about their work so that they can repeat it; otherwise it is a guessing game.

Negative feedback

Giving negative feedback may feel uncomfortable to do, as we fear it may be distressing for the person receiving it. However, persistent failure to give negative feedback may result in:

▪ the tendency for negative feedback to be 'stored up' and, under pressure, explode in a destructive way;
▪ no change in the person's practice because he or she is unaware that it is causing any difficulties;
▪ a continued practice that is less effective.

What are the skills in giving feedback?

1. Clarity. Be clear about what you want to say in advance. In order to achieve clarity, first observe and listen carefully. Second, record observation in concrete and specific terms, ie what as a coach you have seen and heard, eg details of your client's behaviour and reports of its effects. Before delivering feedback verbally, it may help to practise beforehand, possibly with someone else, and/or write down what it is you want to say.

2. Start with the positive. Most people need encouragement, and staff need to know when they are doing something well. Do not take the positive aspects for granted. When offering feedback, it can really help receivers to hear first what they have done well, for example: 'I liked the way you worked with your team on this issue — because you listened, they were prepared to accept the point. *And* I observed that they seemed to wait for something from you.' (Note avoidance of the word 'but' when linking positive and negative feedback, as 'but' tends to devalue what has just been said.) The use of a feedback 'sandwich' has been recommended, where a negative piece of feedback is sandwiched in between two positives.

3. Be specific not general. General comments are not useful in feedback when commenting on a person's behaviour. For feedback to be useful (ie it can be used by the recipient), it needs to be specific. Statements like 'That was brilliant' or 'You were awful' may be pleasant or dreadful to hear but they do not enable the person to learn what was brilliant or awful and act upon it.

4. Select priority areas. Highlight the most significant feedback, especially if it is negative feedback that you are giving. If possible, don't let it build up into one great bundle! Many people can 'take' only one piece of negative feedback at a time, even when sandwiched between two positives.

5. Focus on behaviour rather than the person. Reporting what was seen and heard ensures that the focus is on behaviour rather than the person. For example, the comment 'You dominated there' is potentially damaging and less useful to the recipient than 'I noticed that you interrupted and talked over that staff member.'

6. Refer to behaviour that can be changed. It is not very helpful to give people feedback about something they can do nothing about, eg a personal attribute, dialect or accent.

7. Be descriptive rather than evaluative. Telling the person what has been seen or heard and the effect it had is more effective than saying something was merely 'good' or 'bad', eg 'When X asked the question, I noticed that you looked away without speaking. I felt it would have been more helpful if you had looked at her and responded to her directly with your reply.'

8. Own the feedback. Effective feedback is 'owned', beginning with 'I' or 'In my view' rather than with 'You are...', which may suggest that a universally agreed opinion is being offered about that person. Starting with 'I' means that the coach is also taking responsibility for what he or she is saying.

9. Give the feedback as soon as you can after the event. Clients want feedback as soon as possible, and immediate feedback should be given if possible. The exceptions to this are:
    - if your client is feeling very emotional about the behaviour or the event;
    - if the feedback would not be constructive; and/or
    - if it is inappropriate, eg others do not need to hear it.
10. Feedback should be based on observation rather than inference; it should be based on what is seen, heard or read rather than on interpretations or conclusions made from what is seen or heard, which may contaminate observations and therefore affect the quality of the feedback. For instance, 'You seemed tense this morning – I expect it's because you failed the test last time' is an inference.
11. Feedback should give value to the recipient rather than to the provider of feedback. Coaches may need to check out who this feedback is for. Is it for the benefit of the coach or the client?
12. Feedback should be about what is said rather than why it is said. The aspects of feedback that relate to the what, how, when and where of what is said are observable characteristics. Why something is said relates to the inferred rather than the observable – motive or intent. 'Why' questions can be received interrogatively and lead to defensiveness.
13. Leave recipients with a choice. It is usually more effective for recipients if they have a choice about whether to act on the feedback or not. Making *demands* that they must or *should* change may invite resistance, so feedback should not include imperatives for change, but may include suggestions.
14. Limit negative feedback. Limit feedback to one or two areas if you are giving feedback on weaknesses, as after two pieces of negative information we suggest the receiver may 'switch off' and hear no more of the feedback being offered.

The prospect of receiving feedback often inspires fear, as most people expect negative feedback and are not in a receptive listening mode. The person giving feedback should take into account the receiver's state and check out if the feedback has really been heard and received, possibly ensuring that it is recorded, especially if it is positive.

So having given feedback, can you receive it? We discuss receiving feedback in Chapter 9.

An example of functionalist mentoring is revealed in the organizational programme described in the case study below where mentors were volunteers from within the organization and the purpose was an increase in qualified staff, using senior managers as mentors.

CASE STUDY

A professional awarding body

The awarding body is a self-funding organization dedicated to promoting higher standards of competence and integrity through the provision of relevant qualifications for employees at all levels and across all sectors of the industry concerned. With 90,000 members this organization has been at the forefront in setting professional standards for its industry for over a century. Its broad portfolio of education and qualification services is continually expanding to meet the changing requirements of its customers.

The organization set up a mentoring programme in 1997 to offer educational support to students working towards professional qualifications when government funding cuts had significantly reduced the level of local tuition for these qualifications. The organization was anxious to provide additional resources to the normal face-to-face courses. In addition, the programme was intended to offer opportunities for mature members to enhance their continuing professional development (CPD) plans.

The hoped-for benefits were that students would have a better chance of passing exams whilst at the same time gaining a network of more senior contacts via their local network. For mentors, the benefits included a realization of their membership promise when elected to fellowship of the organization, as well as fulfilling their CPD commitment and, more importantly, helping to engage young members and keep the local network alive.

Mentors opted to join the scheme and were allocated by the local scheme organizer to a member studying for a qualification. Organizers at local level were provided with materials that supported the recruitment and selection of mentors, briefing notes and performance measures, as well as ideas for mentors' meetings and how to deal with difficulties. Mentors were provided with materials describing the role and giving details of the skills (described above) needed to help a student to learn, as well as pro formas for record keeping and reviewing. A brief document defined the role for both mentor and student.

Benefits for the organization

On completion of the programme in 1999, members reported feeling more attached to the organization than was the case previously, feeling part of the local industry community and feeling less isolated. Senior members who acted as mentors benefited from CPD points, which preserved their membership category, and in addition they found that their status in the local industry community was enhanced. The programme resulted in improved pass rates for students who took part, noticeable awareness of mentoring, and increased understanding of the benefits of mentoring on both sides.

ENGAGEMENT MENTORING OR COACHING

We look now at the difficulties that occur when mentors or coaches are created for a functionalist purpose, which may or may not be declared, and a humanistic method is utilized to achieve that purpose. There is potential for disappointment for both mentor/coach and client, and the contractor's purpose may founder. We discuss how potential mentors/coaches can address the issue directly with contractors and communicate congruently with their clients. The skills needed are congruence, assertiveness and questioning, often operating in a 'managing up' situation.

The term 'engagement mentor' was first used by Colley (2003) in her analysis of nine volunteer mentors and eight mentees from a scheme entitled New Beginnings. New Beginnings is defined as a pre-vocational training scheme, providing intensive individual support to re-engage disaffected or socially excluded 16- to 18-year-olds with the labour market in the UK (Colley, 2003: 49). This was achieved by recruiting and training undergraduates from a local university as volunteer mentors.

The characteristics of engagement mentoring/coaching, which we discuss in Chapter 2, are these: the purpose of the mentoring programme for the contractor is re-engagement and the method seeks to transform attitudes, values and beliefs (or dispositions) so that the target group will engage with the required system. We have used the term 'engagement mentoring or coaching' to refer to any mentoring or coaching that carries these characteristics.

Colley's findings for socially excluded young people can be seen to be replicated in organizational engagement mentoring/coaching schemes. For instance, despite the claims of benefits for mentors there is evidence of difficulty both in recruiting and particularly in *retaining* volunteers, which Colley suggests may indicate that the experience is not always a rewarding one for volunteers (Freedman, 1999; Beech and Brockbank, 1999).

In the corporate world, the survival of mentoring schemes is limited, as one in three lasts less than two years (Stott and Sweeney, 1999). We suggest that the problem lies in the limited potential of engagement mentoring schemes to deliver their contractors' objectives.

Mentoring/coaching programmes are typically presented as if the only two parties of interest are the mentor/coach and the client. Two key assumptions are relevant here: that power dynamics of mentoring or coaching exist in a kind of vacuum, separate from the work environment, controlled by mentors/coaches, and that mentors/coaches are the vehicles of empowerment for their clients. In the background, however, is the initiator of the programme: an organizational agent, a senior manager or a board member. That person's objectives are the purpose or function of the programme and will be evaluated on that basis.

Let us examine these assumptions. The power dynamic within the relationship is considered as totally separate from the organizational system in which it is embedded, and this allows the functionalist nature of the programme to remain at worst hidden and at best undeclared. An example of this appears in the case of engagement coaching at Sterling Bank.

CASE STUDY

A sense of engagement

Sterling Bank has been in business for 300 years and operates worldwide employing 100,000 staff. For UK high street branches, the impact of online banking in recent years has affected traditional business detrimentally, and to deal with the situation the bank launched a coaching programme for senior managers. The managers, almost all home-grown, having been in the bank all their working lives, came from a tradition of service in local branches, often playing a significant role in the community. The programme aimed to introduce managers to the idea of coaching their staff in a new role.

The programme was designed, through coaching, to persuade the managers and staff out of their traditional role and into a selling role, where they would be required to 'push' financial services products to their long-term customers. The functionalist agenda was diversification of the product offer but was presented to participants as an additional service offer, together with professional development for themselves as coaches.

Most of the managers (mostly in their 50s and nearing retirement) were horrified at the prospect, believing that, having established themselves as 'pillars of the community', they were being asked to become, and to coach their staff to become, common salespeople.

The coach training was painful and difficult, as trainers found themselves in engagement mode, using humanistic techniques to persuade participants to accept the hidden functionalist agenda. Participants were generally resistant and angry, especially as they realized that there was little choice if they wished to finish their career with Sterling. The programme enabled the bank to argue that managers had been offered the option and, if they didn't manage to cross over to more selling, they were vulnerable to redundancy.

Sterling was a case of engagement coaching where branch bank managers were to be coached out of their traditional role of service to their customers into their new role as salespeople of financial services such as pensions. The purpose was a massive culture change for quite legitimate corporate reasons, ie the demise of hands-on banking due to IT products flooding the market. In the process, the managers as coaches were expected to change their own dispositions, acquire saint-like qualities and present themselves as idealized role models (Beech and Brockbank, 1999). No wonder mentors using engagement approaches were subsequently found to 'become more anxious and more demoralised about mentoring the longer the relationships continued' (Colley, 2003: 103). The same effects were found in business contexts. Terri Scandura reminds us that even the most comprehensive studies of mentoring of every kind fail to address evidence of 'negative and damaging experiences in mentoring' and describes the evidence as the 'dark side' of mentoring (1998: 463). Our recommendation is that engagement programmes like Sterling would be well advised to 'come clean' about their functionalist purposes, but we recognize that in the situation described this would be far from easy. We discuss below the effects of hidden purposes and alternative approaches.

What happens to functionalist mentors' clients in these circumstances? Because the objectives are not theirs, the objectives are unlikely to be achieved. Because there tends to be covert surveillance where the contractor seeks to assess 'progress' by reports from mentors or coaches, clients present an acceptable face to their mentor. Typical ingratiating behaviours include pretending to agree with the mentor, flattering the mentor and false self-presentation. The result of this is an incongruent relationship. We discuss how this impacts on trust in the relationship and ultimately undermines learning in Chapter 3. The prevalence of the assumption that mentors will help their clients with emotional problems is evident. The expectations held by clients about their mentor and the process are widely divergent from what mentors expect to do (Cunningham and Eberle, 1993), and this is confirmed by the authors when expectations are explored at mentoring training events.

What happens to mentors who are trapped between their contractor's purpose or function and their commitment of care to their client? This commitment of care originates in the mythologizing of mentoring activity based on an inaccurate version of Homer's *Odyssey*, which for modern mentors has become the prevailing discourse. In this situation, Colley refers to mentoring as 'an impossible fiction', as mentors 'go round in circles' in their attempts to make progress (2003: 120). Mentors report being trapped into directive mode when it becomes clear that their clients have not assented to the objectives, becoming frustrated and suffering from lack of support themselves (Brockbank, 1994). In addition, the hoped-for benefits to mentors often do not materialize and, far

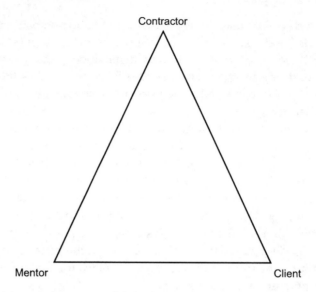

Figure 10.2 *A three-way relationship*

from adding the experience to their CVs, mentors tend to conceal it (Colley, 2003).

How are these difficulties to be addressed? We identify here a three-way relationship with contractor, mentor or coach, and client at the three corners illustrated in Figure 10.2.

The mentor/coach/contractor relationship is where the functionalist objectives are agreed, often with a hierarchical barrier in between. For the mentor/coach, this is a 'managing up' project, so that, while having less power, he or she is able to influence the more senior party, the contractor. Questioning and assertion are the two skills required. The contractor has a purpose that ideally he or she would like the mentor/coach to take on board without comment and ideally without it being articulated. For example, in the Sterling bank situation a board member tells potential coaches that 'this is a matter of the bank's future survival' rather than explaining that the managers to be coached will need to alter their dispositions, ie their values and beliefs. What the contractor is looking for is a simple alteration in behaviour. Mentors or coaches can help themselves by questioning their contractor to the point of clarity so that eventually the functionalist purpose of the programme is revealed, ie the managers will change their traditional role and become salespeople. This offers mentors/coaches a choice. They can assent to the purpose and present it to their clients or they can suggest to their contractor that mentoring/coaching is probably not the best tool for such a massive culture change and, if necessary, decline the role or propose an alternative role. So mentors/coaches can identify function-alist purposes and declare them clearly to their clients or they can propose an evolutionary role for themselves in working with clients, which may well ultimately result in meeting the contractor's objectives but this cannot be guaranteed.

The mentor/coach/client relationship is where the functionalist objectives, if agreed with the contractor, are assented to by the client. If the discussion above has occurred, the mentor/coach is able to be honest about the purpose of the programme and declare the objectives as they really are. Clients may need some time to decide if they are able to accept these objectives for themselves, and mentors/coaches are well placed to enable this process. It may be necessary to roll back to before the board decision and discuss alternative outcomes. When clients have explored alternatives such as downsizing and unemployment they may feel able to consider the proposed programme more readily. If this sounds harsh, it is the reality of business life. Our concern is to make the process transparent.

We move now to the skills needed for evolutionary mentoring, executive coaching and life coaching.

NOTE

1 'Why' questions are likely to be ineffective in coaching situations, unless and until the relationships are resilient. They have been perceived as intrusive, like an interrogation, led by the questioner, for the questioner's benefit, and may cause the learner to lose their train of thought (Dainow and Bailey, 1988).

11 Being an evolutionary mentor or life coach

In this chapter we discuss the skills that you will need if you are acting as an evolutionary mentor or life coach, which aims to achieve reflective learning and transformation. As an evolutionary mentor or life coach, whilst attending to day-to-day performance, you are seeking, through reflective dialogue, to challenge your clients to look beyond their immediate horizon and transform their view of the system in which they live and work. We make the assumption that evolutionary practitioners are already using the skills described in Chapter 10. For ease of reading, we use the term 'mentor' throughout this chapter to mean evolutionary mentor or life coach.

What skills do evolutionary mentors need? 'It is evident that successful mentors are reported as employing a range of enabling strategies and skills within mentoring relationships... it is important to consider the behaviours, qualities and characteristics of those who will be deemed suitable to provide this supportive role for others' (Morton-Cooper and Palmer, 2000: 55).

The skills described in this chapter are:

- mentor presence;
- listening and congruence;
- restatement;
- summary;
- questioning;
- managing emotion;

- advanced empathy (primary empathy is considered in Chapter 10);
- feedback;
- challenge;
- immediacy; and
- confrontation.

We start by assuming that an evolutionary mentor aims to work with their clients' own objectives. Historical meanings of 'mentoring' and some current meanings of 'mentoring' imply a particular model of learning where an individual, as client, seeks the 'advice' of another individual who is perceived as 'expert' in some aspect of the former's activities. In this chapter we depart from the idea of mentor as 'expert' or 'adviser' and maintain that for evolutionary mentoring or life coaching, in order to promote the kind of reflective learning needed for today's organizations, described in detail in Chapter 3, the relationship is a person-centred one.

The characteristics of a person-centred approach to mentoring, based on humanistic principles and recognizing the social and constructed nature of learning, start from the assumption that your client is willing and able to grow and develop. In addition as a mentor using the person-centred approach you will affirm the subjective world of your client, whether you agree with it or not, through empathy and acceptance of the client's emotional experience. We list the essentials of the person-centred approach in Chapter 2, where we note the necessary and sufficient conditions for learning based on Rogers (1983) and discuss the core conditions of congruence, unconditional positive regard and empathy.

However, we note that 'It is easy to embrace the person-centred approach intellectually. However much personal work and practice is needed to eliminate old ingrained patterns – such as the need to be needed, to know best, to control, to solve the problem, to impress – before one can shift towards being truly person-centred' (Silverstone, 1993: viii).

MENTOR PRESENCE

The first thing you bring to a relationship is your presence. You are present to your client by virtue of your posture, gesture, facial expression, and position in relation to your client, even before you use your voice or hearing to communicate. Your non-verbal messages are in the room, like body language, facial expression and voice, which are thought to deliver meaning quite independently of words (Argyle, 1975; Ekman and Freisen, 1975; Pease, 1981; Morris, 1977). In fact, non-verbal and vocal channels often carry a bigger proportion of meaning than the verbal message. For instance, communication of approval has been explored and found to favour the non-verbal channel (90 per cent), leaving the spoken words with only 10 per cent of meaning (Mehrabian, 1971). Where the non-verbal or vocal channels are inconsistent with verbal messages, ie spoken words, receivers accept the meaning carried by the non-verbal channels. A clear example of this is sarcasm, where, whatever the verbal message, the voice tone is the message received. Clearly cultural factors influence how far meanings carried by non-verbal channels are universal, and this point receives a thorough treatment, as do all non-verbal communication issues, in Bull (1983). Of particular interest are the findings on dominance and status and how they are communicated by interpersonal distance and posture (Bull, 1983). Suffice to say that as a mentor you communicate, whether you know it or not, a host of messages through non-verbal and vocal channels and, of course, your client will communicate through the same channels, eg yawning, fidgeting and glazed eyes are all indications that the client has disconnected. Awareness of these non-verbal communication channels is likely to enable you to make sense of responses from clients. For instance, if they keep their head down, avoiding eye contact, and fidget while they talk, they are clearly preoccupied with something, which may relate to their work or personal life, and you may enable them to voice those concerns.

One key aspect of non-verbal behaviour that affects your relationship with clients is your physical stance. We draw on the work of Heron (1993), who has studied the stance and posture of facilitators. He suggests that a facilitator's personal presence enables her to be in 'Conscious command of how she is appearing in space and time' (Heron, 1993: 32). This seems a good thing for a mentor to be. He further suggests that many facilitators crouch in defensive positions, slumped in chairs with ankles crossed and head jutting forward. Heron suggests that if you are in such a position you are likely to be a mentor who is 'About to talk too much, exhibits anxious control, and is missing a lot of what is going on' (1999: 222). This confirms Colley's (2003) account of some mentors' reported difficulty with certain withdrawn clients.

When crouching in the way shown in Figure 11.1a, awareness is reduced, and you are likely to be perceived as a talking head. A simple adjustment to posture with head, neck and spine rearranged with a sense of lift, lengthening and widening the back, pelvis, thighs and legs grounded through contact with the floor, as shown in Figure 11.1b, is suggested by Heron. You move from slouch and impotence into a commanding and potent posture. The body wakes up and is ready to

Figure 11.1a   *Facilitator posture - crouched and defensive*

Source: McGill and Brockbank (2004: 188)

Figure 11.1b   *Facilitator posture - open and potent*

receive energies in the field around it. Such posture projects presence, and the posture *can be learnt*.

MENTOR CONGRUENCE

We define 'congruence' as a way of being genuine, being real, sharing feelings and attitudes as well as opinions and beliefs or judgements. We identified this kind of congruent speech as 'story' and the less congruent version as 'history' in Chapter 9.

As noted in Chapter 9, you as mentor will model self-disclosure within the relationship by being the first to do so. This is essential, as you will model the breadth and depth of appropriate self-disclosure for the relationship. For instance, you may begin by saying that this is a new relationship and, although you are confident of the process as useful for learning, you are unsure about how it will work. The act of self-disclosure is a direct example of trust behaviour, where you take the risk of disclosing and thereby encourage your client to do the same.

As mentor you will also model congruence by demonstrating the crucial characteristic of 'owned' statements (which begin with 'I' or contain 'I' statements). Such statements are likely to be real disclosure whilst use of the distancing 'you', 'they' or 'one' serves to mask disclosure.

As a mentor you are modelling appropriate self-disclosure in the relationship even though this is not designed for yourself. Because self-disclosure is reciprocal in effect, your disclosure gives permission for your client to follow suit and express some positive feeling about what he or she is doing and some negative feeling too. In particular it allows your client to say 'I've never done this before' or 'It feels like counselling.' Note that the example given above, the mentor's disclosure about method, includes some emotional material, namely the mentor's mixed feelings of confidence and unsureness. These feelings, expressed openly, although fairly superficial, are the hallmark of trust-building self-disclosure. We discuss self-disclosure in more detail in Chapter 9.

Where clients refuse or are unwilling to disclose, you may judge that they have made a conscious choice and that their choice should be respected (see sample ground rules in Appendix 3). We would urge you to ensure that your clients are enabled to speak about themselves early in the first session. Many new mentors are surprised to find that their clients are wordless when they first meet, as the relationship is at zero point. The mentoring relationship is embedded in a number of oppressive social systems, eg sexism, racism, ageism etc. If your clients belong to a minority group they may well lack confidence with a mentor from the mainstream. You may like to address the issue when agreeing ground rules at the very beginning.

The significance of congruence or truth telling in evolutionary relationships is revealed in the NCH case study below.

CASE STUDY

NCH: orange cardigans

The children's charity NCH (formerly known as The National Children's Home) is the leading UK provider of family and community centres, children's services in rural areas, services for disabled children and their families, and services for young people leaving care. The charity values the unique potential of all children and young people and promotes the support and opportunities they need to reach it.

A was surprised when asked to consider being a mentor to E, and flattered, while at the same time thinking 'It won't be long before she finds me out.' E sought a mentoring relationship to support her professional development as a manager of people. E was keen to progress to a management role in NCH. E chose A as her mentor because of E's 'really positive view of the way A supported colleagues and worked with people and thought it would be useful to have the opinions and input of a colleague working outside of her direct team'.

The mentoring couple (A mentoring E) both work for NCH where, without a formal mentoring scheme, they had to work it out for themselves. They developed a model based on their reading and research about mentoring, which included a loosely structured agenda, regular lunchtime meetings, a confidentiality clause and a commitment to explore and develop as the need arose.

As the mentoring relationship progressed over a period of one year, A was pleased to find out how much she knew that would be of benefit to E, sometimes because she was older and more experienced but also because she was a different person with a different perspective. A observed that E benefited by simply articulating her own assessment of a situation. Sometimes A could add something, but mostly A simply offered affirmation and recognition of E's self-assessment. In this way A's mentoring helped E to make the most of her own innate skills.

A has little experience in E's field of expertise, and this was not necessary, as the mentoring was not designed to support E's day-to-day work. What A brings to the mentoring relationship is her ability to see E's strengths and affirm them. E hoped to get someone else's 'take' on her management style, her behaviour and how she was dealing with situations. She hoped to learn from A's experience and approach.

Both women saw the relationship as multi-roled in that all the terms, 'mentor', 'coach', 'adviser', 'guide' and 'friend', were relevant at various points in their relationship. They both noted that they reached a stage when they crossed from using a semi-formal agenda to just getting on with it. Both A and E have gained from the relationship, with E gaining in confidence and a promotion to a management position in NCH. E perceives the mentoring relationship as having helped her to see and analyse situations more objectively, and to value development and support so that she is now acting as a mentor herself. A found pleasure in supporting the development of a colleague outside the line manager relationship and has recognized her skill in nurturing others. She has felt refreshed by her contact with E, whom she describes as positive, constructive and committed, and recognizes that they have both found security in being able to 'check out' turbulent situations in the safety of their confidential relationship.

The relationship developed from mentor/coach/adviser into a friendship that includes supporting each other in their commitments to honesty, truth telling, taking shoes off in the office and the wearing of orange cardigans. Their admiration for each other is evident with A's acknowledgement of E's accomplishment and abilities, and E's recognition of A's valuable contributions and continuing support.

For their final comments, A mentions that, 'through my relationship with E, I have realized my yearning for a similar mentor of my own', and E remarks that, 'Since I've had the job, it's just good to have someone there who knows all the little chips I have on my shoulder, the chinks in the armour etc, and can help me deal with them in my new role without judging!'

Here the client generated her own agenda and goals for the relationship. The person-centred approach is revealed by the evident regard and empathy between the two parties. The learning outcome was transformation, and the relationship continues.

LISTENING

We discuss basic listening skills in Chapter 10. As an evolutionary mentor you will need to engage in active listening, and we discuss this in more detail now.

Active listening

We have noted that the message is carried through both audio and visual channels. Effectively attending to the speaker means that as mentor you are in a position to listen carefully to what your client is saying verbally and non-verbally. Egan (1990) describes active or complete listening as follows:

1. observing and reading the speaker's non-verbal behaviour: posture, facial expressions, movement, tone of voice and the like;
2. listening to the whole person in the context of the social groupings of life;
3. tough-minded listening;
4. listening to and understanding the speaker's verbal messages.

Observing non-verbal behaviour

As mentioned above, up to 90 per cent of the message has been shown to be carried by the non-verbal or vocal channels. Over half of the message may be communicated by facial expression or body language, while over 30 per cent travels in the tone, pitch, volume or paralanguage (ums, ahs or grunts) of the voice (Mehrabian, 1971; Argyle, 1975). In relation to non-verbal behaviour it is important to recognize that you want to listen to clients in a way that deepens your understanding of what they are trying to convey in overall terms. It is inappropriate to fix on an expression of non-verbal behaviour and then to create a total impression from that single piece of information.

Listening to the whole person

At this point as mentor you do not form responses to your client, but listen. An example would be when your client is telling what it is like for her, working in an office environment where a manager is continuously baiting her for not adopting the norms of the office, which include late working in a predominately male workforce. While your client is saying what it is like for her as a working mother, coping with her job and her family commitments, you may have some views about how you would cope in such an environment. For example, you may reflect to yourself: 'I could cope with that' or 'It would not be a problem for me.'

In this you are 'playing the doubting game' (Elbow, 1973: 148) and falling into the trap of empathy mis-defined as 'the recognition of self in the other' (Kohut, 1991: 68). As you listen to your own thoughts on *your* way of coping you may detract from how your client is thinking, feeling and being in *her* environment. The key is for you to 'put aside' you own responses to her situation, suspend judgement and listen from your client's standpoint – where she is coming from. Such an approach has been named 'the believing game' (Elbow, 1973: 149). To achieve acceptance without necessarily agreeing, as mentor you must also contain your approval as well as your disapproval, as one implies the other. As we shall see below, even when you respond it is necessary to work with where your client is and not put your solutions forward to her.

In listening to your client's story, you will, if effective, place yourself (as far as is possible) in her social context. You will endeavour to understand what it is like to be a woman in a family situation, to tackle a prevailing norm within which she feels oppressed. Rather than get trapped in your own contextual picture, what is it about *her* picture that you need to understand to enable her to deal with it? In this way you will be endeavouring to get into her personal context – how life is for her, ie in Martin Buber's words 'making the other present' or getting to 'imagine-other' (Buber, 1965, cited in Kohn, 1990: 133). We discuss this more fully under 'Empathy' in Chapter 10.

Issues relating to the social grouping of your client's life may not be part of the verbal message. However, a client who is a member of an ethnic minority may be visibly living with issues of exclusion, and the client's message will convey something of the client's struggle and may be very relevant to his or her learning and reflection. For example, black staff in a mainly white office may be marginalized in group work and informal gatherings. Cultural factors may provide important cues for you, as you will need to be alert to the cultural context of your client and provide what is known as 'transcultural caring' in your responses (Leininger, 1987). 'Cultural care' has been defined as a mentor using the client's notion of care, as defined by the client's culture, and accommodating to it, rather than depending on his or her own notion of care (Eleftheriadou, 1994). We discuss issues in cross-cultural mentoring in Chapter 5.

Tough-minded listening

Tough-minded listening requires that as mentor you place yourself in the frame of your client so that you really understand where the client is coming from. This means that you pick up what is perhaps being distorted or non-verbally leaked by your client. For example, a client may be talking about going for a promotion in the organization and expressing how he or she is well qualified for the promotion. However, the client may also be conveying less explicitly, through voice tone, demeanour and some words, feelings of not being confident to do the job if promoted. This is turn may affect the client's will to apply for the post. It is for you as mentor to pick up this inconsistency and hold it until it is appropriate to offer it as an observation.

Listening to verbal messages

Understanding clients' verbal messages demands that you are able to translate what may be coded messages by recognizing what are known as 'surface structures' and recovering the deep structures in what they say (McCann, 1988). When we transmit a message verbally we often do so in what linguistic experts call 'surface structures' (Chomsky, 1957, 1969). Surface structures are transformations of deep structures by a process of:

- deletion (missing out information);
- distortion (altering meaning);
- generalization (generalizing from the particular).

Example of deletion:
Surface structure: 'The best option is…'
  Deep structure: 'The best option in comparison to the others is…'

Example of distortion:
Surface structure: 'My manager is against me.'
  Deep structure: 'My manager doesn't like me and won't change her attitude to me.'

Example of generalization:
Surface structure: 'People don't understand.'
  Deep structure: 'My colleagues X and Y don't understand.'

It is possible to recover the deep structures that underlie the surface structures in most communications by identifying the deletion, distortion or generalization that has transformed them. In Table 11.1, some deep structures are recovered from surface structures and the transformation identified.

Table 11.1 Recovering deep structures

Surface structure	Deep structure	Transformation
'It's just not possible.'	'I believe it's not possible.'	Deletion
'Nobody tells me anything.'	'My manager has not informed me about the new rates of pay.'	Generalization
'Obviously…'	'It is obvious to me that…'	Deletion
'He never considers my ideas.'	'He did not consider my idea on X and Y occasions.'	Generalization
'He has an attitude problem.'	'I am annoyed by some of his X and Y behaviour.'	Deletion
'They always forget.'	'X and Y forgot on W and Z occasions.'	Generalization

Surface structure	Deep structure	Transformation
'I must get on.'	'I want to be finished by six.'	Deletion
'No one ever talks to me here.'	'My colleagues X and Y didn't talk to me on W and Z occasions.'	Generalization
'They don't like me.'	'I believe that X and Y don't like me.'	Deletion
'He is never here, always on courses.'	'He was not here on days X and Y when he was away on courses.'	Generalization

How can you help your clients to recover their 'lost' structures without being too intrusive? We recommend the technique of restatement described below, as when clients hear what they have just said they may immediately recognize the deletion, distortion or generalization they have used. In most cases the power of restatement is enough. Alternatively, you may choose to formulate your questions in a way that will help clients to realize their deep structure, and we discuss this on page 216.

Whitworth, Kimsey-House and Sandhal (1998) offer a listening model at three levels, and we describe these as follows:

- Level I refers to the state of listening as 'What does this mean to me?', as the listener is attending to him- or herself, which is entirely appropriate for much of the time. In fact it's essential that we attend to ourselves and listen out for what is best for us in terms of survival. So it's acceptable, but not in your role as a mentor. If you find yourself, as mentor, figuring out what to say next or what brilliant intervention to make, this is a clue that you are listening at level I. Your client is at level I, absorbed in him- or herself, and that's the whole point, but not for the mentor, who needs to be at least at level II.
- Level II refers to focused listening where you are focused on your client. The observed behaviour associated with level II listening is leaning forward and eye contact. We noted this under SOLER on page 179. At level II your attention is wholly on your client, his or her words and expressions, and everything your client brings to the session. You are noting your client's demeanour and tone of voice, and what your client says or doesn't say. In particular you listen for

energy, the sign of your client's commitment to what he or she values and wants. This may lead you to level III listening, so be prepared!

■ Level III listening is all-round listening, picking up information from everything around you. Level III listening is holistic, using all five senses, as discussed in Chapter 3, and recognizes the value of intuition, trusting those hunches and senses that pop up in dialogues. As a level III listener you must be receptive and softly sensitive, as the messages are often infinitesimal changes in sound or other stimuli. For example, if your client goes 'cold' you can feel that and 'hear' what it means for him or her. You are listening for signs of life within your client's agenda and also for signs of disturbance or distress.

We would tend to describe level II listening as potentially leading to an empathic response from the mentor, and level III as leading to more advanced empathy, immediacy or even confrontation. We describe these in detail below, beginning on page 222.

RESTATEMENT OF CLIENT'S STORY

When you deem it appropriate to respond, we recommend that before anything else you restate your client's words. We discussed how to do this in Chapter 10. You may wish to start with phrases like 'What I think you said was that you want to decide whether you really want the job or not' or 'If I have understood you properly, you want to discuss how this job relates to your other plans.'

Because of our social tendency to assess and interpret and think what we are going to say even before the speaker has finished, restatement is an important process to disentangle so that you really are attending to clients and not imposing your own view of their reality. In responding, the tone of voice is important. A tone that suggests criticism or uncaring or agreeing is not helpful. The aim is to reflect back what is being said to clients: their words and meaning; their emotions and feelings; and their will or spirit.

The restatement does not have to repeat the words clients used exactly, although use of their key words will be more accurate. It is helpful to paraphrase so that they can respond with, say, 'Yes, that's it' or 'Not quite; I would put it more like this' until there is assent between them and yourself. For instance, when a client expresses concern about a job interview, with a sense of panic in his or her voice, inappropriate responses might be 'You must apply – you're made for the job' or 'Yes, you may not be up to it.' On the other hand, an appropriate response might be 'You seem unsure about applying for the job because of other demands on you.'

The use of repetition is not a regular way of communicating in English. We mention the difference with other languages below under 'Socratic questioning'.

SOCRATIC QUESTIONING

Evolutionary mentors will use the Socratic method to enable their clients to generate their own goals and address the prevailing discourse, their assumptions and the taken-for-granteds (tfgs) in their lives. Questioning comes after contributions have been received with restatement and, if appropriate, empathy (described below) and without judgement, so that some trust and confidence have been established, through the use of the skills and techniques described above.

Enabling questions are different in kind from interrogative questions, but may be equally probing. The main purpose of enabling questioning is for you as mentor to enable your clients to learn and develop, to reflect upon their actions, consider and reconsider their views of reality, and generate their own solutions. In other words, the questioning forms part of reflective dialogue as described in Chapter 4. Using restatement coupled with open questions will enable clients to gain insights into 'forgotten' aspects of their practice, such as avoiding a particular member of staff. Where the Socratic process reveals forgotten material, clients may wish to consider why they have suppressed their memory of behaviour, such as having a 'favourite' member of staff, without realizing it.

Questioning aims to enable clients to struggle with the issue under consideration, challenging embedded paradigms and encouraging consideration of possibilities, without restricting the range of possible solutions and without providing a ready-made solution. This mirrors a style of questioning characterized by the Socrates character in one of Plato's dialogues, *The Meno Dialogue*, where Meno challenges Socrates to demonstrate his maxim that 'All inquiry and all learning is but recollection' (Jowett, 1953: 282).

The use of repetition and restatement is natural in Greek but less acceptable in modern English so for modern mentors the process feels somewhat alien at first.

In addition, Socratic questioning has the potential to take clients into a place where previously held assumptions are threatened. The tfgs are being questioned and reconsidered, and this is far from comfortable. In the dialogue described above, the boy, who is learning a new theorem, struggles with novel ideas, and Socrates' friend Meno observes that the process of learning is uncomfortable for the boy, who is learning something completely new, compared to his previous comfortable state of ignorance: 'What advances he has made... he did not know at first, and he does not know now... but then he thought he knew... and felt no difficulty... now he feels a difficulty' (Jowett, 1953: 282).

The discomfort may lead to a complete reappraisal of previous tfgs, the crossover point in the double loop learning diagram (Figure 3.2 on page 35), so that your client may feel some disturbance, which, in the Socrates story, Meno described as follows: 'We have made him doubt and given him the torpedo's shock' (Jowett, 1953: 282; note this was a late 19th-century translation by Jowett!).

When you question assumptions, eg 'Why do you want the job?', it can feel like an attack and your client may withdraw. Encouraging inspection of taken-for-granted assumptions needs questions that are encouraging rather than threatening, eg 'What is it about the job that attracts you?' The follow-up must also affirm your client, as there is no point in asking insightful questions and then destructively critiquing the answer. Non-verbal responses to answers are notorious here, and you may communicate negative views or even contempt through, for example, sighing, a tired smile, a raised eyebrow, an inflected voice or inappropriate laughter.

We consider now how as a mentor you can work with clients' deep structures without putting them off. We described above the human tendency when speaking to cover up deep structures with surface structures, thereby making effective action difficult (McCann, 1988). The work of Noam Chomsky (1957, 1969) shows how it is possible to recover the 'lost' structures: by calling attention to what is missing in your client's statement (recovering deletion); by analysing a distortion; and by questioning a generalization. We give some examples in Table 11.2.

Table 11.2 Recovering the 'lost' structures

Surface structure	Deep structure	Recovery question
'My manager is against me.'	'My manager doesn't like me and won't change her attitude to me.'	'How is she against you?'
'It's just not possible.'	'I believe that it is not possible.'	'What would make it possible?'

Surface structure	Deep structure	Recovery question
'People don't understand.'	'It seems to me that X and Y don't understand.'	'Who are "people"?'
'Nobody tells me anything.'	'My manager has not informed me about the new rates of pay.'	'What is it that you want to know?'
'The best option is…'	'The best option compared to X and Y.'	'The best option compared to what?'
'Obviously…'	'It is obvious to me.'	'What makes it obvious?'
'He never considers my ideas.'	'He did not consider my idea on X and Y occasions.'	'When did he not consider your idea?'
'They always forget.'	'My colleagues X and Y forgot on W and Z occasions.'	'Who forgot? When?'
'They don't like me.'	'I think they don't like me.'	'What makes you think that?'
'No one ever talks to me here.'	'My colleagues X and Y didn't speak to me yesterday.'	'No one? Who doesn't talk to you? When?'

Another approach to questioning that is becoming popular with mentors and life coaches is the use of clean language.

Clean language

The idea of 'clean language' came from the work of David Grove (1996) when he (re)discovered that questioning clients using no presuppositions enabled them to experience and work with their own patterns, issues and changes. The rediscovery refers to early work by Rogers (1951, 1957, 1961) where he learns from his clients the core conditions that lead to change in psychotherapy, which include staying with the feelings, thoughts and experience of the client, rather than interpreting them and rephrasing them.

David Grove has built on Rogers's seminal work by developing a questioning technique for mentors called 'clean language', which validates the client's experience and brings into awareness symbolic information that is not normally available, and it is claimed that transformation follows.

An example of unclean language would be

> *Client:* I don't know what to do.
> *Mentor:* What do you want to do?
> *Client:* I don't know that either.

An example of clean language (with sample client responses) using the same client statement would be:

> *Client:* I don't know what to do.
> *Mentor:* And what kind of don't know is don't know?
> *Client:* I feel stuck.
> *Mentor:* And what kind of stuck is stuck?
> *Client:* Well, sort of confused.
> *Mentor:* And where does the confused come from?
> *Client:* I'm all mixed up.
> *Mentor:* And that's mixed up like what?
> *Client:* Like when I had to choose a friend to ask to tea.

The process seems peculiar and would sound odd in everyday conversation, especially as Grove recommends that the mentor should:

■ use slower speech time;
■ use a deeper voice tonality;
■ imitate the client's pronunciation and emphasis (even accent).

Grove (1996) also offers a list of nine basic questions for clean language operators, and these include the following (the dotted lines refer to some of the client's words):

■ And is there anything else about ....?
■ And what kind of .... is that ....?
■ And where is ....?
■ And whereabouts?
■ And what happens next?
■ And then what happens?
■ And what happens just before ....?

■ And where does/could .... come from?
■ And that's .... like what?

Mentors will immediately grasp the usefulness of this tool for working with their clients, although they will want to adapt it to their own particular circumstances and may not use it in its pure (therapeutic) form.

MANAGING EMOTION

As mentor you will need to address emotion in the relationship, because of its key role in reflective dialogue, double loop learning and connected or constructivist learning, discussed in Chapter 3. As discussed in Chapter 9, the expression of emotion is socialized on cultural and gender lines, and clients who declare that they feel nothing are likely to 'leak' their feelings in some non-verbal way, often in their body language. As observed earlier, when clients' spoken expression matches their non-verbal messages this is congruent behaviour. Non-verbal expression of emotion may include tone of voice, gesture and body language. Thus, in addition to words, clients express emotion through the vocal and non-verbal channels. As mentors we experience our clients reporting that being able to give voice and express their emotions has been a major breakthrough in tackling a major task in work or in life.

Expression of emotion

Why express emotions in a mentoring relationship? Our discussion in Chapter 4 about connected knowing provides part of the answer. In order to engage in connected knowing, a characteristic of reflective and double loop learning, clients will need to access energy. We discuss in Chapter 3 the motivating power of emotion, which provides the 'fuel' for the adventure of double loop learning. Emotion is an important source of energy to support clients as they swing into the double loop 'orbit' and reconsider the tfgs of their life. In addition, an ability to deal with emotional material is necessary for mentors if they wish to 'unpack' the blocks to learning that emerge in reflective dialogue. But first, what about your feelings?

Awareness of your own emotional state

Awareness of your own emotional states enables you to express clearly in words what it is you are feeling and why. You may have difficulty expressing some emotions or express them indirectly. For example, you may feel frustrated or impatient and, if not expressed, this may be leaked

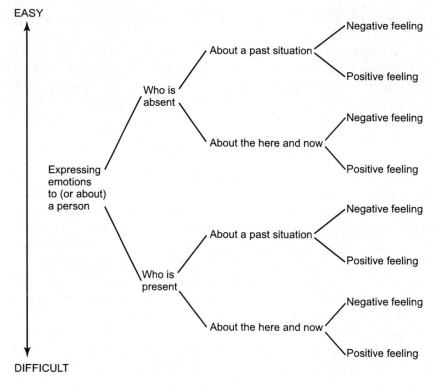

EASY

DIFFICULT

Source: McGill and Brockbank (2004: 196)

Figure 11.2 *Expressing emotion: the difficult-easy continuum*

in your tone of voice. You may be daunted by the seniority or power of your client, and expressing this is preferable to leakage. On the other hand, you may judge that the feeling should be 'parked', and we discuss this below.

We referred in Chapter 9 to the difficult–easy continuum, shown again in Figure 11.2, which is based on the work of Egan (1977) and indicates how awkward we find emotional expression under a variety of circumstances.

Figure 11.2 suggests that we find it easier to express negative emotion, and this is borne out by our lop-sided emotional vocabulary, which tends to incorporate more negative feelings than positive ones, so as a mentor you will need to develop a positive emotional vocabulary. Figure 11.2 also shows that we are able to express emotions about people in their absence more easily than to their face. You may avoid expressing feelings in the here and now. To enable reflective dialogue, you are an important model of emotional expression in the here and now, so how might you express emotions appropriately?

Owning the feeling

Mentoring activity will generate feelings in you, the mentor (and we discuss the reasons for this in Chapter 7). When as mentor you begin to feel impatient with your client, what can you do with that feeling of impatience? You have a choice. You can 'park' it or express it. You can express it like an accusation: 'You are really making me feel impatient' or, by owning the feeling, say: 'I feel impatient somehow – I think it's because I've lost the thread of what you're saying. Could we start again, please?'

With the latter you are taking responsibility for dealing with your own feeling of impatience and trying to identify the cause. This is important. If you make the former statement, your client may feel accused, threatened and defensive, whilst the latter statement relates only to yourself. Why express these feelings – can't they just be ignored?

Storing or parking

Storing up emotions is not helpful generally, for when they eventually erupt they may explode. You need to make a judgement about whether your client can cope with hearing about your feelings and indeed whether they are relevant for your client. Although it is usually better to express feelings as they arise even if they are negative, as a skilled mentor you may decide to park them and take them to a colleague outside the relationship, or your supervisor. We discuss supervision for mentors and coaches in Chapter 13.

As noted above, feelings and emotions as basic human characteristics are neither good nor bad, right nor wrong. As a learnt style of behaviour, we show some of our emotions and not others, eg hurt or anger. As a consequence we may not be able to handle it in others, and this has implications for you as mentor when your clients express their feelings. For instance, if your client becomes tearful, you might feel embarrassed and deal with the situation by pretending it isn't happening or being overly sympathetic. As a skilled mentor you will allow the expression to occur without intervening.

Whatever the emotional expression in a mentoring relationship, how should the mentor respond? In responding to either expressed or leaked emotion in the relationship, as mentor you may use primary empathy, which we described in the previous chapter. Primary empathy responds to feelings and experience that have been expressed explicitly, whilst advanced empathy endeavours to 'read between the lines' or respond to feelings that may have been expressed obliquely. However, because we inhabit an environment that largely devalues feeling and emotion, some advanced empathy skills may be called for where clients are suppressing or denying what they are clearly feeling. This is particularly important when you are dealing with conflict, together with the ability to challenge or confront. We discuss below advanced empathy, followed by feedback, challenge, confrontation and immediacy.

ADVANCED EMPATHY

Advanced empathy differs from primary empathy (described in Chapter 10) in that the feelings to which we respond are not necessarily expressed explicitly. They may be revealed obliquely, through verbal or non-verbal codes. For instance, your client may be talking about a work issue in a puzzled tone of voice. You may 'sense' that the speaker is actually rather worried about the work and not clear about what is needed for the job. We reiterate our understanding of empathy as having both a cognitive and affective component. Our rationale for concentrating on the emotional component here is because you are likely, if Western educated, to be more than competent in the cognitive field and less so in the affective. The definition given below includes both.

The process of advanced empathy is the same as for primary, only in this case, because the feeling is not clearly displayed by clients and, more important, *they may be unaware of the feeling themselves*, then care is needed in communicating what you think you understand about their world. A tentative approach, using qualifiers like 'perhaps', 'it seems', 'I wonder if' and 'it sounds like', means that clients may dissent if they so wish. Offering advanced empathy needs care, so that clients don't feel trampled on.

So for advanced empathy, the definition, as given in Chapter 10 for primary empathy, is valid, with the addition of some hesitancy and caution, as you may be mistaken in your 'sensing' and your response may be based on a hunch. So for advanced empathy, you will, *in a tentative and careful manner*, offer 'an understanding of the world from the other's point of view, her feelings, experience and behaviour, and *the communication of that understanding in full* (Brockbank and McGill, 1998: 195).

For instance, in response to your client above, you might say: 'You have some concerns about the job. I am also wondering about how you see yourself in the job. It seems to me that you might be feeling a little confused about what is required of you exactly.'

An experienced mentor is well placed to 'guess' a lot of what is going on for clients. What is unusual is for clients to be offered empathy before, and possibly instead of, judgement. Clients are often their own harshest judges, and offering empathic understanding may provide them with a basis for tangling with their problems.

You may also have a hunch about your client's feelings, being prepared to be mistaken. In this case, a tentative response may have indicated your hunch as follows: 'You seem very angry, John. Perhaps you are angry about being overlooked at the last promotion round. I know you told me you were shocked when you got your manager's feedback.'

The client concerned may not agree with your hunch and, whatever you think is really going on, you may prefer to return to the 'safe' primary version of empathy, based on expressed feelings, giving the following response: 'You were talking about your work, John, and you sounded puzzled about it.'

The mentor's skill in summarizing also offers an opportunity for advanced empathy, as the sum of a person's statements may reveal a consistent feeling, like resentment or lack of confidence and, in summary, the mentor may be able to draw the threads together and, tentatively, comment on the overall feeling being communicated, albeit obliquely or in code.

SUMMARY

Restatement builds material for a competent summary, so often missing. As a mentor, having restated key points, you will be able, with or without notes, to give a résumé of your client's issue for his or her benefit. Summarizing is a key skill for reflective dialogue and therefore for mentors. You will find it easy to identify the key points in what has been said if you have already done some restatement. Key points are recognizable by the level of energy, either vocal or non-verbal, that is attached to them. For instance, if your client has raised his or her voice or gesticulated you can guess there is an issue of importance there. The key points noted by you may not be the ones that are important to your client, so check.

We should make clear that advanced empathy is different from giving an evaluation of an emerging story.

FEEDBACK

For feedback to be useful, the client needs to be able to:

1. accept it;
2. understand it;
3. use it.

To be helpful, feedback must be delivered by someone who is aware of the emotional charge that can accompany feedback and how this impacts on the receiver. If you as mentor communicate negative emotion, usually via the vocal channel, ie tone of voice, this can have the effect of an emotional exocet for the receiver. If you are angry, this should be owned and declared using congruent words, tone and non-verbal cues so that the receiver can separate the feelings from the feedback itself. For example, when you as mentor are feeling irritated by avoidance, then you should say so and take responsibility for the feeling, which is yours not your client's. You may prefer to say 'Look, I'm sorry, but I am feeling so annoyed with you.' Thereafter you can elaborate by describing what exactly is irritating you, eg 'It seems to me that you are avoiding the issue by saying it's not important', and this information may be valuable feedback for your client.

Positive feedback

Positive feedback is telling clients what they have done and why it was effective. Because feedback holds an emotive element, you are in the 'difficult' part of the continuum in Figure 11.2 on page 220, as you are trying to express a positive emotion directly to someone who is present (your client). In a Western cultural context you may be embarrassed to say something positive to others for fear that it may be misinterpreted or may not seem genuine. You may have been brought up, like millions of others, to think of self-effacement as better than too much self-confidence. Some or all of these reasons may inhibit the giving of positive feedback, which is an important part of learning. Only a mentor is likely to inform clients about what is not evident to them in quadrant 2 (see Figure 9.5 on page 167).

Negative feedback

Mentors may feel uncomfortable about giving negative feedback, as they fear it may be distressing for their client. The fears associated with being the bearer of bad news, whilst archaic, are real. However, persistent failure to give negative feedback may either result in the tendency for negative feedback to be 'stored up' and, under pressure, explode in a destructive way or lead to no change in your client's practice because he or she is unaware that it is causing any difficulties, hence leading to a continuation of less effective practice. Research suggests that helpful and effective feedback enables the receiver to self-assess more accurately and seek feedback again (London, 1997). It is possible to develop feedback skills, by practising, focusing on clarity and simplicity and keeping in mind the dignity and self-esteem of the receiver.

We list the characteristics of effective feedback below and refer readers to Chapter 10 for details and examples.

Giving feedback effectively

First of all, givers of feedback may need to check out who this feedback is for. Is it for the benefit of the giver or the receiver? Thereafter it is possible to give effective feedback by following some simple guidelines:

1. Be clear about what you want to say in advance.
2. Own the feedback.
3. Start with the positive.
4. Be specific, not general.
5. Give one piece of feedback at a time.
6. Focus on behaviour rather than the person.
7. Refer to behaviour that can be changed.
8. Be descriptive rather than evaluative.

As a mentor you might like to ask for feedback from your client. You may be surprised by what you hear about yourself.

CONFLICT, CHALLENGE AND CONFRONTATION

Conflict is inevitable in human interaction. We experience conflict as causing pain and loss of trust. We usually receive no training in dealing with conflict in our lives so we are left with whatever we learn at home. Many people tolerate conflict and can use it productively, but there are those of us who dread it and avoid it at all costs because our early experiences of conflict were frightening and painful. So we can fear conflict but we may also use its benefits to build trust, create intimacy and derive creative solutions. When we deal destructively with conflict, we feel controlled by others, seem to have no choice, blame and compete with others, and hark back to the past rather than grappling with the future.

So to deal with conflict productively we need the courage and the skill to confront. We draw on Egan (1976) to place confrontation into the context of 'challenging skills', an absolute requirement for reflective dialogue. Egan puts three challenging skills together: advanced empathy, confrontation and immediacy. The use of advanced empathy is 'strong medicine', and we discussed its use above.

The manner of using advanced empathy as defined above, ie tentatively and with care, is also the manner needed for confrontation. In addition, Egan stressed the importance of a strong relationship in which to challenge, an established right to challenge (by being prepared to be challenged yourself) and appropriate motivation, ie considering who you are challenging for and whether this is for you or the other person. The state of the receiver should also be considered. Is it the right time? What else may have happened to your client today – does the client look able to receive challenge today? And one challenge at a time, please!

Confrontation

The word denotes 'put in front of', so when I confront I take someone by surprise; hence again I need to do it with care and tentatively, as I might be mistaken. The word 'confrontation' inspires fear due to the common experience of destructive confrontation (Rosen and Tesser, 1970). Experience suggests that a great deal of work time is spent on unresolved conflict due to people being unable to confront and deal with it productively (Thomas, 1976; Magnuson, 1986). Because it is a fearful behaviour, for both confronter and confrontee, we sometimes avoid it and then do it clumsily. For effective confrontation we need to speak directly and assertively and then listen with empathy to the response we get. Note here that confrontation is in the 'eye of the beholder'. Anything can seem confrontational if I'm in that mood, and what may appear low-key to me can seem outrageous to others.

Confronting is the process whereby you as mentor seek to raise consciousness in your clients about some restriction or avoidance that blocks, distorts or restricts their learning. Heron describes the process as 'To tell the truth with love, without being the least judgmental, moralistic, oppressive or nagging' (1999: 182), and for the confronter the test is that 'you are not attached to what you say, you can let it go as well as hold firmly and uncompromisingly to it' (1999: 182).

Note that confronting here has nothing to do with the aggressive, combative account of confrontation that is sometimes applied to legal, political and industrial disputes in Western society. However, the confronting effect of identifying taken-for-granted assumptions can be perceived as threatening, and may be threatening in reality. The transformational nature of breaking paradigms implies a threat to existing models, and this can have real negative repercussions.

Effective confrontation is non-aggressive and non-combative, deeply supportive of your client and with the intended outcome of *enabling learning*. In particular, the power of confrontation for learning lies in its 'surprise' element – the fact that what was previously unknown is now known to your client. If clients can be 'held' and supported in their

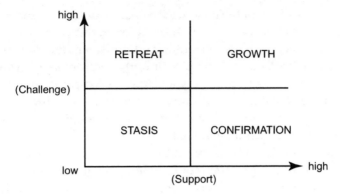

Source: Reid (1994: 38)

Figure 11.3 *Mutual dependence of challenge and support*

'surprise', then they are free to consider how they might use the information. You may like to point out or suggest in the ground rules that your client has a choice, ie to act differently or seek further information from other sources – a second opinion, in effect.

Impending confrontation generates anxiety in the confronter (Rosen and Tesser, 1970). Because confrontation is necessarily revealing that which was previously unknown, receivers will experience shock, even if they are prepared. A simple preamble is a good way of warning clients that a surprise is coming up! Confronting takes nerve to cope with the natural anxiety of causing shock, and this natural anxiety may lead you to avoid confrontation or 'pussyfoot'.

There are two options traditionally available to you as mentor when you want to confront: either *pussyfooting*, being so 'nice' that the issue is avoided; or *clobbering*, being so punitive that the response is aggressive and wounding (Heron, 1999: 183). We are proposing the third option, of skilled, supportive and enabling confrontation. 'The challenge is to get it right. Too much love and you collude. Too much power and you oppress. When you get it right, you are on the razor's edge between the two' (Heron, 1999: 183). This is not an easy task, and we illustrate this in Figure 11.3.

Our earlier comments about challenging pertain here. Who confronts and why? Confronters may like to consider whether they have earned the right to challenge by being open to challenge themselves. Self-disclosure offers the invitation to challenge by others. What motivates my confrontation? Sometimes there are murkier motives operating than the benefits to the client, and you need to be aware of possible contamination along the lines of 'It's for his own good' (Miller, 1983), where discipline is enacted for the benefit of the parent or teacher, masquerading as a concern 'for the good of' the child or, in this case, client.

Has there been sufficient listening and understanding to justify the confrontation? Will the relationship support a confrontation at this point in time? Does the confronter have a history of accepting confrontation him- or herself? Is this the right time or place? Is your client in a good state to receive a confrontation? These are just some of the points to consider before launching into confrontation.

So how is this difficult operation to be done, in the context of a mentoring relationship? We offer some types of confrontation, based on Egan (1976), which might occur in mentoring situations, with some examples:

- Checking previous information, eg 'Correct me if I'm wrong but didn't you say you wanted to go for promotion?'
- Observing discrepancies, eg 'You seem anxious about your interview and you have said you're not good enough; having listened to you talk about your work and appreciated the quality of it, I'm wondering what you are worried about.'
- Observing distortion in what X says, eg 'X, you say that you want to go for promotion, but you haven't applied.'
- Articulating games (perhaps being played unconsciously by Y), eg 'Y, I'm realizing that we've been here before – at our last session you were talking about another job, weren't you?'

We note that confrontation is not always necessarily negative, so:

- Observing strength, eg 'I got a sense of your ability last time we met and I suppose I wonder why it's not in evidence today. I saw then that you were clear about your plans for the job and how you would implement them.'
- Observing weakness, eg 'I know you have a lot on your plate at present. How will you find space for this?'
- Encouragement to act, eg 'Is there any reason why you can't go for it?'

Heron (1986) has offered some ideas on the how-to of confronting, and we offer some examples below:

- Interrupting and identifying the agenda, eg 'Can I just check if you realized, John, that you may be upsetting your colleague when you dismiss her contribution?'

- Open questions and silence, eg 'When can you do this, Karen?'
- Information to your client of which the client may be unaware, eg 'I am getting the impression, Jen, that maybe you don't know about the policy documents that came out this year?'
- Correcting your client if mistaken about a matter of fact, eg 'You mentioned a written warning. Is that correct, Peter? Perhaps you could check.'
- Disagreeing, eg 'I recognize your view here, Mark, and I am aware of finding it difficult to agree with you because...'
- Moving the discourse from 'what and why' to 'how and when' and from 'then and there' to the 'here and now', eg 'James, you are saying what you want to achieve in terms of making a new start and last time you told me why. I'd like to hear today how you intend to do this and when you think that might happen.'
- Mirroring, eg 'You say you want to get promoted within six months.'
- Attending, eg silent attention after your client has spoken can effect a confrontation as the client considers his or her own words in silence.
- Moral aspect, eg 'You said you had mixed feelings about using an idea from one of your staff – perhaps you felt concerned about being unprofessional?'

DEFENCE MECHANISMS

It is important to realize that defence mechanisms are life-preserving and therefore part of a healthy and natural human existence. However, one or more particular defence mechanisms may be counter-productive by inhibiting learning for your client. You will see how that can happen when you read about defence mechanisms below. As an evolutionary mentor your role does not include trying to reveal your client's unconscious defence mechanisms, but a skilled mentor will take account of them, particularly the phenomenon of projection and transference, which we discuss in Chapter 7.

Defence mechanisms include:

- Atonement. Making up for a previous misdemeanour by performing a socially approved act, eg a member of staff staying late to make up for being slack during the day.
- Compensation. Anxiety in one area is balanced by achievement in another, eg failure to achieve academically can be compensated for by excessive sociability or obsessive domesticity.

- Denial. Protection from painful reality by refusing to recognize it, eg believing you're doing OK at work when you are due for a report or final warning.
- Displacement. Transfer of feelings or actions to another person to reduce anxiety, eg if your client is angry with someone at work he or she may displace it to you.
- Fantasy. Creating an imaginary world to meet a desired goal, eg your client's belief that things are better than they are.
- Identification. Trying to 'become' the person we most admire by imitating dress and language. Your client may begin to adopt sayings or gestures of yours.
- Intellectualization. Masking anxious feelings by intellectual and detached discussion, eg discussion of strategy when staff are leaving in droves.
- Introjection. Adoption of someone else's beliefs or attitudes, eg your client believes he or she is no good because a powerful parent said so.
- Projection. Putting undesirable characteristics on to someone else, eg accusing another member of staff of incompetence when it's your own.
- Transference. A particular kind of projection where your client projects on to you aspects of his or her historical relationship with parents or carers, eg adoration or rebellion.
- Rationalization. Creating rational but unreal reasons for your own behaviour, eg staff who blame management for their own lack of motivation.
- Reaction formation. Disguising real feelings or attitudes by the opposite behaviour, eg expressing disgust about someone's behaviour but enjoying gossiping about it.
- Regression. This is reversion to an earlier stage of development, eg a temper tantrum or sleeping a lot under stress.
- Repression. Unconscious exclusion of past memories and feelings to prevent pain anxiety or guilt, eg the person who 'forgets' he or she was bullied at school.

How can you spot defence mechanisms?

Freudian slips are clues to the existence of defence mechanisms. For example, someone denying anger about a colleague's promotion may say, 'I'm so pleased I could hit you' (denial). Other clues to defence mechanisms are non-verbal behaviour such as false smiles, twitching limbs or a sarcastic tone of voice. The feelings that are most likely to be hidden by defence mechanisms are anger, anxiety and hurt. You cannot see your own defence mechanisms because they are unconscious. To bring them into your conscious mind you need to feel very, very safe and that can only happen under special conditions with highly qualified people like therapists, counsellors and some doctors.

IMMEDIACY

Immediacy is an operational form of congruence, and Egan (1976) identifies this as 'you–me' talk, reminiscent of the process of constructing our humanity through interactions of the 'I–thou' kind (Buber, 1994) where realities are forged in relationship and the interplay between you and me.

Immediacy is defined as: 'The ability to discuss with another person what is happening between the two of you in the here and now of an interpersonal transaction' (Egan, 1976: 201).

This skill is crucial for resolving difficult stages, which will occur in every mentoring relationship. We remind readers of the difficult–easy continuum in expression of emotion, given in Figure 11.2, and note that saying a feeling to a person who is present about the here and now is the most difficult and challenging way of expressing emotion. For example, you may say to your client: 'I sense you're feeling resistant to this process, Eddie. I can feel you withdrawing and I feel disappointed.'

Immediacy is a complex skill, and in terms of reflective learning it is 'strong medicine' and may have powerful effects. As mentor, you need to be aware of what is happening internally and externally, and make a judgement about what is appropriate to express and what is appropriate to 'park'. The skill of immediacy takes courage. There is no knowing how your client will react – for many it is a shock – but our experience is that when your client recovers from the shock immediacy is incredibly appreciated and the relationship moves into a new plane. However, it is daunting and you may wait too long.

Another example is: 'I'm aware that you resent me, Peter, although you haven't said so. I see by your look and your tone of voice that you are angry. I feel confused and I would prefer you to say how you feel out loud.'

Really, immediacy is high-level self-disclosure and feedback wrapped together – what-is-happening-to-me-right-now disclosure, which relates to the relationship and the purpose of the mentoring relationship.

REVIEWING THE LEARNING

As mentor, it is your responsibility to conduct a review of each session, making sure that sufficient time is left for it, as described in the cyclical model described in Chapter 7.

Reviewing the learning means that clients have the opportunity to reflect on each session. This has been identified as clients' reflection-on-reflection or the process of learning about their learning. As mentor you may additionally need to become a recorder, ensuring that actions are noted and agreed.

The material for the review relates to *the learning process* as it has been discovered in the couple's dialogue. For example, your client may have identified, in dialogue, that he or she does not in fact wish to apply for promotion and would rather wait for a more challenging opportunity. When reflecting on the learning process your client may see that this realization came from the dialogue process itself, and questioning, empathy and confrontation enabled him or her to get there. In this way your client learns about his or her own learning process.

Your clarification and summary of what has been said is an opportunity for your client to take part in reflection-on-reflection. The mentor's role includes ensuring that a record is kept (not necessarily by the mentor) of the review, as conclusions represent evidence of reflective learning and your client may wish to record such evidence for CPD purposes and the like.

Towards the end of the learning review, as mentor you will ensure psychological safety by a closing-down process where your client may express any feelings that remain and he or she wishes to voice. Such a close-down, which may take no more than a few minutes, is likely to be important as a time for 'healing'. Through reflective dialogue, clients may discover inadequacies in themselves or others and may be hurt, angry or disappointed. These feelings may be expressed obliquely, so you will need to have advanced empathy skills at the ready, as unfinished business can block the future learning process. You should allow all the fears and worries *relating to the session or the relationship* to be expressed and received, but at this point stop discussion about other issues or other people.

In this chapter we have described the skills needed for mentors as a requirement for engaging in reflective dialogue leading to reflective transformatory learning.

DEVELOPING MENTORS AND SUPPORTING THEM

Many mentors take on the role serendipitously in that they are asked to take part in a programme in their organization and find themselves acting as mentors. Where the programme is planned and structured in advance, there may be the possibility of training mentors for the programme, and we recommend this. The offer of training is almost always taken up by aspiring mentors, and the ongoing support ideally included as part of the training, ie being a member of a group of mentors, is an opportunity for support and reassurance. We discuss how the training programme can be tailored to organizational requirements in Chapter 12.

12 Training and development of mentors and coaches

We now examine the rationale for preparing mentors and coaches for their role, the initial stages of the relationship in terms of agreeing a contract and goal setting, and the development of trainee skills through a range of experiential exercises. The exercises cover basic coaching skills used by all mentors and coaches, and also the advanced skills needed by evolutionary mentors and life coaches. Why is mentor and coach training necessary?

REASONS FOR MENTOR TRAINING

Why train mentors? The traditional model assumed a willing and informed senior with the necessary skills and qualities to 'bring on' a junior colleague. The contract mentor may be a different matter. It is common in the UK to submit the potential client to assessment, and limit assessment of the mentor to a 'health check', taking the mentor's readiness and skills for granted (Parsloe and Wray, 2000: 171).

In the UK, an early practitioner in the field of mentoring was David Megginson (1988) of Sheffield Hallam University, who devised a questionnaire for managers to test their behaviours as more or less 'mentoring' in style. His results revealed that managers perceived their behaviour as more mentoring than their staff or senior manager perceived them (Megginson, 1988). This supports the need for proper assessment of potential mentors, training and ongoing support. A variety of assessment instruments such as a selection questionnaire (Cohen, 1995) and checklists for mentor motivation, readiness and skills (Zachary, 2000) can be found in the US literature.

David Clutterbuck emphasized in 1991 the necessity of training for successful mentoring programmes and recommended preparation for mentors, clients, line managers and peers. Subsequent research highlighted the need to prepare mentors properly for their task: 'Mentors need to be skilled in defining what they will and will not offer... dealing with ground rules and boundaries and managing the relationship' (Brockbank, 1994: 88).

The discrepancy between mentors' expectations and those of their client has been established, as well as their perceptions of the relationship (Brockbank, 1994; Beech and Brockbank, 1999).

Another difference that has emerged is how mentors and clients view the relative importance of skills and characteristics. For example, in a study of 13 Canadian government employees who acted as mentors, the results were as follows: 'Mentors indicated that their most important skills and characteristics should be security, confidence and the ability to trust, while clients on the other hand, felt that mentors should be patient, tolerant and accessible' (Cunningham and Eberle, 1993: 64) and 'Mentors indicated that the most important skills or characteristics of clients are their desire to learn and their positive orientation to people, while clients felt that goal orientation and conceptual ability were most important' (Cunningham and Eberle, 1993: 64). In addition, mentors did not share a common view of the key ingredients of a healthy mentor/client relationship: 'Mentors felt that the atmosphere of shared responsibility was most important, while clients emphasized frequency of meetings and mutual respect, focus and flexibility' (Cunningham and Eberle, 1993: 64). Clearly with these discrepancies in place the prospects for healthy and satisfying mentoring relationships are remote.

Ragins, Cotton and Miller, researching over 1,000 US employees, established that 'the degree of satisfaction with the mentoring relationship accounted for more of the unique variance in work attitudes than the type of relationship (*formal or informal*)' (2000: 1190, our italics).

Not only this but the study also found that for individuals in unsatisfactory relationships the outcome was worse than for non-mentored individuals. So to offer people a mentor who has inadequate skills in building satisfactory relationships is doing more damage than leaving them mentorless. Some of these findings echo earlier work where clients ended unsatisfactory mentoring relationships themselves and found alternative peer relationships (Beech and Brockbank, 1999).

Recent findings confirm the significant importance of relationship quality to productive mentoring activities, and suggest that there is a 'need to train managers on the art of giving quality feedback and relationship maintenance' (Nielson and Eisenbach, 2005). Our recommendations for such training are laid out below together with some ideas for workshops.

Nevertheless when training is provided, the failure of some mentoring relationships could be related to a number of mentors who failed to complete the training, having not grasped the difficulties of the role (Brockbank, 1994): hence the importance of clarifying what mentoring is on offer from the start. We analyse four different approaches in Chapter 2, functionalist, engagement, revolutionary and evolutionary, in terms of the purpose, the process and learning outcomes. The process is key to building the relationship, and we have recommended for evolutionary mentoring a robust and radical humanistic approach modelled on the core conditions of Carl Rogers, fully discussed in Chapters 3 and 6.

Accreditation of mentors is available through the European Mentoring and Coaching Council, which supplies at a very reasonable rate a workbook for self-assessment, guidance and submission towards accreditation as a mentor. The only drawback here is the absence of third-party observation, which good training courses will include, as well as review procedures. We discuss such training courses below.

REASONS FOR COACH TRAINING

What about coach training? We have placed coaching (unless it is life coaching) within the functionalist quadrant, particularly in organizational contexts, where the coaching may be part of a line management role, or senior management responsibility, with the purpose of promoting organizational objectives. For coaches working in organizations with their staff, 'Coaching is a process that enables learning and development to occur and thus performance to improve. To be a successful coach requires a knowledge and understanding of the process as well as the variety of styles, skills, and techniques that are appropriate to the context in which the coaching is taking place' (Parsloe and Wray, 2000: 42).

There is a plethora of training offers available for coaches, life coaches or executive coaches, usually aimed at independent consultants who are adding coaching to their offer. NLP organizations have full-blooded programmes to train their coaches, who are then called 'master practitioners', qualified to practise NLP.

A vast choice of training is on offer, as more providers enter the field, not always of high quality. Jenny Rogers remarks that 'anyone promising the full, once-and-for-all authoritative guarantee that they can turn you into a fully-fledged coach within a few short days will be misleading you' and 'four days of face-to-face training is the minimum for serious learning about coaching' (2004: 178–79). We reported on the outcomes from such training offers in Chapter 6 where the process of using an untrained coach was described as 'putting your life in their hands' (Burt, 2005), and there is potential for damage to vulnerable clients from either coaches who 'tell' or coaches who 'pathologize'. We discuss the difference between coaching and therapy in Chapter 13.

For ordinary managers, who are given the coaching role as part of their job, there may be an assumption that they know what is involved in the role and have the skill set required.

Here the training is even more essential, as it is likely that managers are being asked to adopt an engagement approach, ie use humanistic techniques and skills to promote a functionalist agenda. Such a process is problematic for skilled trainers, and to ask inexperienced (in this field) managers who are embedded in a 'command and control' mentality to achieve such a dramatic change in their style is asking the impossible. For managers to transform themselves in this way would involve the managers themselves being offered evolutionary mentoring or coaching, and innovative organizations will do just that. Where managers are given a day's training or left to get on with it the outcome is predictably disappointing.

One of the leading providers of coach training is the Chartered Institute of Personnel and Development (CIPD), whose courses range from frankly functionalist programmes led by industrial practitioners to blended programmes that include coaching theory. Our hope is that readers of this book will be enabled to identify which courses they want, be they functionalist, engagement or evolutionary. On inspection of the CIPD course outlines, the terms 'senior' and 'advanced' do not necessarily guarantee an evolutionary approach. NLP practitioners use the terms appropriately, and NLP life coaches are trained to work in an evolutionary way. The CIPD do offer the possibility of accreditation, and this will enable the activity of coaching to become more regulated, as has happened with the therapy profession (Jarvis, 2004).

TRAINING IDEAS FOR MENTORS AND COACHES

We now present some training ideas for practitioners who are seeking to offer potential mentors and coaches some insights into the theory and techniques of mentoring or coaching.

Mentors and coaches: creating a contract with your client

As discussed in Chapters 5 and 6, mentors and coaches may need to explore their expectations of the role and so must their clients. There is evidence that these are very different, with clients expecting mentors who are patient, tolerant and accessible, while mentors expect clients who are motivated to learn and have a positive orientation to people (Cunningham and Eberle, 1993). We can detect here the early beginning of unrealistic expectations, which are likely to influence the emerging relationship. The idea of formally writing down what has been agreed is not congenial for some trainee mentors or coaches, and the training is where the contract is presented as an ethical matter, as clients who are mentored or coached without a contract may be vulnerable to deleterious effects. The contracting process involves a degree of negotiation, and we offer a negotiation checklist in Appendix 1.

A full sample coaching contract is presented on pages 174–176. A full sample mentoring contract is presented on pages 120–121.

We maintain that mentors or coaches who are clear about which quadrant they are operating in, namely functionalist, engagement or evolutionary, will be confident and effective. When they have clarified in training who owns the purpose and the intended learning outcome, the process and skills needed become evident.

Mentors and coaches: setting goals

In order to clarify purpose it is necessary to agree on the goals or objectives of the mentoring or coaching programme. We discuss goal setting for mentors in detail in Chapter 7. For training coaches we recommend using the GROW model (described in Chapter 8), as the first part of the acronym is 'G' for 'goal setting'.

At this point trainee mentors or coaches will need to identify what they are doing. Are they aiming to fulfil a function prescribed by the organization? Are they working with their client's own goals? If the former, the job of goal setting includes ensuring that the client assents to the goals prescribed. For this to happen the functionalist objectives must be clearly stated, as unclear goals spell coaching disaster. If the objectives are likely to meet with resistance, then some preparatory work needs to be done. For instance, where clients are being coached into new competences, as in the Addaction case study in Chapter 6, the clients will need to appreciate what the benefits of such competences will be for them. These may include promotion prospects, an improved CV or financial reward. The fear of downsizing and unemployment is a last resort. Where the client's values are significantly opposed to the organization's intentions, basic coaching in-house is insufficient, as the agreement will founder at the goal-setting stage. In such circumstances we recommend an evolutionary approach using an external mentor or executive coach.

MENTORING AND COACHING SKILLS

As the quality of relationship has been identified as the most significant indicator of effective mentoring or coaching, the skills required are those that build rapport, trust and a solid I–thou relationship. Even functionalist mentoring or coaching must start with some kind of relationship; engagement mentoring or coaching calls for a wider range of skills; and evolutionary mentoring demands a sophisticated skill portfolio. We begin therefore with training techniques and workshop exercises for basic coaching skills (which mentors and life coaches will also use) for functionalist or engagement purposes and continue with practicums to assist in the development of the evolutionary skills needed by mentors, executive coaches and life coaches. We list here again the key coaching and mentoring skills:

- listening;
- restating;
- questioning;
- empathy;
- summarizing;
- reflection;
- feedback.

The workshop exercises are listed below:

1. listening and restatement in pairs;
2. Socratic questioning in groups;
3. coaching triad and summary;
4. the non-verbal channel of communication;
5. the vocal channel;

6. empathy circle;
7. mentoring trios;
8. the training six: a practicum;
9. handling defence mechanisms;
10. codes of practice.

Exercises 1, 2, 3, 4 and 5 are appropriate for basic coaching or functionalist mentoring. Exercises 1, 2, 3, 4, 5 and 6 are appropriate for engagement mentoring. Exercises 1, 2, 3, 4, 5, 6, 7, 8 and 9 are appropriate for
evolutionary mentoring or life coaching. The diversity workshop and
Exercise 10 are needed by all coaches and mentors of whatever type.

Exercise 1: listening and restatement

The purpose of this exercise is to enable participants to practise listening
and restatement to achieve accuracy in their responses. Most trainee
mentors or coaches will tell you how important listening is so this exercise needs hardly any justification but will reveal a great deal to
participants about how accurate their listening may be.

Timing: 20 minutes.

Method: Work in twos taking turns as speaker and listener.

Speaker to recount his or her journey to the workshop, giving all
factual details. Aim to speak for about five minutes and add five minutes
for the listener to respond, giving 10 minutes each. Listener to restate as
accurately as possible what the speaker has said, changing 'I' to 'you'.
Note that the restatement involves changing the volunteers' 'I' statements into 'you' statements. For example, the volunteer might say 'I
caught the train and arrived just in time' and a restatement of this becomes 'You caught the train and you arrived just in time.' Stop the
speaker every so often so that you can restate what you have heard. Do
this mechanically at this stage – it's an exercise – and then check out with
the speaker if you've got it right. Speaker to clarify if necessary or confirm. Pair to discuss the process briefly and report back in plenary.

Exercise 2: Socratic questioning in small groups of four or five

Purpose: To enable coaches to practise the Socratic method of questioning using open rather than closed questions. Establish what an open
question is and offer Kipling's rhyme to help:

I had six honest serving men
They taught me all I knew

Their names were what and why and when
And how and where and who.

(Rudyard Kipling)

Refer to Chapter 11 for detail of the ancient origins of Socratic questioning as an aid to learning.

Timing: 20 minutes.

Method: The use of open questions can be illustrated by reference to goal setting, the first part of the GROW model described in Chapter 8. One member of the small group agrees to present for discussion a real goal that the person has in mind for him- or herself. The rest of the small group work to generate open questions, which aim to set the goal effectively. One member to record the questions and report back in plenary. After the initial questions there will be follow-up questions, and these must also be Socratic.

The characteristics of goals that are likely to be achieved can be identified in terms of a mnemonic, SMART:

S – Is the goal **s**pecific?   What exactly do you want to achieve?
M – Is the goal **m**easurable?   How will you know you have
                                                       succeeded?
A – Is the goal **a**chievable?   How will you do it?
R – Is the goal **r**ealistic?   What could block your goal?
T – Is the goal **t**ime-bounded? When will it be done?

Exercise 3: coaching triads – summary

This exercise combines the four key skills and allows participants to practise giving feedback to each other.

Purpose: To offer coaches an opportunity to practise listening, restatement, questioning and summary and receive feedback from an observer.

Timing: one hour (20 minutes for each coach).

Method: This exercise involves an observer, and this is an opportunity for trainee coaches to practise giving and receiving feedback, which we discuss in detail in Chapters 9, 10 and 11. We recommend that the trainees as a group, guided by their trainer, formulate some 'rules' for giving and receiving feedback before the exercise. Either allocate or suggest that trainees form trios to work independently. Decide on who will take what role initially.

Client brief

Choose an issue, relating to your work, that you are willing to share with two other people (your issue will not be discussed outside your triad). Speak naturally, explaining the issue in your own way and taking your time so that everything you want to say is included. Don't be afraid to add extra information as it comes to mind.

Coach brief

Position your body so that you are opposite the client and ensure that you can hear and see him or her. Look at the client. Try to concentrate on what the client is saying, excluding everything else around you. Put your own thoughts, ideas and feelings on one side until after the exercise.

First, listen and respond, restating what the client has said, as accurately as you can. Where the client uses 'I', eg 'I am stuck with my staffing rota', you should respond using 'you', eg 'You are stuck with your staffing rota.' This is verbal mirroring, and you can also mirror non-verbally, using a similar tone and volume as well as your body.

Second, summarize what the client has said as best you can. Try to use some of the speaker's own words and include key points *as indicated by the client*, eg points raised by the client with negative or positive energy (these are likely action points).

Third, question the client, using open rather than closed questions: what, why, when, how, where and who.

Fourth, listen again, identifying action points and restating them to the client.

Fifth, summarize again, including action points with agreed timescales if possible.

Repeat the five stages as required. Take 20 minutes.

Observer brief

Your function is to provide feedback to the coach, having observed his or her non-verbal behaviour, stance and verbal responses. Observe the body position and stance of the coach, facial expression, eyes and head orientation. Particularly note movement or stillness in the coach. Listen carefully to the client, and check the accuracy of the coach's restatement. Note down anything the coach 'missed', even if you don't think it was important (check this out later with the client). Note the contents of the coach's summary, again noting down 'missing' points. Record the coach's questions as 'O=open' or 'C=closed'. Note the coach's restatement of action points. Check the final summary for accuracy, particularly agreed action points and timescales. Offer effective feedback in a skilful manner. Observers may also record process comments to be reported in plenary – no details but general learning points.

Rotate roles.

Exercise 4: the non-verbal channel of communication

Coaches may not be aware of the non-verbal aspects of their own communications with clients so this exercise is relevant and useful even for experienced managers. First, it is necessary to call attention to the three channels of communication, namely verbal, non-verbal and vocal. The first is overemphasized in our education system, as discussed in Chapter 3; the second is known to carry more of the message than words and is difficult to disguise; the third is largely neglected except by voice coaches and actors.

Purpose: to enable coaches to experience giving and receiving non-verbal messages.

Timing: short 15-minute exercise – often good for after lunch as the participants move around.

Method: Ask participants to form two circles, an inner circle and an outer circle. They are going to walk around in their circle in the opposite direction from those in the other circle. Participants in the outer circle are given a card each with a description on it of a non-verbal behaviour. They do not show their card to anyone. As they walk around they adopt the description on their card towards whoever is opposite them in the inner circle. The cards should be a mixture of the negative and positive messages sometimes known as 'strokes', because they echo the stroking we experienced as infants, that are essential for our well-being (Harris, 1997). We list these below. The circles should then swap over and do it again.

Some of the positive non-verbal messages or 'strokes' that mentors and coaches may use to communicate to clients are:

- smile;
- nod;
- eye contact;
- wave or gesture;
- touch;
- handshake;
- body turned towards client, head up;
- equal height and appropriate distance.

Some of the negative non-verbal messages or 'strokes' that mentors and coaches may use to communicate to clients are:

- frown;
- lack of eye contact;
- body turned away, head down;
- tightly held body – no touch;
- cold distance or superior height.

The benefit of the exercise comes in the debrief when those in the inner circle comment on how they received the messages from the outer circle. Some messages will have more power because of the cultural context, and this needs to be attended to. For instance, the degree of touch that is acceptable in the workplace is culturally specific and may need to be discussed and agreed.

Exercise 5: the vocal channel

This important channel of communication is often overlooked.

First, participants are asked to brainstorm what is in the vocal channel that will be received as part of their communication. They will identify some of the following:

- volume;
- pitch;
- speed;
- tone;
- pauses;
- paralanguage (example(s) of).

Purpose: To allow participants to send and receive a message in one word.

Timing: 5–10 minutes involving movement.

Method: Invite two or three participants to be 'receivers'. The remaining participants form a line and approach the receiver one at a time. They are asked to say the word 'yes', but to load it with an emotional message of their choice, using the factors above to do this. For example, the first in line may say 'yes' in a frightened way, the second may shout 'yes', the third may say 'yes' happily, the fourth may say 'yes' rather sadly, etc. The process can be repeated and replicated with the word 'no'. The value again is in the debrief of both 'senders' and 'receivers'.

The basic skills are needed by mentors and coaches in every quadrant, ie functionalist, engagement and evolutionary. The evolutionary skills of the next section are in addition to the basic skills above. However, we recognize that many mentors or coaches will have and use the skills we have called 'evolutionary'.

EVOLUTIONARY SKILLS

We now consider the skills needed for mentors or coaches who are taking an evolutionary approach. For reflective dialogue, which leads to double loop learning and transformations, mentors or coaches will need to be able to deal with emotional material, as this is the fuel needed to leave the taken-for-granted groove, challenge the prevailing discourse and engage in transformational learning (see Chapter 3 for details).

Therefore the exercises that follow take trainees from a group situation, through mentoring trios to the training six, and include exercises to develop awareness of defence mechanisms, diversity and ethical issues.

Exercise 6: empathy circle with guides[1]

This exercise is designed to allow potential mentors or coaches to develop or enhance their use of empathy with clients.

Purpose: The circle method offers the possibility of trainee mentors or life coaches learning from each other in a non-threatening way. A client is needed, and this may be a trainer if there are two of you or, if only one trainer is present, a participant who is willing to volunteer. For the empathy circle we strongly recommend a co-trainer as client. The skills of listening, restatement and summary are also practised in this exercise, but the main focus is empathy, which we discuss fully in Chapter 10, and we recommend the use of the empathy template given on page 188 and repeated in the box below.

'You feel... because...' or
'You feel... when... because...'

For ease of reading, we describe participants as 'mentors'.
Timing: 40 minutes.

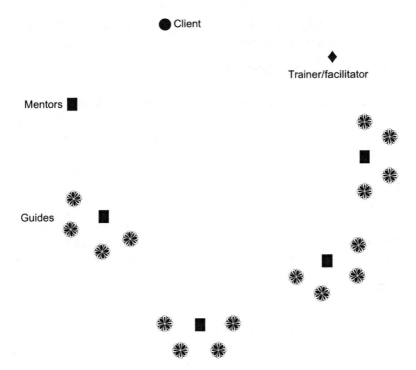

Figure 12.1   *The empathy circle*

Method: Participants form a semicircle of mentors around the client as in Figure 12.1. The client (usually the trainer, acting as speaker/client) is to describe a recent professional issue that holds an emotional charge, eg a downsizing programme or redundancies. Participants form a circle of up to six mentors around the client and four or five 'guides' sit behind each mentor. Another trainer needs to act as overall tutor, controlling the timing, as well as recording the material given by the client. See Figure 12.1. (Note that up to 30 participants can do this.)

After one or two sentences, ask the client to stop and invite mentors, with the help of their guides, to restate the client's material. Let all six mentors in turn have a go (helped by guides) and if necessary go round again to get all the information. The trainer/facilitator controls who speaks when and for how long. After another one or two sentences, invite the mentors to summarize what has been said so far. Then allow the circle of six mentors to reflect back as accurately as they can the feelings expressed by the client, helped by guides. Mentors are to respond particularly to feelings and the behaviour or experience that causes them. If the circle completes without accuracy, trainer/facilitator models correct empathy. If you have only one trainer then a volunteer participant has to be the client.

The empathy circle: description of roles

- Client. Client presents as directed, using real material from his or her own experience, speaking freely and openly as he or she judges appropriate to the exercise. The client receives responses without comment.
- Mentor. Mentors attend to speaker using SOLER, described in Chapter 10; they listen and restate what they have heard, as accurately as possible. Each mentor, helped by one to five guides (depending on numbers), will be asked to respond to the client in turn by the trainer/facilitator. For this exercise each mentor should try to use the formula for empathy or something like it, concentrating on the feelings expressed, either verbally or non-verbally, by the speaker/client. Mentors in this exercise offer empathy only; therefore no questioning is allowed.
- Guides. Any number of guides from one to five is possible. The guides cluster around each mentor, offering advice, ideas and support, to assist with restating to the client, especially with accuracy. In this exercise the guides are likely to offer their mentor ideas about feelings expressed obliquely by the speaker or, indeed, about directly articulated feelings expressed verbally.
- Trainer/facilitator. The trainer/facilitator is responsible for timing and controlling the exercise, giving each mentor a chance to 'have a go' at responding to the speaker. The mentor should confer with guides for advice and support. If the material offered by the client runs out, then the trainer/facilitator will ask him or her to continue.

Processing session in plenary: Discuss what has been learnt or gained as well as difficulties that arose in the empathy circle exercise, without revisiting the detail. Participants report being surprised by how many different 'versions' emerge of the volunteer's account.

Exercise 7: mentoring trios – reflective dialogue

As discussed in Chapter 3, for transformational learning to occur a process known as 'reflective dialogue' is necessary, where the learner or client begins to question the tfgs, challenge the prevailing discourse and reframe his or her view of the world. This exercise offers mentors a model of reflective dialogue to work from (see Figure 12.2).

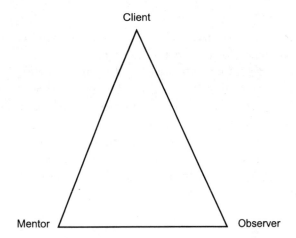

Figure 12.2 *Mentoring trios: the roles of mentor, client and observer*

Purpose: to offer trainee mentors the opportunity to practise reflective dialogue, mentoring and observing as well as experiencing what it feels like to be a client.

Timing: one and a half hours.

Method: For this activity choose your role – descriptions of each role are given below. The client and mentor dialogue for 20 to 30 minutes ending when appropriate. The mentor has the first opportunity to comment on the process, for five minutes initially, and the observer gives feedback for 10 minutes. After discussion, the trio decide on issues for the plenary.

Check out confidentiality before beginning the exercise. The plenary session will discuss process issues only.

Client

Consider your own professional work and the standards defined by your profession. Identify a current or recent instance where it is important for you to make a professional judgement. With your mentor, spend 20 to 30 minutes in reflective dialogue with a view to coming to clarification, some resolution and/or first steps toward action. The client should speak directly from his or her own experience, using 'I' statements and disclosing as much as he or she feels appropriate. The background and details should lead to a clear statement of the issue. The client is supported by the mentor but retains responsibility for the learning outcome of the dialogue.

Mentor

The mentor's purpose is to enable the client to engage in a challenging and reflective dialogue about his or her professional issue, exploring it from a variety of perspectives, enabling the client to move towards an outcome that may or may not be final. The mentor should listen first, until the client stops or reaches clarification, and then summarize. The mentor should question and summarize in turn, offering empathy where appropriate, and using open or probing questions. The mentor should encourage the client to move towards closure, be it action or intent, without taking away the responsibility for the learning outcome, which remains with the client.

Observer

The observer's purpose is to offer feedback after the dialogue between mentor and client, to the mentor primarily, about what skills enabled the client most effectively. A checklist for giving feedback is provided below, and this is what the observer should attend to. The observer should offer constructive feedback directly to the mentor on the basis of what he or she has seen and heard, not what he or she has interpreted or speculated. The observer does not act as another mentor, but reports only the process that has been observed and how the dialogue was enabled.

The process review

The trio may wish to discuss the observations and review those parts of the process that were conducive to enabling the client to work productively with his or her professional issue. On the basis of this discussion, the observer is asked to record conclusions that the trio wish to convey to the plenary group.

MENTORING TRIOS: A CHECKLIST FOR GIVING FEEDBACK TO BE USED BY THE OBSERVER

■ Skills and criteria:

- listening and attending;
- SOLER;
- facial expression and stance;
- silence.

- Restating:

    - accurate use of speaker's words;
    - stopping the flow;
    - natural style of interruption.

- Empathy:

    - use of feeling word if used;
    - use of feeling word if non-verbal;
    - use of formula (or other method), eg 'I get a sense of...';
    - addition of 'because' or 'when'.

- Questioning:

    - open: what, why, how, where, when and who;
    - probing: can be closed;
    - not multiple or rhetorical.

- Summarizing (essential at end of 'mentoring' session):

    - complete as far as possible, including process (what has occurred between the pair);
    - drawing on restated material;
    - restatement of positives and some disclosure;
    - affirmation of unstated positives.

- Challenge:

    - hypothetical questions: 'What if...?'
    - the worst and the best outcome?
    - 'Perhaps you feel...'
    - 'What other ways...?'
    - 'What went well/not so well and why?'
    - 'What would you now do differently?'
    - use of silence as challenge.

Exercise 8: the training six – a practicum[2]

The training six may be used for developing the skills of mentoring or life coaching or bringing to awareness the effects of particular behaviours. For instance, the training six allows mentors to practise in their role and discover where they are more effective and less effective with clients. The process enables six people to learn from one person's experience, and good practice is analysed and understood, taking some of the mystery out of the mentoring role. All conversations in the training six should be audible to the six participants, who take the following roles:

■ speaker;
■ mentor (or life coach);
■ guide to speaker;
■ guide to mentor;
■ observer to mentor;
■ observer to speaker.

A trainer or facilitator will normally oversee the exercise, taking responsibility for timing and debriefing.

The mentor has a 'guide' to assist with the mentoring task, and this process should be audible to all participants. Additionally, the speaker has a guide who will talk openly with the speaker about what is happening during the interactions, material not normally available to the mentor. Mentor and speaker confer with their guides when the facilitator 'pauses' the exercise or when they wish to pause it themselves for whatever reason. One observer records the skills used by the mentor and the mentor's guide whilst the second observer records the skills used by the speaker's guide, as well as the speaker's own communication process. The facilitator keeps time and controls the exercise. The facilitator will 'pause' the process as appropriate and allow guides to confer with mentor and speaker, whilst all six participants listen.

When necessary the second observer may also act as facilitator. The six participants arrange themselves as shown in Figure 12.3.

The training six: description of roles

1. Mentor or coach (for ease of reading, 'mentor' is used hereafter). This role uses listening, restating, summary and empathy, as well as questioning and summarizing.
2. Speaker. The speaker should relax and enjoy being listened to! Choose an issue that you are happy to share with others. Speak

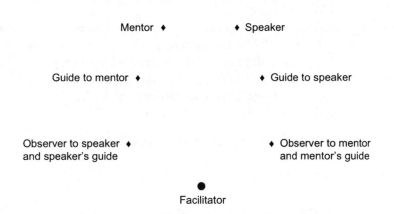

Figure 12.3 *Training six: arrangement of participants*

openly and honestly, pausing to give your mentor a chance to respond. The facilitator will intervene occasionally, 'pausing' the proceedings while guides and mentors confer.
3. Guide to mentor. This role is supportive and advisory, giving the mentor ideas or working with the mentor on his or her responses to the speaker. The guide role is an enabling role and demands the same skills being used by the mentor. This role enables the guide to practise the very skills needed for mentoring, and the observer should record the guide's skilled behaviour.
4. Guide to speaker. This role is also supportive, but no advice is necessary. Your role is to enable the speaker to articulate what is helpful or effective in the interaction, as it occurs, and is an opportunity to practise the skills needed for mentoring.
5. Observer to mentor and guide. The observer's role is to record what he or she sees and hears in respect of skilled behaviour on the part of the mentor and offer feedback to the mentor at the end of the exercise. The observer also listens to the interaction between guide and mentor, and may offer the guide feedback on his or her skilled behaviour.
6. Observer to speaker and guide. The second observer's role is to record what he or she sees and hears in respect of skilled behaviour on the part of the speaker's guide and offer feedback to the guide at the end of the exercise. The observer may also offer the speaker feedback if appropriate.

Facilitator

The facilitator takes responsibility for timing the exercise, pausing the process, and intervening, should it be necessary. Additionally, the facilitator may record what he or she sees and hears for the benefit of all participants, whose skills he or she has observed. The facilitator will normally be responsible for debriefing the training six in the following order: mentor, guides, observers, speaker, having initially agreed with participants on ground rules for giving feedback. A typical set of ground rules generated by participants is given below.

Typical ground rules for giving feedback in practicum analysis

- Mentor or coach focused.
- Skills focused.
- Not reconnecting with problem or issue.
- Confidentiality.
- Structure: mentor or coach first.
- Respect.
- Acknowledge it is our perception.
- 'I' statements.
- Framing, eg 'perhaps', 'maybe'.
- Model/techniques.
- Recognize good things.
- Dealing with difference.
- Honesty.
- Be clear about point of feedback (who is it for?).

Feedback structure

1. Mentor speaks first.
2. Mentor pauses and asks for feedback.
3. Guides' feedback to mentor and speaker – two points only.
4. Observers' feedback to guides – two points only.
5. Guides' feedback – additional points.
6. Observers' feedback – additional points.
7. Speaker feedback on how it was for the speaker. (This is not recommended but should be optional – see ground rules.)

To run the training six practicum, participants need to be willing to take part, and our experience is that most trainee mentors and coaches are. Careful facilitation is essential, and the review process of giving feedback should be strictly adhered to, without becoming a free-for-all. Other participants who may be observing the practicum should be invited to speak when the exercise proper is finished, the six have been debriefed and the points of interest can be focused on general issues rather than individuals.

Exercise 9: handling defence mechanisms

We list defence mechanisms (discussed in Chapter 11) below and reiterate that in general our own are invisible to us. However, with practice we can spot other people's and this may be valuable in mentoring or coaching relationships.

Purpose: To enable trainee mentors or coaches to discover how to 'spot' unconscious defence mechanisms operating in their client.

Timing: 40 minutes.

This exercise offers trainee mentors or coaches an opportunity to explore the significance of defence mechanisms in mentoring or coaching relationships. First, explore with participants what a defence mechanism is and why it is altogether part of being human, and its original development for psychological safety. We list below the defence mechanisms that may emerge in a reflective learning situation like mentoring or coaching:

■ compensation: anxiety in one area balanced by achievement in another, eg failure to achieve academically can be compensated for by excessive sociability or obsessive domesticity;
■ denial: protection from painful reality by refusing to recognize it, eg believing you're doing OK at work when you are due for a report or final warning;
■ displacement: transfer of feelings or actions to another person to reduce anxiety, eg youngsters who are angry with their parents often displace it to teachers, managers etc;
■ fantasy: creating an imaginary world to meet a desired goal, eg a manager's belief that things are better than they are;
■ intellectualization: masking anxious feelings by intellectual and detached discussion, eg discussion of strategy when staff are leaving in droves;
■ introjection: adoption of someone else's beliefs or attitudes, eg a young person who believes that he or she is 'no good' because a powerful parent said so;

- projection: putting undesirable characteristics on to someone else, eg accusing another member of staff of incompetence when it's your own;
- rationalization: creating rational but unreal reasons for your own behaviour, eg staff who blame management for their own lack of motivation;
- repression: unconscious exclusion of past memories and feelings to prevent pain, anxiety or guilt, eg the person who 'forgets' he or she has been abused.

Method: Refer to the list above of defence mechanisms, invite participants to work in pairs and follow the instructions below.

Pick out a slip of paper and try to identify the potential defence mechanisms that may be operating. There is no right or wrong answer. The items below are transferred to slips of paper, folded and put in a basket for participants to choose from:

1. An elderly lady, waiting at the bus stop, is watching two teenage boys joking around, playing at fighting. She remarks to her neighbour that 'Young folk today don't know their place.'
2. A young woman manager is appraising her staff and comments that her deputy is 'rather pushy'.
3. A middle-aged mother tells her friend, 'I'm always here for my family – I've never wanted a career like these youngsters.'
4. A senior manager has a reputation for picking up ideas from his juniors and presenting them as his own.
5. Line managers often refer to the HR department as 'those touchy-feely people at head office'.
6. An assistant manager gives his staff a bad time after a tough meeting with his boss.
7. Good friends sometimes pick up each other's mannerisms and dress alike.
8. A junior executive finds that his meetings with the senior buyer always end up in a shouting match.
9. After counselling a member of staff, the manager went home feeling tired, low and depressed.
10. One member of the team was always arguing and disagreeing for the sake of it.
11. A senior manager finds that a particular member of staff winds him up and he finds himself punishing her for no reason.
12. After being disciplined at work, John went home in a thoroughly bad mood and everyone suffered.

13. My aunt used to say, 'I always go by first impressions and I'm never wrong.'
14. The headteacher said, 'I never trusted her. Right from the start, I knew there was something wrong about her.'

Exercise 10: code of practice

A mentoring code of practice is provided by the EMCC (European Mentoring and Coaching Council) and we present it in Chapter 7. A coaching regulatory code is provided by the International Coaching Federation at www.coachfederation.org/regulatory/default.asp.

From our experience of training coaches and mentors, the best code is the one participants devise for themselves and compare for completeness with professionally provided codes. This exercise enables them to do this.

Purpose: To establish the need for a professional code of ethics for practising mentors and coaches.

Timing: 40 minutes.

Method: Participants work in small groups to generate items for a mentoring or coaching code of practice. This exercise is developmental for trainees and allows the ethical issues to be raised and discussed, as well as the need for appropriate supervision for both mentors and coaches. Ethics and guidelines are discussed further in Chapter 13.

This completes the series of experiential exercises listed earlier. We consider now how practitioners can select mentors and choose coaches.

SELECTION OF MENTORS

Who gets mentors? For true classical mentoring, the relationship happens organically as mentors 'take a shine' to a junior colleague. A survey of over 600 government mentors found that mentors' choice of client was influenced more by their perceived ability or potential than their perceived need for help (Allen, Poteet and Russell, 2000). Those launching contract mentoring in organizations are now aware that line managers do not make ideal mentors, but tend not to allow the mentor and client to choose each other. Mentoring programmes in the UK often use psychometric tests to 'match' mentors with clients, rather than offering clients a choice of mentor, a practice sure to lead to collusion, and the kind of self-deception discussed in Chapter 3. The outcome of such 'arranged marriages' is known to be limited as: 'Individuals in mentoring relationships prefer to let the process evolve naturally, and to select their own mentors/protégés… it seems that any formalized mentoring programme should allow both mentors' and protégés' input into the matching process and some mechanism for exit if an assigned mentoring relationship does not work out' (Scandura, 1998: 451).

To allow both mentors and clients to have a say about their match, it is necessary first to select a pool of mentors from which clients may make a choice of their best three, say, and then to assign the clients' choices to mentors, who make their final choice. Mentors are selected by means of a questionnaire, not a psychometric test, which reveals the mentors' attitude to adult learning and their potential skills level. The whole process of arranging choice on both sides is discussed in the CILT case study in Chapter 5.

CHOOSING A COACH

Jessica Jarvis has provided a very thorough guide for practitioners who are seeking external coaches, and this is available online from the Chartered Institute of Personnel and Development (Jarvis, 2004). The person specification for an external or executive coach, which we would define as 'evolutionary', offered here includes the following:

- coaching experience;
- relevant business experience;
- references;
- background;
- supervision;
- breadth of tools and techniques;
- understanding of boundaries;
- relevant qualifications and training;
- membership of professional bodies;
- professional indemnity insurance.

For training and development purposes, new mentors and coaches should be provided with a booklet outlining the role they are required to take, the objectives of the programme and guidance on setting up the relationship. A typical booklet would contain the following:

1. definition of role and relationship;
2. why me?
3. mentoring functions and what to do;

4. mentoring skills;
5. dos and don'ts;
6. benefits for the mentor;
7. the first meeting;
8. mentor accreditation;
9. mentoring code of practice;
10. pro formas:

   – negotiation checklist;
   – mentoring agreement (sample);
   – mentoring sessions;
   – development plan;
   – evaluation.

Typical pro formas for mentoring and coaching schemes can be found in Appendix 1.

DIVERSITY TRAINING

Mentors and coaches will need to address issues of diversity in their training. The training process should be designed to bring unconscious assumptions about 'out-groups' into consciousness without blame, so that mentors and coaches are able to work with their stereotypes or prejudices. We present some typical workshop material below.

Workshop case studies in diversity for mentors and coaches

This is a group exercise. Participants are divided into small groups of three or four and asked to prepare a response to the following situations. They go into the roles suggested by the case and engage in the response before reviewing in plenary. The facilitator then leads a plenary discussion after the role play, having asked the group for their reflections upon the case.

Note that, to use these case studies, the emphasis should be on re-educating perpetrators of poor practice rather than asking the victims to deal with the situation. Clutterbuck and Ragins (2002) offer a list of beliefs about the out-group, shown below, to use as a personal diagnostic – and this can also be used for discussion afterwards:

■ All are...
■ All tend to be...
■ Most are...

- Most tend to be…
- Many are…
- Many tend to be…
- Some are…
- Some tend to be…
- A minority is…
- A minority tends to be…

1. At a coaching workshop, the facilitator is introducing the organization's code of practice on diversity to the participants. A white member of staff who has been working in the department for the last 10 years asks why this is necessary because: 'As far as I'm concerned, there's no problem. To me all people are just people, and I treat them all the same.' As a fellow mentor at the workshop, how might you respond?

2. A male manager is rounding off the discussion at the open day for men and women applicants to the department and talks very understandingly and confidently about 'how difficult it will be for women applicants to make the choice between having children and a career once they have graduated, particularly in our profession'. As a colleague, how will you respond?

3. At the next management team meeting you report that you have been on one of the diversity workshops. In part of your verbal report back you comment that one of the things that you are most concerned about is the need to ensure that any cases of sexual harassment are treated very seriously. Before you are finished one man interjects: 'What harassment? Tell us more!' Another man interjects: 'No one's harassed me' and sniggers. Another adds: 'Nor me, unfortunately.' How will you respond?

4. In a hospital context a white patient is attending the clinic where your client, an Asian medical student, is undertaking clinical practice. When the patient sees the client, he asks: 'Are you properly qualified?' The client brings the matter to the attention of the mentor. As the mentor, what will be your response?

5. In a discussion about how mentoring can influence the diversity of staff, two colleagues are saying things like: 'Oh, we are keen to recruit more women, more black people etc, if only they'd apply.' As another colleague in the discussion, how would you respond?

6. At a meeting going through the identification of suitable mentors for staff, one colleague comments, 'She looks as if she satisfies the criteria for entry – the only trouble is she's disabled.'

7. A female member of staff meets her coach for the first time, a male senior manager, also her line manager, who walks into the departmental office and says, cheerfully: 'You're new here, petal. Aren't you lucky you've got me?' Before she can reply, he says brusquely: 'Let me have that report by lunchtime – I need it this afternoon.' As a colleague who has observed this interaction, what would be your response?

8. A white colleague at a departmental meeting says to the only black member of staff in the group, 'I don't notice your colour – I see you as one of us.' As another colleague at the meeting, what would be your reaction and response?

9. You are considering potential mentors with another colleague, who makes the following comment: 'Well, he's certainly a strong applicant, more so than most, but he is a bit camp. We don't want him seducing the young graduate trainees, do we?' How would you respond to this comment?

10. You are having coffee in your office with a female colleague who has been on maternity leave, and a manager (who is also her coach) pops his head round the door and says 'Hello, girls' and then addresses the colleague: 'So, your first day back... I expect you'll find it a bit confusing at first, what with all the pressure here etc. But don't you worry, you take it at your own pace – I'm sure you'll get used to it all eventually, won't you?'

11. You are selecting potential clients for the company career mentoring scheme. Your colleague says about a woman candidate: 'As a single parent, do you think she will be able to cope with the demands of this work?' How will you respond?

12. Toward the end of their first mentoring session, the black client asks the mentor: 'It says in the details we have been given that you're committed to the company's diversity policy. Can you give me an idea of what this means, in fact – what does it mean for our mentoring?'

We have discussed why training and preparation are needed for a successful mentoring or coaching scheme and identified the necessary skills to be developed. We have provided a range of experiential exercises that practitioners can use and adapt, offered some guidance on selecting mentors and coaches and, finally, offered workshop material that can be used for diversity training for mentors and coaches.

NOTES

1 We acknowledge this idea as originating from our work with One Plus One.
2 We acknowledge this idea as originating from our work with One Plus One.

Part IV

BOUNDARIES AND ETHICS

13 Mentoring, coaching or therapy?

The boundary is explored between mentoring or coaching and therapy, that is, psychotherapy or counselling. The literature can be confusing, as neither counselling nor psychotherapy is a clearly defined concept. It is important to be aware of where the boundaries lie, as most mentors and coaches are anxious not to stray into a therapeutic situation without professional support and training in the field. However, the training of mentors and coaches rarely addresses their own emotional material, and when this is triggered without awareness it may result in dysfunctional mentoring with all its negative outcomes (Scandura, 1998). We discuss the boundary between mentoring or coaching and therapy, present guidelines for coaches (or mentors) and draw attention to the value of therapeutic ideas, including the requirement for supervision to support coaching and mentoring activity.

Attempts have been made by practitioners to define the different activities of mentoring, coaching and therapy that we now address (Neenan and Dryden, 2002; Rogers, 2004). We have noted in the preceding chapters that the terms 'mentoring' and 'coaching' are used to describe a wide variety of helping interventions. We have suggested that the key to understanding what is being offered is to identify the purpose of the intervention, whose it is, the process adopted to promote the intervention, and the ultimate learning outcome. This 'map' gave us three main categories: functionalist mentoring or coaching; engagement mentoring or coaching; and evolutionary mentoring or life coaching.

The terms 'counselling' and 'psychotherapy' have suffered from a similar difficulty in definition as practitioners sought to establish a clear difference (or not) between them. The practice of counselling was defined 20 years ago by the professional body, the British Association for Counselling (now the British Association for Counselling and Psychotherapy – BACP), as 'to give the client an opportunity to explore, discover and clarify ways of living more resourcefully and towards greater well-being' (BAC, 1985). More recently, there has been a misdirected tendency to 'sentence' wrongdoers in the community to counselling instead of it being seen as a voluntary contract between free agents (Hodson, 2000).

For many practitioners and clients, counselling is chosen because the term 'psychotherapy' has echoes of the medical diagnostic model and believed links with mental illness. Another way of differentiating them is to describe counselling as brief and psychotherapy as in-depth and long-term when in fact there is a huge overlap and 'the most intensive and successful counselling is indistinguishable from intensive and successful psychotherapy' (Syme, 2000). Here we have a parallel with the mentoring or coaching debate. The purpose, process and learning outcome identify the activity whatever its name and therefore we use the term 'therapy' for both.

THE BOUNDARY

Functionalist mentoring and coaching are unlikely to come up against the boundary, discussed below, as their purpose is prescribed and therefore limited, the learning outcome being improvement without radical change so as to maintain the existing equilibrium. The relationship is less intense and the mentor or coach is using basic skills in order to achieve the agreed objectives. Engagement mentoring or coaching is likely to engender a stronger relationship but is still working to prescribed objectives so the client's personal goals are unlikely to be part of the process. Where functionalist and engagement mentors or coaches find themselves straying into therapy (usually by mentors or coaches asking clients how they feel), then the contract is failing to support the process and should be revised to include a clear line between the mentoring or coaching and referral to a therapist. When more advanced skills are used, as in evolutionary mentoring, executive coaching or life coaching, the relationship is likely to be more powerful and emotional material becomes part of the process, taking it into the evolutionary quadrant, and this is where the boundary with therapy may be encountered by mentors or coaches.

The executive coach role (which we have defined as evolutionary) has been described as psychologically risky, as 'clinical work with leaders shows that a considerable percentage of them have become what they are for negative reasons' (Kets de Vries, 1995: 221). This, together with the fearful belief in business circles that 'only sick, weak or crazy people get therapy' (Peltier, 2001: xix), makes it tough for executives to admit to visiting a therapist. Hence executive coaching becomes an acceptable form of therapy for isolated leaders with hubristic tendencies.

Where does mentoring or coaching end and therapy begin?

David Clutterbuck includes counselling in his collection of learning alliances (1998) that make up the mentoring role and he maintains that, 'in the role of helping a learner, counselling is an essential part of the helper's toolkit'. However, he also warns that 'the most dangerous person in the organisation is the one who is unaware of his or her limitations' (Clutterbuck, 1998: 53). Evaluation of prospective mentors should weed out this kind of would-be helper. Further to this, he lists as the most crucial behaviour for a workplace mentor 'acting as a gateway to other forms of professional help… where the learner has specific needs beyond the counsellor's competence' (Clutterbuck, 1998: 53). We concur with these observations and would recommend including 'how to refer your mentoring or coaching client for counselling' in a training course for mentors or coaches. In addition, we have designated the term 'using counselling skills' for the activity often described as 'workplace counselling', as this indicates a set of behaviours rather than a likely-to-be misunderstood role. We note here that the counselling skills of listening, restatement and empathy are also used by therapists, mentors and coaches. Questioning differentiates them, as person-centred therapists rarely question their client.

Medical terminology is used by Weafer (2001: 77), who describes *contraindications* to coaching, where the client should be referred to a therapist, as 'addictive or dependency issues, marital issues, financial issues, family or personal issues'. These do appear to make up the human condition but the serious point is the necessity for referral where clients present with 'signs of depression, anxiety attacks, alcohol or drug addiction, personality disorders, and paranoia… persistent anger or aggression, expressing suicidal ideas, self-destructive impulses or behaviours and extreme dependency' (Hart, Blattner and Leipsic, 2001: 233).

Jenny Rogers (2004) suggests that coaching owes a debt to the therapeutic profession that is largely unacknowledged. On the other hand, therapists express concern about 'the very real dangers of executive coaching' (Berglas, 2002). Some general advice can be given to coaches concerning signs that a client may need referral, and these are listed as follows:

- Client cries frequently, intensely and uncontrollably.
- Client returns over and over to one relationship in his or her life.
- Client appears dominated by one major fear.
- Client has experienced a major trauma in his or her life.
- Client is unable to move on.
- Client says 'if only…' a lot.
- Client has experienced a bereavement that has not been processed.
- Client has low self-esteem.
- Client adopts the victim role.
- Client describes him- or herself as depressed or as having anxiety attacks, obsessive-compulsive disorder, agoraphobia, self-harm or eating disorders.
- Client denies reality.
- Client uses drugs or alcohol to addiction.
- Client behaves inappropriately, eg flirting.

(adapted from Rogers, 2004: 22)

Rogers describes the boundary between coaching and therapy as 'the coach needs to know about earlier life and the impact of these important relationships but does not need to dwell on them. If they need to be dwelt on, then you will refer the client to a trusted psychotherapist' (Rogers, 2004: 14).

When mentors or coaches wish to refer their clients for therapy they may like to keep the details of the British Association for Counselling and Psychotherapy (http://www.bacp.co.uk/) to hand. This organization holds a data bank of their members and registered practitioners, and they will send enquirers a list of therapists in their local area on request. Another professional organization which offers a similar service is the United Kingdom Council for Psychotherapy (www.ukcp.org.uk/). In addition, clients may choose to seek help from their GP.

Many coaches would find some of the behaviours above disturbing to deal with, and this feeling is a good guide to referral. When coaches (or mentors for that matter) feel out of their depth, they probably are. We recommend that coaches and mentors address only feelings *that have been expressed either verbally or non-verbally by their client*. We discuss empathy in Chapters 10 and 11 and warn against making enquiries about your clients' feelings. Asking clients how they feel invites a move into therapeutic areas. Any self-respecting coach or mentor should be aware of how a client is feeling or at least be able to make a guess, as in advanced empathy (see Chapter 11).

How to identify the appropriate emotional level for working with clients

The purpose of the work should indicate the level required. Functionalist mentoring or basic coaching will normally keep its focus on that functionalist purpose, using the models in Chapters 7 and 8 to structure the process. For engagement mentoring or coaching, expressed feelings are likely to be at a level of intensity that is typical of day-to-day life, such as frustration, satisfaction, annoyance, contentment, resentment and disappointment. Feelings at this level are relevant to the work in hand, and can be affirmed by offering your client empathy *at that level*, which keeps the mentoring or coaching activity within the professional boundary. Evolutionary mentoring, executive coaching or life coaching may move into areas that are close to the boundary with therapy, and this is why training and supervision are so important. When clients generate their own objectives, they are likely to come with feelings attached. Evolutionary mentors and coaches need to be comfortable with deeper feelings, such as hurt, happiness, anger, determination, self-doubt and the intense pleasure that comes from success. They will need *advanced empathy* and immediacy skills to handle where their clients may take them.

Criteria for the appropriate level were proposed nearly 30 years ago, and we adapt them here as follows:

■ to intervene at a level no deeper than that required to produce enduring solutions to the problems at hand, which fits functionalist mentoring and basic coaching as it stays with the prescribed objective or problem;
■ to intervene at a level no deeper than that indicated by the client's expressed feeling, which fits engagement mentoring or coaching;
■ to intervene at a level no deeper than that at which the energy and resources of the client can be committed to transformational change, which takes us into evolutionary mentoring, executive coaching or life coaching.

(adapted from Harrison, 1978: 555)

These criteria imply that the mentor or coach concerned is able to relate to the emotional world of the client, and we discuss this capacity in

Chapters 10 and 11. The fear that inhibits coaches and mentors from dealing with emotional matters is likely to come from their feeling of incompetence in this area, a predictable and cultural outcome in the Western world, which we discuss in Chapters 10 and 11. We would encourage coaches and mentors to be bolder in their work with clients, as emotions are the key to their learning and development, whilst at the same time taking note of discomfort in themselves, as that feeling is likely to indicate the presence of one of the 'contraindications' described above.

We relate an instance of a colleague working on the boundary in the case study below.

CASE STUDY

On the boundary

Helene Donnelly, an award-winning forensic paper conservation expert, is the founder/director of Data and Archive Disaster Control Centre (DADCC). The company specializes in worldwide emergency rescue and restoration of fire-, flood- and bomb-damaged documents. It also provides disaster management training for organizations wishing to produce or improve their disaster plans.

A seasoned visitor to disaster sites all over the world, Helene offers her clients advice and guidance before, during and after disaster incidents, which has become essential in today's world.

Recently Helene has found herself in a helping role after a high-value residence fire, where she was concerned to find that the insurance company did not always attend to the emotional and physical well-being of the house owner, Rachel, who tended to be ignored while the insurance company personnel dealt with the value of the contents insured. Rachel makes the point that a support team of insurance specialists, police and fire and security experts all appeared out of the blue but no one was present actually to assist the victim and deal with her post-event state of mind. Rachel is an international high-profile businesswoman, with a busy schedule, used to dealing with tough business operational situations and, more importantly, clients who expect the very best service.

This particular case followed a horrific fire that destroyed much of Rachel's home and left her pretty traumatized and functioning on automatic. Then she was advised to speak to Helene who agreed to meet Rachel in her (Helene's) office. From the beginning Helene made it clear that she did not offer counselling.

In the first one-and-a-half-hour session, Helene allowed Rachel to recall the details of the event and the ensuing weeks, while she noted key points on a flip chart and in a notebook. Helene asked for details of Rachel's behaviour, as it is her experience that people believe they are behaving erratically when, in fact, screaming, fainting and being angry are normal reactions to an event that is not under their control or within their experience. The validation this gave to

Rachel was confirmed by her as follows: 'It made me feel that all the emotions that I was experiencing were entirely normal.'

When Helene had summarized what Rachel had been through she constructed a diagram of Rachel's experience in the aftermath of the incident and, from this, put to Rachel a perceptive question: 'You do not have to answer this question out loud to me, but can you recount what was going on in your life at the time of the incident?' Rachel was more than willing to answer this question. However, this is where Helene explained that she was interested only in the incident and not in some past Freudian episode. Both were able to laugh at this point.

Rachel found the question and discussion that followed soul-searching, intriguing and really inspirational. Helene believes that, after a disastrous event that involves the near-destruction of a person's home, there is serious loss of the person's schema, which can have negative chemical and physical effects. So Helene recommended that Rachel should take high-strength vitamins to support her recovery and do physical training. The vitamins were named and so were the types of exercises recommended.

Rachel told Helene that it was the first time she had been able to talk about the incident without crying, and has nothing but praise for the relationship, saying 'I needed to talk to someone who understood where I was at that time.'

Helene has struggled to define the nature of this type of relationship, which includes aspects of mentoring and coaching, particularly the use of counselling skills, like listening, restatement, summary and empathy. Helene is clear that she is not counselling – these are ordinary people in extraordinary circumstances. Helene believes a service of this kind is essential in residential or organizational disaster contexts, and she recommends that individuals are debriefed properly during the recovery period. The recovery period may last up to three months. The individuals may also just want to speak on the phone, by e-mail or over coffee.

Most people never experience the loss of a home or their place of work. However, friends, family and loved ones may want to help by saying things like 'At least you did not lose your life'. These words do not help but only confuse the person more because the person does not understand what is happening to his or her world. Helene recognizes it is not the 'things' people miss but the daily schema and emotional values connected to their homes and workplaces. Once these have gone, they take time to rebuild, and someone has to help with the new building materials for the body and mind.

Helene Donnelly
DADCC

Here the activity (whether coaching, mentoring or using counselling skills) entailed working with ordinary feelings triggered by an extraordinary event. The boundary was attended to by Helene's disclaimer, and she ensured that the relationship remained focused on its original purpose and didn't wander into areas of Rachel's life that were not relevant.

WHAT CAN MENTORS OR LIFE COACHES LEARN FROM THERAPY?

Evolutionary mentors and life coaches are so busy making sure that people understand that they are not therapists that they may fail to realize that they could usefully borrow from this related profession. For instance, 'there are a number of issues in coaching, the understanding of which could be enriched by close examination of similar issues in the counselling field' (Bachkirova and Cox, 2004). An understanding of the relationship, which characterizes therapy, is an ethical requirement for evolutionary mentors or life coaches, and their training should reflect this requirement. In addition, mentoring and coaching lack some of the underpinning theory that supports therapists in their work and enables them to work productively and safely. This book is an attempt to remedy this lack. It is likely that mentors and coaches are operating with their own implicit theory, and they owe it to their clients to articulate it so that clients may choose to accept or reject such mentoring or coaching. Bachkirova and Cox (2004) have suggested that mentoring and coaching should 'borrow' theory from the therapeutic world and adapt it to mentoring and coaching, as well as encouraging the development of a body of theory to support their practice. In addition, when coaches offer their services to clients they have a duty to identify their own personal issues, some of which may intrude on the coaching relationship with potential damage to their client. When coaches find themselves experiencing strong emotions about a client or the client's behaviour, it behoves them to check out the connections within their own life and history, internally or with a supervisor. This is standard practice in therapy, and the process of self-questioning can transfer to coaches and mentors within their training, which should include an understanding of boundaries and diversity issues, which we discuss in Chapters 4 and 5.

More recently, Geoffrey Ahern (2001) has stipulated two 'commandments' for executive coaches: first, follow the individual client's agenda; and second, maintain absolute confidentiality from the company. Specific guideline provisions that emerge from these two commandments include principles that protect a client from breaches of confidentiality as a result of sponsoring and contracting arrangements. In addition, coaches are exhorted to engage in continuing professional development to maintain minimum psychological competence and to take up regular supervision. We would add to these the requirement for professional liability insurance, which the CIPD guidance recommends for all coaches (Jarvis, 2004). Some of these 'commandments' are similar to requirements for practising as a registered therapist.

SUPERVISION AND SUPPORT FOR MENTORS AND COACHES

Supervision in the helping professions is very different from the old-style supervisor who monitored and checked the worker, and could sometimes hire and fire. The supervision that coaches need (Rogers, 2004; Carroll, 2004; Hawkins and Shohet, 1989) is a place where professional matters are brought for consideration with the purpose of maintaining professional practice. Supervision has been identified by the Chartered Institute of Personnel and Development as one of their requirements of a professional coach (Jarvis, 2004). As part of the guidelines for coaches given above, Ahern (2001) includes supervision with an approved qualified supervisor, for two hours a month. At this point there are very few dedicated coach supervisors available and again coaches may have to resort to their therapeutic colleagues. The development of coach supervisors is proceeding and will provide a bank of suitable personnel in the near future (Carroll, 2004).

The appropriate model for supervising coaches is the person-centred one, where the coach brings his or her agenda and the supervisor works with it. The process has been described as one that 'allows discussion of issues in a safe and supportive context, offering a setting in which to look at work that is not going well' (Barrett, 2002). We note that the supervision process is a particular case of reflective practice for the coach as client, and is typified as a process in which to explore ourselves by reflecting on our experience in order to become more self-aware and self-evaluative, primarily through reflective dialogue, which we discuss in Chapter 4. However, the supervisor also carries a responsibility for monitoring professional standards and alerting the coach client to potential breaches of those standards. The full range of functions and tasks of supervision have been well described elsewhere (Inskipp and Proctor, 1988) and are outside the scope of this book.

We have explored the boundary between mentoring or coaching and therapy, as the danger of crossing the boundary is what worries many coaches and mentors, who are anxious not to stray into a therapeutic situation without professional support and training in the field. We have examined where mentoring or coaching begins and ends, giving advice and guidelines to follow in relation to the intensity of the relationship and where referral is indicated. In addition, we have urged the fledgling profession of coaching to draw on therapeutic ideas, including the requirement for supervision to support evolutionary coaching and mentoring activity.

14 Conclusion

We embarked on this book because of our experience, in common with many of our colleagues, of mentoring and coaching as rather vaguely defined activities. We have aimed to remedy this by adopting a 'map' that places the activity, be it mentoring or coaching (the name is irrelevant), in relation to answers to these questions:

- Whose purpose?
- What process?
- Which learning outcome?

The naming of a mentoring or coaching activity is a matter of choice, and different environments will use the terms differently. Our concern is an ethical one, that, whether the activity is named as 'mentoring' or 'coaching', potential clients are made aware of what they are being offered in terms of purpose, process and learning outcome. For potential clients, contractors, purchasers and designers, these questions are important diagnostic tools that can inform their choices.

THREE DIFFERENT APPROACHES

For functionalist mentoring or basic coaching we note that the purpose will be prescribed, often by the parent organization or sector of society. The process tends to be Socratic in style with a problem-solving focus. The learning outcome for this activity is improvement, an important result for performance but maintaining the status quo for the client and his or her environment. We have identified engagement mentoring or coaching as functionalist in disguise, using a person-centred approach to persuade and achieve client consent. The learning outcome for this activity remains improvement, as clients work with goals, either implicitly or explicitly, that have been prescribed. Evolutionary mentoring, executive coaching or life coaching starts from the client's ownership of his or her goals, generated within the relationship. The process is deeply person-centred, involving each party in a relationship focused on change, with the potential for transformation.

Our framework offers a comprehensive definition of mentoring and coaching activity, with the necessary and sufficient conditions clearly set out for functionalist, engagement and evolutionary purposes. We trust that colleagues will welcome a more rigorous framework for their mentoring and coaching work, and one more clearly defined and fit for its purpose. Our intention is that this framework will make a potentially significant contribution to the professional practice of mentoring and coaching.

CODE OF ETHICS

Mentoring and coaching are presently an unregulated activity, and many think they should remain so. However, the existing free-for-all is unlikely to generate respect and recognition for the important work being carried out in the burgeoning number of mentoring and coaching relationships. In addition, clients who experience below-standard service are unlikely to recommend the activity to others.

We acknowledge the professional standards for mentoring and coaching provided by, among others, the European Mentoring and Coaching Council and the International Coaching Federation. We recommend that those interested should set up a process of creating separate ethical codes that address the particular issues that may arise in the different approaches. In functionalist activity, the code should include clarification of purpose and potential learning outcome; in engagement programmes, there is an ethical requirement to inform clients of the possibly hidden goals and to be clear about the process in use; in evolutionary mentoring and coaching, which move nearest to the boundary with therapy, a code is needed to maintain that boundary and maintain psychological safety for clients. In summary, the ethical codes for each activity will reflect their different purposes, processes and learning outcomes.

Appendix 1:
Pro formas for mentors and coaches

1 FUNCTIONALIST MENTOR OR COACH: NEGOTIATION CHECKLIST

Issue for discussion	Agreed
What kind of role will I take in the mentoring relationship?	
How will we deal with issues of confidentiality?	
Who will make contact?	
How often will we meet or make contact?	
How much time is to be allocated?	
How will mentoring sessions be recorded?	
What is the agreed duration of the relationship?	
How can the mentoring agreement be concluded if other than the specified time?	
Any others?	

2 SAMPLE EVOLUTIONARY MENTORING AGREEMENT

Mentor and client agreement between Martin (mentor) and Peter (client)

We are voluntarily entering into a mentoring relationship that we expect to benefit both of us. We want this relationship to be a rewarding experience with most of our time together focusing on client development. We have noted these features of our relationship:

Confidentiality

Duration of the relationship

Frequency of meetings

Time to be invested by Martin (mentor)

Time to be invested by Peter (client)

Role to be taken by Martin (mentor)

An individual development plan will be maintained by Peter (client).

Records of mentoring sessions will be maintained by Martin (mentor).

Records of mentoring sessions will be copied to Peter (client).

We agree to a no-fault conclusion of this relationship, for whatever reason.

Signed:

_____ (mentor)
_____ (client)
Date _____
Date _____

3 EVOLUTIONARY MENTORING SESSIONS OUTLINE

Every mentoring session should consist of a beginning, a middle and an end.

Beginning

1. Agree a mutually acceptable meeting place and time when you will not be interrupted.
2. Agree an end time and stick to it.
3. Review the relationship and check for any problems or concerns the client may have.

4. Review matters arising since the last meeting, including revisiting action points if any.

Middle

5. Focus on client's chosen issue.
6. Take time to explore it in depth, using listening, reflecting back and empathy.
7. Agree actions or non-actions and record them.

End

8. Summarize the session and record details.
9. Refocus back to day-to-day matters.
10. Arrange the date and time of the next meeting and reiterate action points.

4 DEVELOPMENT PLAN FOR COACHING CLIENT

Many CPD programmes include a personal and professional development planner, and we recommend that this is used to record the objectives, achievements, career details, and development reviews generated in coaching sessions. The planner includes a personal log section, which can be used to record achievement. A sample development plan is given below.

Development plan (sample)

Name:
Address for correspondence:
Telephone:
Fax:
E-mail:

Overall development goal:

Objectives	Action steps	Target date	Resources	Status

5 MENTORING EVALUATION

The programme will be reviewed and evaluated after 12 months, and an interim review will be carried out after 6 months. In addition to the formal group review, we would value individual views on the mentoring programme in practice. On completion of the programme, please take a few minutes to complete the questionnaire and return it to [name of recipient] by [date].

Mentor's review

Name:
Address for correspondence:
Telephone:
E-mail:

How long have you been a mentor?
How many people have you mentored?
Why did you choose to become a mentor?
How would you describe your mentoring relationship(s)?
How helpful was the training you received?
On reflection, what additional training or support would you have liked?
What benefits do you feel you have gained from mentoring?
At the start of this mentoring relationship, did you agree any terms of reference or ground rules?
What review process have you used with your client(s)?
Are you willing for this information to be written up for future mentors?

Thank you for completing this questionnaire.

Client's review

Name:
Address:
Telephone:
E-mail:

How long have you had a mentor?
How did you choose your mentor?
How would you describe the relationship?
What benefits do you feel you have gained from the mentoring?

At the start of this mentoring relationship, did you agree any terms of reference or ground rules?

Are you willing for this to be written up for future mentors and clients?

Thank you for completing this questionnaire.

Source: Adapted from Whittaker and Cartwright (2000)

6 PERSONAL ACTION PLAN FOR CLIENTS

Name:
Position/project:
Date:

Personal objective	Action	Timescale

7 COACHING RECORD

Name:
Position/project:
Start date:

Date	Goal agreed	Action	Date completed

Appendix 2:
Self-coaching:
keeping a journal

Why keep a journal?

Just as babies do, we take in new things all the time. We are affected by what we take in, and there is sometimes a mixed-up period while we get used to a new thing in our lives. This is known as the 'learning curve', and is a normal and positive sign of development. The learning journal helps us in this mixed-up stage to sort out what's gone on and to confirm the important things before they get lost. The journal charts the development of your learning and is therefore an important source of evidence about your learning.

What is a learning journal?

A learning journal is a collection of your thoughts, feelings, speculations and maybe dreams. It is like a map of your learning journey.

What are the benefits of a journal?

- It's always available.
- It never answers back.
- It can be revisited.
- It keeps information private.
- The continuous relationship with the journal and therefore the self.
- It accepts unconditionally.
- The repetition – telling the story over and over – the journal never tires of hearing the same thing.
- Writing in the moment – likely to be truthful.

- A chance for communication with the self.
- The clarity through writing down.
- Validation – your journal never disagrees.
- The record of learning and development.

What does it look like?

You can use all sorts of writing or drawing, pens or papers, as no one else will read your journal. Some people use a ring binder, which takes lots of different shapes and sizes.

Who will read it?

It is for your eyes only but you can extract parts of it to present to mentors, coaches or appraisers.

What style will I use?

Your own.

What subjects will I write about?

Anything that occurs at work or in your personal life that you have energy about; interactions with others; your reactions to information or readings; changes in your beliefs, attitudes, relationships or practice; anything else you want to get off your chest.

How do I start?

Try using the journal template to begin with – you will soon find your own preferred way of doing it.

Journal techniques

'Journal writing is a purposeful and intentional use of reflective or process writing to facilitate psychological, emotional and intellectual development and to further behavioural goals' (a definition based on Adams, 1990).

Some techniques in journal writing:

- five-minute sprint;
- significant clustering;
- captured moment;
- lists of 100;
- perspectives;
- dialogues;
- free writing;
- unsent letters.

Details are given below of the first six as likely to be used in a mentoring or coaching context:

1. Five-minute sprint – an exercise to begin your journal.
   Take five minutes to answer three questions.
   Questions:

   – Who am I?
   – Why am I here?
   – What do I want?

   Take another five minutes to process and reflect upon your answers:
   Process/reflect:
   When I read this:

   – I notice…
   – I feel…
   – I'm surprised…

2. Significant clustering: eight stepping stones in my life.
   List the eight items and then move on to:

3. Captured moment.
   Choose an event from your past and relive the chosen event and attendant feelings. Take seven minutes.

4. List of 100 (take 20 minutes).
   Make a list under one of these headings:

   – 'what I need';
   – 'what I want';
   – 'how I feel';
   – 'why not?';
   – 'things to do';
   – 'people to see'.

   OK to repeat – theory suggests that around the 80 or 90 mark something significant emerges.

5. Perspectives (take 20 minutes).
   See things from an altered point of view, eg:

   – A year from today…
   – Turn it on its head…
   – Roads not taken – what if?

6. Dialogues (take 20 minutes).
   Writing two sides of a conversation with anything or anyone or with different parts of the self. This technique circumnavigates the internal censor.

NB All the exercises above should be followed by some form of processing, either as above in item 1 or in dialogue with mentors or coaches.

What time should I write a journal?

Any or every time; when you want to.

The most creative times are believed to be when your brain is tired, late at night or in the night, so many people keep their journal handy by their bed.

Timing is vital, as if it is left too long the event or happening may have lost its impact, having gone past its 'sell by' date. Alternatively, if writing too soon, the event may be too recent for an effective focus. Only the writer can judge the best time.

Journal template

The template below is a guide – you may not want to use it but if you do it may be photocopied and filled in when convenient.

Stage 1: describe what happened

What occurred?

What did you notice about yourself?

What did you notice about others?

How did you feel?

How do you think others felt?

What would you have liked to do differently?

How would you have liked to behave?

How will you use this next time?

What do you hope to achieve by this?

Stage 2: now step back and consider
Use the entries in your journal to identify the following:

What you have discovered about yourself.

What you now know about learning and development that you didn't know before.

What you realize about your own learning and development.

How your new understanding will influence your future work or behaviour at work.

Your feelings about all this.

Calming the mind: a mindfulness exercise
Perfect for busy people, this takes just one minute.

Timing: one minute.

Sit in front of a clock or watch that you can use to time the passing of one minute. Your task is to focus your entire attention on the passing time. Notice what happens when you focus your mind on the clock or watch. You may find your mind wandering. When this happens, just gently draw your attention back to watching the clock.

Acknowledgement: We are grateful to Margaret Landale for granting permission to publish this exercise.

Appendix 3: Examples of ground rules

Example 1

1. Confidentiality.
2. Safe environment.
3. Respecting each other's cultures.
4. Non-judgemental.
5. Respecting each other's opinions.
6. Acceptance.
7. Supportive in sharing experiences and ideas with each other.
8. Commitment.
9. Accessibility.
10. Enjoyment and fun.
11. Mobile phones off.
12. Telephone or e-mail contact arrangements.
13. Flexible approach.
14. Disclose.
15. 'I' statements.
16. Ownership.
17. Boundaries.
18. Honesty.
19. Don't be afraid to ask questions.
20. Don't be afraid to challenge.
21. Both parties recognized as a resource (sharing).
22. Reliability.

23. Plan to succeed – dare to fail.
24. Valuing diversity.
25. Respecting difference.
26. Equal opportunities.

Example 2

1. Confidentiality, ie assume that the shared material is confidential unless told otherwise.
2. Respect for difference.
3. Openness and risk taking.
4. Being prepared to 'talk it out'.
5. Constructive/supportive criticism.
6. Non-judgemental behaviours and statements: no assumptions.
7. Listening, not interrupting; giving space; active listening.
8. Taking personal responsibility for participation and seeking clarification.
9. Sharing tasks.
10. Hold boundaries, ie timekeeping and mobile phones.
11. Mediation approach.
12. Safe environment.
13. Check out assertions.
14. Asking for what you need/want.

Example 3

1. Review the ground rules.
2. Confidentiality – not to share outside the mentoring relationship anything that identifies an individual or the individual's organization.
3. Timekeeping.
4. Attendance.
5. Questions for clarification.
6. Tolerance – the right to a different opinion. Respect for the other's right to a different opinion.
7. Listening.
8. Opportunity to speak.
9. Be prepared to disclose.
10. Respecting diversity and learning from diversity.
11. Learning about each other to build trust (differences).
12. Freedom of disclosure – depth at discretion of discloser.

13. Respecting silence.
14. Right to say 'I don't understand'.
15. 'I' statements.

Example 4

1. Disclose as much or as little as you feel comfortable with.
2. Safety: freedom to speak constructive criticism.
3. Willing to be open and honest.
4. Supportive and constructive criticism.
5. Ability to say 'no' or renegotiate.
6. Respect for each other's views.
7. Challenging actions/statements, not the person.
8. To be supported in exploration of attitudes or skills.
9. Being able to be open; non-judgemental.
10. Timekeeping: turning up and on time.
11. Following through to a new point of decision.
12. Confidentiality.

Appendix 4:
Passionate learning: a case of reflective learning

Purpose of session

To enable participants to realize their learning through holistic story-telling. The title 'passionate' refers to the third, rather neglected, domain of learning, the emotions. The session invites participants to access their feeling domain before considering the other two domains of doing and thinking. This departs from most learning experiences in the Western world where thinking and doing come before emotion or even exclude it.

Session objectives

On completion participants will have:

1. told a story about their experience;
2. engaged in reflective dialogue about their experience;
3. realized their learning from that experience.

Method: Participants will work in pairs, taking turns as 'learner' and 'reviewer'.

The session is designed to offer participants a brief insight into the significance of reflective dialogue in deep learning. Participants are invited to realize their learning in the three domains of feeling, thinking and doing, through holistic storytelling. Working in pairs, as learner and reviewer, learners revisit an experience, first through the feeling evinced by the event, second through the new understanding that occurred and third through their actions. Hence the three learning domains of feeling, knowing and doing are explored through the process of reflective dialogue with a reviewer. Session details and guidance to reviewers are given below.

Passionate learning: session details

Timing: one hour.

Participants work in pairs of their choice, taking turns as 'learner' and 'reviewer'.

Method: Each learner to take a total of 30 minutes, 15 minutes for a negative and 15 minutes for a positive feeling as outlined below:

Negative feeling (bad, angry, sad, mad, hurt, uncomfortable, disturbed etc). Each learner to take 15 minutes: 3 minutes in telling a brief story about his or her experience beginning with the words: 'I felt [negative feeling] when…', whilst the reviewer listens. This is followed by 5 minutes' reflective dialogue with the reviewer to identify what if anything the learner now understands about him- or herself or another, beginning with the words: 'I have realized…' The reviewer continues to dialogue with the learner for 5 minutes so as to enable the learner to articulate his or her subsequent or planned actions, beginning with the words: 'Now I will…' Reverse roles for a further 15 minutes.
The process is now repeated as below:

Positive feeling (glad, joyful, happy, excited, positive, warm, loving etc). Each learner to take 15 minutes: 3 minutes in telling a brief story about his or her experience beginning with the words: 'I felt [positive feeling] when…', whilst the reviewer listens. This is followed by 5 minutes' reflective dialogue with the reviewer to identify what if anything the learner now understands about him- or herself or another, beginning with the words: 'I have realized…' The reviewer continues to dialogue with the learner for 5 minutes so as to enable the learner to articulate his or her subsequent or planned actions, beginning with the words: 'Now I will…' Reverse roles for a further 30 minutes.
Individually record your reaction to the whole exercise.

Reflective dialogue: instructions to reviewer

1. Listen and summarize.
2. Respond without questioning until clarity is achieved or the learner stops.
3. Open questioning – what, how, where, when, why and who.
   Feeling domain:
   - 'Why were you there?'
   - 'What else happened?'
   - 'How did you feel then?'
   - 'Who else was involved?'

Thinking domain:
   - 'What surprised you?'
   - 'What was different?'
   - 'What did you think?'

Action domain:
   - 'What will you do differently?'
   - 'When will you do this?'
   - 'Who can help you?'

4. Respond as in 2, including empathy in response where appropriate.
5. Summarize.

Appendix 5:
Questions for reflective dialogue

Questions for task focus

1. What is your understanding of the task?
2. What were the aims of the task?
3. Can you give a detailed description of the task?
4. How did you feel about the task?
5. What happened?
6. What did you do?
7. What did another do?
8. How do you feel about that?
9. Where did the task occur?
10. Describe the environment where the task occurred.

Questions for process focus

1. How well prepared were you for the task?
2. How did you carry out the aims of the task?
3. How did you feel while you were doing it?
4. List your successes in the task.
5. List your disappointments in the task.
6. How do you feel now about what happened?
7. What helped you to complete the task?
8. What would have helped you to complete the task better?
9. What enabled you to complete the task?

10. What didn't enable you to complete the task?
11. How did the environment help/hinder you?
12. How satisfied are you with the outcome? If not, why not?

Learner language (used by client)

- I think...
- I want...
- I realized...
- I know...
- I found out...
- I thought I knew...
- I was unaware...
- I knew...
- I felt...
- I was overwhelmed by...
- I went blank...
- I wanted...
- I am feeling...
- I am wondering about...
- I will...
- I was surprised...
- I am surprised...
- This feels difficult because...

Reviewer language (used by mentor or coach)

- Tell me about...
- What did you know...?
- What did you do...?
- How did you feel...?
- How did it happen...?
- What occurred...?
- Where did it happen...?
- When did it happen...?
- Can you remember...?
- What were you aware of...?
- What could you do...?
- How would you know...?
- It sounds as though...
- You seem to be feeling...

- You look...
- How does that make you feel...?
- What would make a difference...?
- When can you...?
- What do you think is important here...?
- What can you do...?
- What do you want...?
- What helped you...?
- What got in your way...?
- What will you do...?
- How will you...?
- Tell me what you have learnt...
- How did you learn...?
- What else...?
- Who helped...?

Questions for learning review

1. How would you like us to conduct this review? For example, what approach? Style? Stance?
2. How do you feel about doing a learning review at this point in our relationship?
3. What is your understanding of the purpose of this review?
4. How can we make the review as productive as possible for you?
5. What do you hope to gain from the review in terms of learning?
6. Please tell me what I need to know in order to conduct this review effectively.
7. What is your understanding of the three levels of learning?
8. What is to be included in/excluded from this review?
9. Who is responsible for what?

   - Moving levels.
   - Summarizing each level.
   - Final summary.
   - Note taking.

10. How would you like to record this review?

Questions for learning-to-learn focus

1. How did we get here together?
2. How did the task emerge?
3. Why did the task emerge?

4. What was the task for?
5. Who devised the task?
6. How did you get ownership of the task?
7. Why did you get ownership of the task?
8. Why are you satisfied?
9. Why are you dissatisfied?
10. What do you now know/realize that you didn't before?
11. Name one thing that would help in future tasks like this.
12. What does the task mean to you now?
13. How relevant is the task now? If not, why not?
14. What has helped you in this review to learn about yourself in relation to the task?
15. What has inhibited you?
16. What now needs to happen for you to benefit from your learning?
17. How can you get the support you need?
18. Where can you get support?
19. Who can support you?
20. What assumptions did you begin with?
21. How have you revised those assumptions?
22. What new understanding has emerged from this review?
23. What are the implications for you? Another? The organization?
24. What have you learnt about the review process?

Acknowledgement: Ron Ford

Appendix 6:
Case study exercises

Case studies

Two case studies are given below. Can you identify the type of mentor described? Can you estimate the purpose, whose purpose, the process and the learning outcome?

Mentor A

Jack met Walter when he started work as an apprentice in a large manufacturing firm. Jack had left school without qualifications, wanting to earn money early, as theirs was a single-parent family. He was clever and quick and soon attracted the attention of Walter, not his line manager but a senior manager in the next department. Although nearly 20 years apart in age, Walter and Jack became good friends, with the older man often strolling through the workshop to give Jack the 'time of day', as he called it. Walter encouraged Jack to study at night school and get his technical qualifications, enabling him to apply for a better position. Jack went from strength to strength and was moved to another company within the group, in another part of the country. The two men continued to keep in touch by phone, and more recently by e-mail, even as Jack was headhunted by another organization.

Mentor B

When James joined an electronic company with another 10 graduate trainees, the personnel officer informed him that he had been 'allocated' a mentor, one of the senior managers in his section, who was not his line manager. James received a telephone call on his first day from the mentor, Roger, who told him that he, Roger, could be relied upon to 'put him straight' about anything he didn't understand and that he should 'give him a bell' if he needed help. As James understood nothing and was unsure about what he was supposed to be doing, he was unable to express any needs at this point. After a fortnight James had a lot of questions, but was unable to raise Roger, who didn't return his calls. Eventually James e-mailed Roger and asked for a meeting. When the two men met, it turned out that they had rather different approaches to life, with James being a vegetarian non-drinker and Roger being a real ale fan. Roger took charge of the meeting: told James how to handle his boss, warned him about some of his colleagues and regaled him with stories of his, Roger's, successes in the company. James never contacted Roger again, and the personnel department never asked how the mentoring had progressed.

Mentoring situations

Three mentoring situations are given below. Can you speculate about the sort of mentoring that might result in these situations and what the parties could do to minimize difficulties?

Situation 1

Diana is assistant personnel director of a large telecommunications company whose mission includes a statement about developing employees to reach their potential. She influences the appointment of a training manager, Jo, who reports directly to the personnel director, and it is agreed that Diana will mentor Jo. The early stages of Jo's appointment are intoxicating. She turns out to be a very effective manager, as well as being a charismatic and talented trainer. Diana quickly realizes that Jo could easily take or get her (Diana's) job. Diana is single; Jo is partnered.

Situation 2

Joan is a board member of a small company that offers personnel services to businesses seeking to outsource their personnel function. She is responsible for mentoring one of the consultants who deliver the services the company offers, whose name is Alison. Joan has a lot of experience in the personnel function, and Alison came to the company with a lot of line management experience with a multinational company. Joan is the only woman member of the board and is careful not to upset any of her male board colleagues. Alison wants action on how the company is operating, as she can see ways to improve the bottom line. Both women are married.

Situation 3

David is a talented scientist working for a medical research company. He is highly qualified with a first-class degree from Oxbridge and a PhD. He is asked to mentor a young woman, Mary, who has been recruited for her experience in a competing and very successful company. She is qualified in her field (from one of the new universities) but she opted to go straight into the business world rather than continue her academic career. David has been married for 20 years. Mary is single.

References

Achterberg, J (1985) *Imagery in Healing*, Shambhala Publications, Boston, MA

Adams, K (1990) *Journal to the Self*, Warner Books, New York

Ahern, G (2001) Individual executive development: regulated, structured and ethical, *Occupational Psychologist*, **44**, pp 3–7

Albom, M (1997) *Tuesdays with Morrie*, Doubleday, New York

Allen, TD, Poteet, ML and Russell, JEA (2000) Protégé selection by mentors: what makes the difference?, *Journal of Organisational Behaviour*, **21**, pp 271–82

Alvesson, M and Willmott, H (1992) On the idea of emancipation in management and organisation studies, *Academy of Management Review*, **17** (3), pp 432–64

Anthony, K (2000) Counselling in cyberspace, *Counselling*, **11** (10), pp 625–27

Antonacopoulou, E (1999) Developing learning managers within learning organisations: the case of three major retail banks, in *Organisational Learning and the Learning Organisation*, ed M Easterby-Smith, J Burgoyne and L Araujo, Sage, London

Argyle, M (1975) *Bodily Communication*, Methuen, London

Argyris, C and Schon, D (1996) *Organisational Learning II: Theory, method and practice*, Addison-Wesley, Wokingham

Arkin, A (2005) Hidden talents, *People Management*, 14 July

Bachkirova, T and Cox, E (2004) A bridge over troubled water: bringing together coaching and counselling, *International Journal of Mentoring and Coaching*, **2** (1), www.emccouncil.org [accessed 4 January 2005]

Ball, SJ (1990) *Foucault and Education*, Routledge, London

Bandler, R and Grinder, J (1979) *Frogs into Princes: Neuro linguistic programming*, Real People Press, Utah

Barna, LM (1997) Stumbling blocks in intercultural communication, in *Intercultural Communication: A reader*, 8th edn, ed LA Samovar and RE Porter, pp 337–46, Wadsworth, Belmont, CA

Barrett, R (2002) Mentor supervision and development, *Organisations and People*, **9** (2), pp 25–34

Baum, HS (1992) Mentoring, *Human Relations*, **45** (3), pp 223–45

Beech, N and Brockbank, A (1999) Power/knowledge and psychosocial dynamics in mentoring, *Management Learning*, **30** (1), pp 7–25

Belenky, MF *et al* (1986) *Women's Ways of Knowing: The development of self, voice and mind*, Basic Books, New York

Berger, PL and Luckmann, T (1966) *The Social Construction of Reality*, Penguin, Harmondsworth

Berglas, S (2002) The very real dangers of executive coaching, *Harvard Business Review*, June, pp 86–92

Bierema, L and Merriam, SB (2002) E-mentoring: using computer mediated communication (CMC) to enhance the mentoring process, *Innovative Higher Education*, **26** (3), pp 214–21

Biggs, J (1999) *Teaching for Quality Learning at University*, Open University Press, Buckingham

Bogen, JE (1969) The other side of the brain: an appositional mind, *Bulletin of the Los Angeles Neurological Society*, **34**, pp 135–62

Bohm, D (1996) *On Dialogue*, Routledge, London

Boud, D, Keogh, R and Walker, D (1985) *Turning Experience into Learning*, Kogan Page, London

Bourdieu, P and Wacquant, L (1992) *An Invitation to Reflexive Sociology*, University of Chicago Press, Chicago, IL

Bowlby, J (1969) *Attachment*, Hogarth Press, London

Boyd, EM and Fales, AW (1983) Reflective learning: key to learning from experience, *Journal of Humanistic Psychology*, **23** (2), pp 99–117

British Association for Counselling (BAC) (1985) *Definition of Terms in Use with Expansion and Rationale*, British Association for Counselling, Rugby

Brockbank, A (1994) Expectations of mentoring, *Training Officer*, **30** (3), pp 86–88

Brockbank, A and McGill, I (1998) *Facilitating Reflective Learning in Higher Education*, SRHE/Open University Press, Buckingham

Brockbank, A, McGill, I and Beech, N (2002) *Reflective Learning in Practice*, Gower, Aldershot

Brookfield, S (1987) *Developing Critical Thinkers*, Open University Press, Buckingham

Brookfield, S and Preskill, S (1999) *Discussion as a Way of Teaching*, Open University Press, Buckingham

Buber, M (1965) *Between Man and Man*, Macmillan, New York

Buber, M (1994) *I and Thou*, T&T Clark, Edinburgh

Bull, P (1983) *Body Movement and Interpersonal Communication*, John Wiley, Chichester

Burgstahler, S and Nourse, S (1999) *Opening Doors: Mentoring on the internet*, http://www-cod.csun.edu/conf/1999/proceedings/session 0032.htm [accessed 7 August 2002]

Burley-Allen, M (1995) *Listening: The forgotten skill*, John Wiley, New York

Burr, V (1995) *An Introduction to Social Constructivism*, Routledge, London

Burrell, G and Morgan, G (1979) *Sociological Paradigms and Organisational Analysis*, Heinemann, London

Burt, K (2005) Your life in their hands, *Guardian Weekend*, 15 January, p 15

Bushardt, SC, Fretwell, C and Holdnak, BJ (1991) The mentor/protégé relationship, *Human Relations*, **44** (6), pp 619–39

Cardow, A (1998) Mentoring at light speed, *Mentoring and Tutoring*, **5** (3), pp 32–39

Carkuff, RR (1969) *Helping and Human Relations*, Vols 1 and 2, Holt, Rinehart & Winston, New York

Carroll, M (2004) Coaching managers to be managers, Private communication

Carruthers, J (1993) The principles and practice of mentoring, Chapter 2 in *The Return of the Mentor: Strategies for workplace learning*, ed BJ Caldwell and EMA Carter, Falmer Press, London

Caruso, R (1992) *Mentoring and the Business Environment*, Dartmouth, Aldershot

Caruso, RE (1996) Who does mentoring?, Paper presented at the Third European Mentoring Conference, London

Chomsky, N (1957) *Syntactic Structures*, Mouton, The Hague

Chomsky, N (1969) *Aspects of the Theory of Syntax*, MIT Press, Cambridge, MA

Clarkson, P and Shaw, P (1992) Human relationships at work in organisations, *Management Education and Development*, **23** (1), pp 18–29

Clinchy, BM (1996) Connected and separate knowing: towards a marriage of two minds, in *Knowledge, Difference, and Power*, ed NR Goldberger *et al*, Basic Books, New York

Clutterbuck, D (1991) *Everyone Needs a Mentor*, 2nd edn, Institute of Personnel Management, London

Clutterbuck, D (1998) *Learning Alliances*, IPD, London

Clutterbuck, D and Megginson, D (2005) Create a coaching culture, *People Management*, 21 April, pp 44–45

Clutterbuck, D and Ragins, BR (2002) *Mentoring and Diversity*, Butterworth-Heinemann, London

Cohen, Norman H (1995) *Mentoring Adult Learners: A guide for educators and trainers*, Krieger, Malabar, FL

Colley, H (2000) Exploring the myths of Mentor: a rough guide to the history of mentoring from a Marxist feminist perspective, Conference paper, British Educational Research Association, Cardiff University, September

Colley, H (2003) *Mentoring for Social Inclusion: A critical approach to nurturing mentor relationships*, Routledge-Falmer, London

Cooper, CL (1983) *Stress Research: Issues for the 80s*, John Wiley, London and New York

Cooper, R (1997) Applying emotional intelligence in the workplace, *Training and Development*, December, pp 31–38

Coopey, J (1995) The learning organisation: power, politics and ideology, *Management Learning*, **26** (2), pp 193–213

Covey, S (1989) *Seven Habits of Effective People*, Simon & Schuster, London

Cox, RW (1981) Social forces, states and world orders: beyond international relations theory, *Millennium*, **12** (2), pp 129–30

Cozby, Paul C (1973) Self-disclosure: a literature review, *Psychological Bulletin*, **79**, pp 73–91

Cramer, P (2000) Defence mechanisms in psychology today, *American Psychologist*, **55** (6), pp 637–46

Cross, S (1999) Roots and wings: mentoring, *Innovation in Education and Training International*, **35** (3), pp 224–30

Cunningham, JB and Eberle, T (1993) Characteristics of the mentoring experience: a qualitative study, *Personnel Review*, **22** (4), pp 54–66

Dainow, S and Bailey, C (1988) *Developing Skills with People*, John Wiley, London

Daloz, L (1986) *Effective Teaching and Mentoring: Realising the transformational power of adult learning experiences*, Jossey-Bass, San Francisco, CA

Damasio, A (1995) *Descartes' Error*, Harper Collins, New York

Darling, LAW (1984) What do nurses want in a mentor?, *Journal of Nursing Administration*, **14** (10), pp 42–44

Darling, LAW (1986) What to do about toxic mentors, *Nurse Education*, **11** (2), pp 29–30

Darwin, A (2000) Critical reflections on mentoring in work settings, *Adult Education Quarterly*, **50** (3), May, pp 197–211

Department for Education and Employment (DfEE) (2000) *The Connexions: Strategy document*, ref CX2, DfEE Publications, Nottingham

Downey, M (1999) *Effective Coaching*, Orion Business Books, London

Dreher, GF and Ash, RA (1990) A comparative study of mentoring among men and women in managerial, professional and technical positions, *Journal of Applied Psychology*, **75** (5), pp 539–46

Dulewicz, V and Higgs, M (1998) Soul researching, *People Management*, 1 October

Egan, G (1973) *Face to Face: The small group experience and interpersonal growth*, Brooks-Cole, Monterey, CA

Egan, G (1976) *Interpersonal Living: A skills/contract approach to human relations training in groups*, Brooks-Cole, Monterey, CA

Egan, G (1977) *You and Me: The skills of being an effective group communicator*, Brooks-Cole, Monterey, CA

Egan, G (1990) *The Skilled Helper: A systematic approach to effective helping*, 4th edn, Brooks-Cole, Pacific Grove, CA

Ekman, P and Freisen, W (1975) *Unmasking the Face*, Prentice Hall, Englewood Cliffs, NJ

Elbow, P (1986) *Embracing Contraries: Explorations in learning and teaching*, Oxford University Press, New York

Elbow, P (1998) *Writing without Teachers*, 2nd ed, Oxford University Press, New York

Eleftheriadou, Z (1994) *Transcultural Counselling*, Central Book Publishing, London

Fairclough, N (1992) *Discourse and Social Change*, Polity Press, London

Fineman, S and Gabriel, Y (1994) Paradigms of organisations: an exploration in textbook rhetorics, *Organisation*, **1** (2), pp 375–99

Flaherty, F (1999) *Coaching: Evoking excellence in others*, Butterworth-Heinemann, Oxford

Flood, R and Romm, N (1996) *Diversity Management*, John Wiley, Chichester

Foucault, M (1976) *The History of Sexuality*, Vol 1, Penguin Books, London

Freedman, M (1999) *The Kindness of Strangers: Adult mentors, urban youth and the new voluntarism*, Cambridge University Press, Cambridge

French, R and Vince, R (eds) (1999) *Group Relations, Management and Organisation*, Oxford University Press, Oxford

Friedman, M (1985) *The Healing Dialogue in Psychotherapy*, Jason Aronson, New York

Gallwey, T (1974) *The Inner Game of Tennis*, Bantam, New York

Geertz, C (1986) The uses of diversity, *Michigan Quarterly Review*, Winter, pp 105–23

Giddens, A (1992) *The Transformation of Intimacy*, Polity Press, Cambridge

Goldberger, NR *et al* (eds) (1996) *Knowledge, Difference, and Power*, Basic Books, New York

Goleman, D (1995) *Emotional Intelligence*, Bloomsbury, London

Gqubule, Thandeka (2005) Horse-whispering: follow the lead, *Financial Mail*, http://www.tomorrowtoday.biz/inthemedia/040806_finmail_horsewhisper.htm

Grenfell, M and James, D (1998) *Bourdieu and Education*, Routledge-Falmer, London

Grove, D (1996) And... what kind of a man is David Grove? An interview by Penny Tomkins and James Lawley, *Rapport*, **33**, August

Habermas, J (1974) *Knowledge and Human Interest*, Heinemann, London

Halfpenny, P (1985) Course materials, MSc in Applied Social Research, University of Manchester

Hall, L (2005) IT support, *People Management*, 24 March, pp 34–37

Harris, TA (1997) *I'm OK, You're OK*, Pan Books, London

Harrison, R (1978) Choosing the depth of organisational interventions, in *Organisation Development and Transformation*, ed W French, CY Bell and R Zawacki, pp 354–64, McGraw-Hill, Boston, MA

Hart, V, Blattner, J and Leipsic, S (2001) Coaching versus therapy: a perspective, *Consulting Psychology Journal: Practice and research*, **53**, pp 229–37

Hawkins, P and Shohet, R (1989) *Supervision in the Helping Professions*, Open University Press, Buckingham

Hay, J (1995) *Transformational Mentoring: Creating developmental alliances for changing organisational cultures*, Sherwood Publishing, Watford

Hay, J (1998) Mentoring: traditional versus developmental, *Organisations and People*, **5** (3), pp 22–26

Heirs, B and Farrell, P (1986) *The Professional Decision Thinker: Our new management priority*, 2nd edn, Garden City Press, Hertfordshire

Heron, J (1977) *Catharsis in Human Development*, Human Potential Research Group, University of Surrey, Guildford

Heron, J (1986) *Six Category Intervention Analysis*, Human Potential Research Project, University of Surrey, Guildford

Heron, J (1991) *Helping the Client: A creative practical guide*, Sage, London

Heron, J (1993) *Group Facilitation*, Kogan Page, London

Heron, J (1999) *The Complete Facilitator's Handbook*, Kogan Page, London

Hodson, P (2000) Counselling: in the public eye, *Counselling*, **11** (5), pp 268–69

Inskipp, F and Proctor, B (1988) *Skills for Supervising and Being Supervised* (private publication)

International Coaching Federation (2005) Coaching definition, International Coaching Federation, http://www.coachfederation.org/aboutcoaching/index.asp [accessed 31 May 2005]

Jacobson, E (1929) Electrical measurements of neuromuscular states during mental activities: imagination of movement involving skeletal muscle, *American Journal of Physiology*, **91**, pp 597–608

Jacoby, M (1984) *The Analytic Encounter*, Inner City Books, Toronto

James, K and Baddeley, J (1991) The power of innocence: from politeness to politics, *Management Learning*, **22** (2), pp 106–18

Jarvis, J (2004) *Coaching and Buying Coaching Services*, CIPD, London, http://www.cipd.co.uk

Jarvis, P (1987) *Adult Learning in the Social Context*, Croom Helm, London

Jenkins, R (1992) *Pierre Bourdieu*, Routledge, London

Jensen, E (1995) *Brain Based Learning and Teaching*, Turning Point, Del Mar, CA

Jourard, SM (1971) *The Transparent Self*, Van Nostrand Reinhold, New York

Jowett, B (1953) *The Dialogues of Plato*, Vol I, Book XVII, *Meno*, Oxford University Press, London

JS International (2005) *About NLP*, http://www.js-International.com [accessed 9 June 2005]

Kagan, N (1980) Influencing human interaction: 18 years with IPR, in *Psychotherapy Supervision: Theory, research and practice*, ed AK Hess, John Wiley, New York

Kahn, DG (1981) *Fathers as Mentors to Daughters*, Working paper, Radcliffe Institute, Cambridge, MA

Kates, J (1985) In search of professionalism, *City Woman*, **8** (1), pp 34–42

Keep, E (1992) Corporate training strategies: the vital component?, in *Human Resource Strategies*, ed G Salaman, Sage, London

Keller, EF (1983) Women, science and popular mythology, in *Machine ex Dea*, ed J Rothschild, pp 131–35, Pergamon Press, New York

Kelly, GA (1955) *The Psychology of Personal Constructs*, Norton, New York

Kemmis, S (1985) Action research and the politics of reflection, in *Reflection: Turning experience into learning*, ed D Boud, R Keogh and D Walker, pp 139–63, Kogan Page, London

Kets de Vries, M (1995) *Life and Death in the Executive Fast Lane*, Jossey-Bass, San Francisco, CA

Kim, B (2001) Social constructivism, in *Emerging Perspectives on Learning, Teaching and Technology*, ed M Orey, http://www.coe.uga.edu/epitt/SocialConstructivism.htm [accessed 8 August 2005]

King, ML, Jr (1968) *A Testament of Hope: The essential writings and speeches of Martin Luther King Jr*, ed JM Washington, Harper Collins, New York

Kohn, A (1990) *The Brighter Side of Human Nature: Altruism and empathy in everyday life*, Basic Books, New York

Kohut, H (1991) Empathy and self boundaries, in *Women's Growth in Connection: Writings from the Stone Centre*, ed J Jordan *et al*, pp 67– 80, Guilford Press, New York

Kolb, D (1984) *Experiential Learning*, Prentice Hall, Englewood Cliffs, NJ

Kram, K (1988) *Mentoring at Work*, University Press of America, Lanham, MD

Krantz, J (1989) The managerial couple: superior–subordinate relationships as a unit of analysis, *Human Resource Management*, **28** (2), pp 161–75

Kukla, A (2000) *Social Constructivism and the Philosophy of Science*, Routledge, New York

Landale, M (2005) Working with somatisation, Private communication

Lapierre, L (1989) Mourning potency and power in management, *Human Resource Management*, **28** (2), pp 177–89

Leininger, MM (1987) Transcultural caring: a different way to help people, in *Handbook of Cross-cultural Counselling and Therapy*, ed P Pederson, Praeger, London

Lessem, R (1991) *Total Quality Learning*, Blackwell, Oxford

Levinson, DJ and Levinson, J (1996) *The Seasons of a Woman's Life*, Ballantine Books, New York

Levinson, DJ *et al* (1978) *Seasons of a Man's Life*, Alfred A Knopf, New York

London, M (1997) *Job Feedback*, Lawrence Erlbaum, Mahwah, NJ

Luft, J (1984) *Group Processes: An introduction to group dynamics*, Mayfield Publishing, Mountain View, CA

McCann, D (1988) *How to Influence Others at Work*, Heinemann, Oxford

McGill, I and Brockbank, A (2004) *The Handbook of Action Learning*, Routledge, London

McGuire, GM (1999) Do race and gender affect employees' access to and help from mentors? Insights from the study of a large corporation, in *Mentoring Dilemmas: Developmental relationships within multicultural organisations*, ed AJ Murrell, FJ Crosby and RJ Ely, pp 105–20, Lawrence Erlbaum, Mahwah, NJ

McKeen, CA and Burke, RJ (1989) Mentor relationships in organisations: issues, strategies and prospects for women, *Journal of Management Development*, **8** (6), pp 33–42

McKenna, YA and Bargh, JA (1998) Coming out in the age of the internet: demarginalisation through virtual group participation, *Journal of Personality and Social Psychology*, **75** (3), pp 681–94

Magnuson, E (1986) A serious deficiency: the Rogers Commission faults NASA's flawed decision-making process, *Time*, March, pp 40–42

Margulies, A (1989) *The Empathic Imagination*, WW Norton, New York

Marton, F, Dall'Alba, G and Beaty, E (1993) Conceptions of learning, *International Journal of Educational Research*, **19**, pp 277–300

Maslow, A (1969) *The Psychology of Science: A reconnaissance*, Henry Regnery, New York

Maturana, H and Varela, FJ (1987) *The Tree of Knowledge*, Shambhala Publications, Boston, MA

Mayer, J (1999) Emotional intelligence, *People Management*, 28 October

Megginson, D (1988) Instructor, coach, mentor: three ways of helping for managers, *Management Education and Development*, **19** (1), pp 33–46

Megginson, D and Clutterbuck, D (1995) *Mentoring in Action*, Kogan Page, London

Megginson, D and Garvey, B (2004) Odysseus, Telemachus and Mentor: stumbling into, searching for and signposting the road to desire, *International Journal of Mentoring and Coaching*, **2** (1), www.emccouncil.org [accessed 20 February 2005]

Mehrabian, A (1971) *Silent Messages*, Wadsworth, Belmont, CA

Mezirow, J (1994) Understanding transformation theory, *Adult Education Quarterly*, **44** (4), pp 222–44

Miller, A (1983) *For Your Own Good: Hidden cruelty in child-rearing and the roots of violence*, trans Hildegarde and Hunter Haanum, New American Library, New York

Morris, D (1977) *Manwatching*, Cape, London

Morton-Cooper, A and Palmer, A (1993) *Mentoring and Preceptorship*, Blackwell Science, Oxford

Morton-Cooper, A and Palmer, A (2000) *Mentoring and Preceptorship*, 2nd edn, Blackwell Science, Oxford

Neenan, M and Dryden, W (2002) *Life Coaching*, Brunner-Routledge, Hove

Nelson-Jones, R (1986) *Relationship Skills*, Holt, Rinehart & Winston, London

Nielson, TR and Eisenbach, JR (2005) Not all relationships are created equal: critical factors of high-quality mentoring relationships, *International Journal of Mentoring and Coaching*, **1** (1), www.emccouncil.org [accessed 4 January 2005]

Noddings, N (1984) *Caring*, University of California Press, Berkeley, CA

Orbach, S (1994) *What's Really Going On Here?*, Virago, London

Page, S and Wosket, V (1994) *Supervising the Counsellor: A cyclical model*, Routledge, London

Parsloe, E (1995) *The Manager as Coach and Mentor*, IPD, London

Parsloe, E and Wray, M (2000) *Coaching and Mentoring*, Kogan Page, London

Paulston, Rolland (1996) *Social Cartography: Mapping ways of seeing social and educational change*, Garland, New York

Pease, A (1981) *Body Language*, Sheldon Press, London

Pedler, M, Burgoyne, J and Boydell, T (1990) *Self Development in Organisations*, McGraw-Hill, London

Peltier, B (2001) *The Psychology of Executive Coaching*, Brunner-Routledge, Hove

Perry, W (1970) *Forms of Intellectual and Ethical Development during the College Years: A scheme*, Holt, Rinehart & Winston, New York

Phillips-Jones, L (1982) *Mentors and Protégés: How to establish, strengthen and get the most from a mentor/protégé relationship*, Arbor House, New York

Pointon, C (2003) A life coach in two days?, *Counselling and Psychotherapy Journal*, **14** (10), pp 20–23

Pollard, P (1997) *Reflective Teaching in the Primary School*, 3rd edn, Cassell, London

Prosser, M and Trigwell, K (1999) *Understanding Learning and Teaching*, Open University Press, Buckingham

Quinn, Robert (2000) *Change the World*, Jossey-Bass, San Francisco, CA

Ragins, BR, Cotton, JL and Miller, JS (2000) Marginal mentoring: the effects of type of quality of relationship, and program design on work and career attitudes, *Academy of Management Journal*, **43** (6), pp 1177–94

Reeves, T (1994) *Managing Effectively*, Butterworth-Heinemann, London

Reid, B (1994) The mentor's experience: a personal perspective, in *Reflective Practice in Nursing: The growth of the professional practitioner*, ed A Palmer, S Burns and C Bulman, Blackwell Science, Oxford

Reynolds, M (1997) Learning styles: a critique, *Management Learning*, **28** (2), pp 115–33

Rich, A (1979) *On Lies, Secrets and Silence: Selected prose 1966–78*, Norton, New York

Rigano, D and Edwards, J (1998) Incorporating reflection into work practice, *Management Learning*, **29** (4), pp 431–46

Roberts, A (1998) Androgynous mentor: bridging gender stereotypes in mentoring, *Mentoring and Tutoring*, **6** (1/2), pp 18–29

Roberts, A (1999a) Androgyny and the mentoring role: an empirical study to examine for prominent mentor expectations, *Mentoring and Tutoring*, **7** (2), pp 145–222

Roberts, A (1999b) An empirical study to examine for androgynous mentoring behaviour in the field of education, *Mentoring and Tutoring*, **7** (3), pp 203–22

Roberts, A (2000) Mentoring revisited: a phenomenological reading of the literature, *Mentoring and Tutoring*, **8** (2), pp 145–70

Rogers, CR (1951) *Client-centred Therapy*, Constable, London

Rogers, CR (1957) The necessary and sufficient conditions for therapeutic personality change, *Journal of Consulting Psychology*, **21**, pp 95–103

Rogers, CR (1961) *On Becoming a Person: A therapist's view of psychotherapy*, Houghton Mifflin, Boston, MA

Rogers, CR (1979) *Carl Rogers on Personal Power*, Constable, London

Rogers, Carl (1983) *Freedom to Learn for the 80s*, Merrill, New York

Rogers, CR (1992) *Client Centred Therapy*, Constable, London

Rogers, Jenny (2004) *Coaching Skills: A handbook*, Open University Press, New York

Rose, C and Nicholl, MJ (1997) *Accelerated Learning for the 21st Century*, Piatkus, London

Rosen, S and Tesser, A (1970) On reluctance to communicate undesirable information: the MUM effect, *Sociometry*, **33**, pp 253–63

Rosinski, P (2003) *Coaching across Cultures*, Nicholas Brealey, London

Rothschild, B (2000) *The Body Remembers*, WW Norton, New York

Ruddick, S (1984) New combinations: learning from Virginia Woolf, in *Between Women*, ed C Asher, L DeSalvo and S Ruddick, pp 137–59, Beacon Press, Boston, MA

Russell, G (2001) Computer mediated school education and the web, *First Monday*, **6** (11), http://www.firstmonday.org/issues/issue6_11/Russell/index.html [accessed 8 August 2002]

Ryle, G (1983) *The Concept of Mind*, Penguin, Harmondsworth

Saljo, R (1979) *Learning in the Learner's Perspective I: Some common-sense conceptions*, Report No 76, Department of Education and Educational Research, University of Gothenburg, Gothenburg

Scandura, TA (1998) Dysfunctional mentoring relationships and outcomes, *Journal of Management*, **24**, pp 449–67

Schön, D (1987) *Educating the Reflective Practitioner*, Jossey-Bass, London

Schwaber, E (1983) Construction, reconstruction and the mode of clinical attachment, in *The Future of Psychoanalysis*, ed A Goldberg, pp 273–91, International Universities Press, New York

Silverstone, L (1993) *Art and the Development of the Person*, Autonomy Books, London

Skynner, R and Cleese, J (1983) *Families and How to Survive Them*, Methuen, London

Smail, D (2001) *The Nature of Unhappiness*, Constable, London

Sperry, RW and Gazzaniga, MS (1967) Language following surgical disconnection of the hemispheres, in *Brain Mechanisms underlying Speech and Language*, ed FL Darley, pp 108–21, Grune & Stratton, New York

Stacey, R (1993) *Strategic Management and Organisational Dynamics*, Pitman Publishing, London

Steinaker, N and Bell, R (1979) *The Experiential Taxonomy: A new approach to teaching and learning*, Academic Press, New York

Stott, T and Sweeney, J (1999) More than a match, *People Management*, 30 June

Syme, G (2000) Psychotherapy, counselling – what's the difference?, *Counselling*, **11** (6), pp 332–33

Tarule, J (1996) Voices in dialogue, in *Knowledge, Difference, and Power*, ed NR Goldberger *et al*, Basic Books, New York

Thomas, KW (1976) Conflict and conflict management, in *Handbook of Industrial and Organisational Psychology*, ed MD Dunnette, Rand McNally, Chicago, IL

Warren, C (2005) Quantum leap, *People Management*, 10 March, pp 34–37

Weafer, S (2001) *The Business Coaching Revolution*, Blackhall, Dublin

Weil, SW and McGill, IJ (1989) *Making Sense of Experiential Learning*, Open University Press/SRHE, Milton Keynes

Whitely, W, Dougherty, TW and Dreher, GF (1991) Relationship of career mentoring and socioeconomic origin to managers' and professionals' early career progress, *Academy of Management Journal*, **34** (2), pp 331–51

Whitmore, J (1996) *Coaching for Performance*, Nicholas Brealey, London

Whittaker, M and Cartwright, A (2000) *The Mentoring Manual*, Gower, Aldershot

Whitworth, L, Kimsey-House, H and Sandhal, P (1998) *Co-active Coaching*, Davies-Black Publishing, Palo Alto, CA

Wikipedia (2005) Coaching, Entry in Wikipedia, http://www.answers.com/coaching [accessed 2 June 2005]

Williams, D and Irving, J (2001) Coaching: an unregulated, unstructured and (potentially) unethical process, *Occupational Psychologist*, **42**

Wright, RG and Werther, WB (1991) Mentors at work, *Journal of Management Development*, **10** (3), pp 25–32

Zachary, L (2000) *The Mentor's Guide*, Jossey-Bass, San Francisco, CA

Index

With over 42 years of publishing, more than 80 million people have succeeded in business with thanks to **Kogan Page**

www.koganpage.com

KoganPage